489 KAH
Kahane, Renee
Spoken Greek

rebound 4/97

Vail Public Library
292 West Meadow Drive
Vail, CO 81657

Henry and Renée Kahane and Ralph L. Ward

SPOKEN GREEK

BOOK ONE

Spoken Language Services, Inc.

This is one of a series of self-teaching textbooks in more than thirty languages prepared under the aegis of the American Council of Learned Societies and the Linguistic Society of America, distributed by Spoken Language Services, Inc. There are four hours of recordings keyed to the printed text.

Library of Congress Cataloging in Publication Data

Kahane, Henry, (date)
  Spoken Greek.

  (Spoken Language Series)
  CONTENTS: Book 1
  1. Greek language--Conversation and phrase books.
  I. Kahane, Renée and Ward, Ralph L., joint authors. II. Title.
  PA1059.K16   74-150404
  ISBN 0-87950-100-6

© Linguistic Society of America 1945, 1946
© Spoken Language Services, Inc. 1972, 1974, 1976

Published by
Spoken Language Services, Inc.
P.O. Box 783
Ithaca, New York 14850

No part of the material covered by these copyrights may be reproduced in any form without written permission of the publisher.

CONTENTS

PART ONE

UNIT   *Page*

1. GETTING AROUND. Greetings and general phrases. Places and directions. Comment on the *Aids to Listening*. Asking for things. Price. Time. The numbers 1-10. The Greek accent; the Greek vowels; the Greek consonants.   1

2. MEETING PEOPLE. The vowels in combinations of words; the sound *s* in combinations of words. The three kinds of Greek nouns. "A" child and "one" child. Singular and plural. About verbs.   31

3. WHAT'S YOUR TRADE? The vowels *i, e, o;* the sound *n* in combinations of words. The definite article. The indefinite article. About nouns. A verb in *-me*. How to ask questions, and how to say yes or no.   62

4. WHERE ARE YOU FROM? Shift of accent in nouns. Personal substitutes. How to express 'my', 'your', 'his', etc. Verbs with the accent on the last syllable. 'I was living'.   92

5. LET'S TALK ABOUT THE WEATHER. The sounds *kh*, *ch*, *gh*, and *y*. The neuter noun. The plural of the masculine and feminine nouns. Greek adjectives.   119

6. REVIEW.   144

VAIL LIBRARY

* 114037*

VAIL PUBLIC LIBRARY

PART TWO

UNIT	Page

7. GETTING A ROOM. The sounds *t*, *k*, and *p* after *n*; the sounds *ts*, *ks*, and *ps* after *n*. The verb *ksipnó*. The verb *kimúme*. *-o* verbs and *-me* verbs. How to express in Greek 'I want to', 'I have to', 'I may', 'I can', etc. How to say 'no one (nobody)', 'nothing', and 'never'. How to say 'one o'clock', 'three o'clock', and 'four o'clock'. — 151

8. SPRUCING UP. *p*, *t*, and *k*; *k* before *e* or *i*; *l* before *e* or *i*; Greek *r*. More about the important word *na*. How to find the perfective stem of verbs of the *-o* type. — 177

9. LET'S EAT. The position of the accent. Adjectives of the type *varís*. How to say 'much' and 'many'. The words for 'this' and 'that' before nouns. *tróo* 'I eat'. — 202

10. SEEING THE SIGHTS. Some more numbers. The indirect object. How to say 'I'll come', 'I'll see', etc. The forms of the Greek numerals. *akúo* 'I hear'. — 226

11. SHOPPING. Something more about words that are run together. How to command and how to forbid. How to say 'one and a half', 'two and a half', etc. How to express time. — 250

12. REVIEW. — 275

INTRODUCTION

1. What We Are Trying to Do. This course in spoken Greek is designed as a general introduction to the Greek language. It contains all the essential grammatical materials for learning to speak everyday Greek, and its vocabulary, though small, is built around a number of the most useful common situations and current topics. It is based on the principle that you must *hear* a language if you are to understand it when spoken, and that you must practice speaking it in order to master its sounds and its forms.

A teacher of Greek will seldom be available for those for whom this book is written. So the course has been made as nearly self-teaching as possible. This Manual covers the course completely and requires the use of no other reference material. It explains in detail, step by step, how the work is to proceed, and sets the stage for the listening and talking which you are to do.

2. The Greek Language is spoken by about seven million people in Greece; and it is widely understood around the Eastern Mediterranean. This Manual presents the daily speech of the fairly well educated Greeks. You must not be surprised, however, if you sometimes hear words which, in pronunciation or formation, are different from those used in this Manual. There are two reasons for these variations: first, Greek is considerably less fixed in its details than many other languages, and different persons use often different forms of the same words; secondly, the dialects play a great rôle, especially in the country areas, and even educated people use dialect words in their daily speech. But the Greek taught in this Manual is understood everywhere, and in order to understand the people in a certain region, you have to listen carefully, to have people repeat, and to imitate. They, in turn, will do their best to pronounce so that they can be understood. Incidentally, the use of gestures is strongly developed in Greece; they are a normal accompaniment to the language; use the gestures yourself, if you can imitate them.

Finally, don't be surprised if you open a Greek newspaper and discover that the language used there is entirely different from the language taught here. This situation is a peculiar feature of Greek culture: there is one language (the one that you are going to learn) which is popular and used by everybody in daily speech (and in poetry, modern novels, and short stories); and there is a second language, a kind of scholastic Greek surviving from the Middle Ages and adapted to the intellectual life of Western Europe. It is the language of the administration, the courts, scientific books, and newspapers. The borderline between these two languages is not too well defined, and there are many expressions of the learned language, especially scientific or official terms, which have been taken over by the popular language. They are often treated in a way slightly different from really popular words; we will draw your attention to each case that may come up.

3. How to Use This Manual. To help you in learning to speak Greek, this course makes use of two tools: a native speaker of the language, and this book. The two must be used together, as neither one is of any use without the other.

This Manual has been so organized that it can be used to study by yourself or in a group. The group may or may not have a regular teacher; if you have no regular teacher choose one of your own number (called the *Group Leader*) to lead the others and to direct their work.

4. A Native Speaker is the only good source of first-hand knowledge of the pronunciation and usage of any language. The method used in this Manual requires the use of a native speaker of Greek, preferably a person who can be on hand through the course, or next best the voice of a native speaker recorded on phonograph records which are supplied with this Manual. But even when a native speaker is present during the course, the records can always be used for additional study.

The native speaker of Greek is referred to as the *Guide;* if you can get a Guide, use him as a source of information throughout the course. The Guide's job is to act as a model for you to imitate, and as a check on your pronunciation; it is *not* his business to be a teacher or to "explain" the language to you. The Guide should be, if possible, a person who speaks more or less the type of Greek found in this Manual, not merely the dialect of a particular region; but he should speak this type of Greek naturally and without affectation. He should be neither overeducated nor too uncultured.

5. The Book is divided into five major parts, each containing five *learning units* and one unit devoted to review. Each Unit contains several sections, usually the following:

A. Basic Sentences (with Hints on Pronunciation, in Parts I, II, and III, and Hints on Spelling, in Part III)
B. Word Study and Review of Basic Sentences
C. Review of Basic Sentences (Cont.)
D. Listening In
E. Conversation
F. Conversation (Cont.)

These six sections are followed in each learning unit by a *Finder List* containing all the new words in the particular Unit. At the end of the Manual there is an Appendix comprising the following parts: 1. Supplementary Word Lists; 2. Idiom List; 3. Survey of

Inflectional Endings; 4. Greek-English Vocabulary; 5. English-Greek Vocabulary; 6. Grammatical Index.

6. The Basic Sentences in each Unit are arranged so as to give you a number of new words and a number of new ways of saying things; first broken up into words or short phrases, and then combined in complete sentences. On the printed page they are presented in parallel columns, which contain on the left the English equivalent, in the center and on the right the Greek material. The Greek material is given both in the *Aids to Listening* in the second column and in the *Conventional Spelling* in the third column.

When you have your book open at whatever Unit you are going to study, and when the Guide is ready to begin speaking the words for you, or the Group Leader is ready to start the phonograph records, you can start working on the Basic Sentences for that Unit. If the Group Leader is working with the Guide, the Leader will read the English out loud, and the Guide will pronounce the Greek twice, each time allowing enough time for you to repeat the Greek after him. If you are using the phonograph records, two voices on the records will act as Leader and Guide for you. While you are listening to the Guide, follow with your eyes the Aids to Listening. When you repeat the words and sentences after the Guide or phonograph records, repeat them loud—good and loud. Never mumble. It is absolutely essential that you repeat after the Guide or phonograph record each time, and that you imitate as closely as you can, and learn by heart what you have imitated.

7. The Aids to Listening present a simplified version, in our ordinary letters, of the Greek spelling, which is designed to help you in remembering how the Greek words *sound*. In the Aids to Listening, each Greek sound is represented by one letter or group of letters. Every letter (or group of letters) always stands for the same sound. Concentrate your attention first on the Aids to Listening, especially through Parts I and II; from Part III on you should pay more attention to the Conventional Greek Spelling.

8. The Hints on Pronunciation are given you to help you improve your speech in Greek. No language has sounds exactly like those of any other; and in Greek you will find some sounds which are quite absent from English, and others which are somewhat but not exactly like English sounds. After you have been through the Basic Sentences of the Unit at least once, read through the Hints on Pronunciation carefully, having the Guide repeat or playing on the phonograph the words and sounds which are being discussed. Then go back and listen again to the Basic Sentences, always repeating them after the Guide or phonograph as you did before. Try to hear and imitate more precisely the sounds to which your attention has been called.

9. Pronouncing to Be Understood. Pronunciation is important for a number of reasons: if you expect to be understood when you speak a foreign language, you will have to pronounce it more or less the way the people are used to hearing it. If you are too far off from the usual way of talking the language, people won't be able to understand you at all. Furthermore, the nearer you get to pronouncing the precise sounds, the easier it will be for your ear to catch the sound as spoken by a native, and the more rapidly you will pick up new words and phrases and make progress in learning the language.

Learning to pronounce is really not hard, if you go about it in the right way. If you follow the suggestions and instructions given in this Manual, and work carefully through all the hints, practices, and drills, you can expect to acquire the kind of pronunciation you need. Many students who are good mimics and who get into the spirit of speaking Greek will learn to talk like natives.

The only way to learn to pronounce like a native is to imitate. You must get a native to pronounce the words, then say them right after him, mimicking everything, even to the tone of his voice. This Manual will make it easier for you by pointing out the sounds you need to observe, and by describing their peculiarities.

10. The Native Speaker Is Always Right. There may be instances where this Manual or the phonograph records indicate one pronunciation and the native speaker will pronounce something a little different. Always imitate the pronunciation of your Guide rather than that of the phonograph records or of the Aids to Listening.

11. Each Word Study shows you new uses and new combinations of materials studied up to that point; you are taught how to take apart the words and phrases which you hear and how to make new words and phrases on the same model. Read each part of the Word Study carefully, and make sure you understand thoroughly everything which is said in them; then go back over the Basic Sentences with the Guide or phonograph, exactly as you did before. By this time you can start going through the Basic Sentences with your book closed, and you should now be able to understand the sentences without looking at the English equivalent.

12. The Listening In section gives you a number of conversations or stories, which use the vocabulary and constructions you have learned in each Unit and in all those preceding. Its purpose is to give you practice in listening to and understanding the foreign language as you might overhear it in normal conversation among Greek-speaking people, and to furnish you with models for your own conversation practice.

13. The Conversation Practice represents the central aim of the course. In order to converse well, you should know well everything that has been introduced in the Unit you are working on, and everything that you have learned in previous Units as well. When you take part in a conversation, do so as easily and naturally as you can. Don't try to bring in new words and phrases that you haven't learned in the material you have studied in this course; stick to what you have learned and practice it thoroughly.

14. Talking Greek. In speaking Greek you should not first figure out what you want to say in English and then translate it into Greek, word for word. This will get you nowhere. You should apply, instead, the words and expressions you already know to the given situation. If you cannot immediately rattle off a word or expression to fit a particular situation, go on to another, or ask a question, but under no circumstances attempt to compose. As soon as you do, you lapse into English speech habits and stop learning Greek and Greek speech habits.

When people speak to you, they will frequently use words and expressions you do not know. If you can't guess their meaning, try to find out by asking questions in Greek, or by asking them to repeat slowly, or to explain in simpler terms. If you (and they!) are good natured, and reasonable about it, you won't have any trouble. On the contrary you will constantly learn more and will practice the Greek you already know in the process.

Your learning of the language will not stop, therefore, when you have mastered this material. You will, rather, be able to get around among the people, practice what you know, and steadily pick up more and more words and phrases. Try to learn them thoroughly. Carry along a notebook to jot down what you want to remember; you·can then review this material from time to time.

You should not wait until you have finished this Manual before you start using the language. Start practicing at once. When you have done the first Unit, try out the expressions on as many people as possible. When you try out your Greek at this early stage, make it slide off your tongue as smoothly as possible. Be careful not to slip back into a careless English-like pronunciation. Listen closely to what the person says in response, trying to catch as much as you can. The first few times it may be hard to catch even the words you know, but you will improve rapidly if you keep on practicing every chance you get.

KEY TO PRONUNCIATION

—SIGNS*—	—NEAREST ENGLISH SOUNDS—	—SIGNS*—	—NEAREST ENGLISH SOUNDS—
a	*a* in f*a*ther	kh	see description on p. 14
ch	see description on p. 14	o	*o* in cl*o*th
dh	*th* in *th*is	r	see description on p. 15
e	*e* in l*e*t	th	*th* in *th*in
gh	see description on p. 15	u	*u* in tr*u*ce
i	*i* in mach*i*ne		

*The signs not listed here are pronounced more or less as they are pronounced in English.

KEY TO THE GREEK SPELLING*

GREEK LETTERS		—NEAREST ENGLISH SOUND—	GREEK LETTERS		—NEAREST ENGLISH SOUND—
Capital	Small		Capital	Small	
A	α	*a* in f*a*ther		γγ	g; *ng*, as in fi*ng*er, often within a word
	ᾳ	*a* in f*a*ther		γκ	
	αι	*e* in l*e*t	Δ	δ	*th* in *th*is
	αυ	*af; av*	E	ε	*e* in l*e*t
B	β	*v*		ει	*i* in mach*i*ne; *y*
Γ	γ	gh** before *a, o, u*, and consonants; *y* before *e, i*		ευ	*ef; ev*
			Z	ζ	*z*
	γει		H	η	*i* in mach*i*ne; *y*
	γι	*y*		ῃ	*i* in mach*i*ne
	γυ			ηυ	*eav* in l*eav*ing
	γυι				

*This key presents a list of the Greek letters and the sounds they stand for. In Part III Greek spelling will be discussed in detail.   **For the pronunciation of this sound see p. 15.

Θ	θ	*th* in *th*in	T	τ	*t*
Ι	ι	*i* in mach*i*ne; *y*		τς	*dz*
Κ	κ	*k*	Υ	υ	*i* in mach*i*ne; *y*
Λ	λ	*l*		υι	*i* in mach*i*ne; *y*
Μ	μ	*m*	Φ	φ	*f*
	μπ	*b*; *mb* often within a word; *mp* sometimes within a word	Χ	χ	*kh* before *a, o, u,* and consonants; *ch* before *e, i,* and *y***
Ν	ν	*n*	Ψ	ψ	*ps*
	ντ	*d*; *nd* often within a word; *nt* sometimes within a word	Ω	ω	*o* in cl*o*th
				ῳ	*o* in cl*o*th
Ξ	ξ	*ks*	' ʼ		these signs have no value in pronunciation
Ο	ο	*o* in cl*o*th			
	οι	*i* in mach*i*ne; *y*	´ ` ˆ		these signs generally indicate stress
	ου	*u* in tr*u*ce	;		?
Π	π	*p*	·		; or :
Ρ	ρ	*r**			
Σ	σ	*s*; *z* before certain consonants			
	ς at end of words	*s*			

---

*For the pronunciation of this sound see p. 15.   **For the pronunciation of these sounds see p. 14.

PART ONE

GETTING AROUND

UNIT

To the Group Leader: Each *Unit* of this course is divided into six *Sections*. It is suggested that the group spend not less than fifty minutes on each Section.

Before you get the group together to work on this first Unit, read carefully the following material up to the heading *Useful Words and Phrases* on page 4. When the group meets, read the material aloud to them or have some other member of the group do the reading. The students will follow the reading with their books open. Be sure that your Guide, or the phonograph and records, are ready before the group meets for work on Section A. See that the Guide is supplied with a copy of the manual Ὁδηγίες γιὰ τὸν Ὁδηγό, which tells him just what he is to do and gives him the Greek he is to speak to the group.

You should look through all of the Sections of the Unit, reading the directions carefully, so that you will have in mind the general plan of the work. Always get clearly in mind the directions for a Section before you take that Section up in group meeting.

This Unit gives you the most immediate and necessary expressions that you will need in meeting people, asking your way, buying things, and counting. The amount of learning and memorizing required for the first Unit is considerably greater than that for any later Unit. You are given such a large dose at the start because this Unit is meant to be a kind of "language first aid" which gives you enough useful expressions to enable you to make ordinary wants known and to carry on a simple conversation in Greek from the very start.

All but a few of these words and phrases are selected from the phonograph records for the *Greek Language Guide* (Introductory Series) (TM 30–350). If you have worked with these records, the present Unit will serve as a review.

SECTION A—USEFUL WORDS AND PHRASES

In the list of *Useful Words and Phrases* which follows, the English equivalent of these words and phrases is given at the left of the page. Opposite, in the middle column, is a simplified spelling of the Greek, in English letters, which will help you in getting the sounds. In the third column is the ordinary or *conventional* Greek spelling. The *Leader* of the group will first read the *English Equivalent* and pause for the *Guide* to speak the Greek. Every member of the group then repeats after the Guide. The Guide will then say the Greek a second

[1–A]

time and everybody will repeat after him as before. The Leader will then read the next English equivalent and the Guide and group will follow the procedure indicated.

If no Guide is available, the *phonograph records* provided for the course should be used. When the group is ready, the Leader will begin playing the appropriate record and the group will repeat right after the Greek speaker during the silences on the record. The phonograph records can be used with profit even in cases where a Guide is available because they can be heard between meetings of the group, whenever it is convenient to you; they furnish additional practice in hearing Greek; you may listen only to those portions which you have found difficult; and the records may be played as often as you wish. In case the speaker on the record has a Greek pronunciation different from that of your Guide, use the records only for listening and understanding and not for imitating.

Whether you are working with a Guide or only with the phonograph records, you must repeat each Greek word and phrase in a loud, clear voice, trying at all times to imitate the pronunciation as closely as you can. Keep constantly in mind the meaning of the Greek you are about to hear, glancing at the English equivalent whenever you need to remind yourself. When you are hearing the Greek, keep your eyes on the *Aids to Listening*. But whenever the written form seems to you to differ from the spoken sound, follow the spoken sound always.

Learning to understand and pronounce a language is not really hard. Every one of us learned to do this as a child, and all over the world children learn to speak all kinds of languages without any trouble. The difficulty that an adult faces in learning a foreign language as you are now learning Greek, is that the adult already has a set of habits for pronouncing his own language and this makes it harder for him to learn new ones than for a child who is starting from scratch. That is why it is so important that you should not be afraid of mimicking even when what you hear may sound strange to you. Don't be afraid to let yourself go. You will never learn to speak a language if you don't plunge right in as soon as you can. Never mind if you do make mistakes at first. The important thing is for you to try to say the words and phrases. Imitate your Guide with the same spirit and enthusiasm that you use in mimicking a person whose speech sounds peculiar to you. You will find that if you do this, your Guide will not think you are making fun of him; instead he will probably smile because what you have said to him sounds like Greek.

In the first five Units, do not attempt under any circumstances to pronounce the Greek before you have heard it. You will only make trouble for yourself if you try to guess the pronunciation by "reading" the *Aids to Listening* or the conventional Greek spelling.

If you are working with a Guide who does not understand English, ask the Leader of your group to demonstrate for you and the Guide what hand signals are to be used to let the Guide know when you want him to read more slowly or to repeat. They are as follows:

1. Index finger raised: BEGIN
2. Hand raised, palm toward the Guide: STOP
3. Palm down, hand moved slowly in semi-circle: SLOWER
4. Beckoning with index finger: REPEAT
5. Hand held palm up and moved quickly up and down: LOUDER

Remember that each phrase you say has a real meaning in Greek and hence you should always act as though you were really saying something to someone else. You will learn fastest if, when your book is open, you follow these steps:

1. Keep your eyes on the *Aids to Listening* as you listen to the Greek being spoken.
2. Repeat immediately what you have heard.
3. Keep in mind the meaning of what you are saying.

Begin the words and phrases as soon as your Guide is ready or when the Leader of your group is ready to play the first phonograph record.

To the Group Leader: Give the members of the group a chance to ask questions about the instructions. Make sure that everyone understands just what he is to do. Then have the students go through the list of *Useful Words and Phrases* once with the books open, repeating in unison after the Guide. Following this first practice, read with the group the *Comment on the Aids to Listening* on page 7. Make sure that everyone understands it.

Now go through the list a second time, mucn as you did before. And finally, go through it a third time, but let the students take turns repeating individually after the Guide—a sentence to a student. Indicate the order in which the repetitions are to go, who is first, who next, and so on. Continue this individual repetition as long as the fifty-minute period permits. Then, just before dismissing the group, read with them the paragraph headed *Check Yourself* on page 8.

Here are some hints that will make the work of the group more effective:

1. Insist that everyone speak up. Don't allow any mumbling! Each member of the group must be able to hear what is being said at all times.
2. Indicate to the Guide that he is to repeat whenever the pronunciation is bad and to keep on repeating until he gets a pronunciation that sounds like Greek.
3. Urge everyone to mimic to the limit every sound, every inflection, even the mannerisms of the Guide.
4. Keep the work moving. Don't let it drag at any time. See that everyone is listening, not only to the Guide, but to himself and to the others as they repeat after the Guide.
5. Go through all the work yourself. Repeat with the others and take your turn at the individual repetitions.

Record 1A, beginning. 1. **Useful Words and Phrases**

Here is a list of useful words and phrases you will need in Greek. *You should learn these by heart.*

> **NOTE:** Words enclosed in brackets [ ] are not expressed in the Greek. Words enclosed in parentheses ( ) help to explain the meaning of the Greek but are not necessary in English. Words enclosed in single quotation marks ' ' are literal or word-for-word equivalents.

Greetings and General Phrases

ENGLISH EQUIVALENTS	AIDS TO LISTENING	CONVENTIONAL SPELLING
Good morning.	kaliméra-sas.	Καλημέρα σας.
Good evening.	kalispéra-sas.	Καλησπέρα σας.
Good night.	kalinίkhta-sas.	Καληνύχτα σας.
Hello *or* good-bye.	chérete.	Χαίρετε.
sir*	kírie	κύριε
the gentleman**	o-kírios	ὁ κύριος
madam*	kiría	κυρία
the lady**	i-kiría	ἡ κυρία
miss*	dhespinís	δεσποινίς
the young lady**	i-dhespinís	ἡ δεσποινίς
(the) Peter	o-pétros	ὁ Πέτρος
what?	tí	τί
you do	kánete	κάνετε
How are you, Mr. Christophorou?	ti-kánete kírie-khristofóru?	Τί κάνετε, κύριε Χριστοφόρου;

*When speaking to the person. **When speaking about the person.

very	*polí*	πολύ
well	*kalá*	καλά
Very well.	*polí-kala.*	Πολὺ καλά.
I thank	*efkharistó*	εὐχαριστῶ
Thank you very much.	*sas-efkharistó-polí.*	Σᾶς εὐχαριστῶ πολύ.
you	*esís*	ἐσεῖς
And you?	*k-esís?*	Κ' ἐσεῖς;
you excuse	*sikhoríte*	συχωρεῖτε
Excuse me.	*me-sikhoríte.*	Μὲ συχωρεῖτε.
Yes.	*né.*	Ναί.
or	*málista.**	Μάλιστα.
No.	*óchi.*	Ὄχι.
Did you understand?	*katalávate?*	Καταλάβατε;
I understood.	*katálava.*	Κατάλαβα.
I didn't understand.	*dhén-gatálava.*	Δὲν κατάλαβα.
speak!	*milíte*	μιλεῖτε
slowly	*sighá*	σιγά
I beg	*parakaló***	παρακαλῶ
Speak slowly, please.	*milíte-sighá**** *parakaló.*	Μιλεῖτε σιγά, παρακαλῶ.
you said	*ípate*	εἴπατε
What did you say?	*ti-ípate?*	Τί εἴπατε;

*More polite. **Both 'please' and 'you're welcome'. ***On the record, the first time, *arghá*, which can also be used.

[1–A]

Places and Directions

where?	pú	ποῦ
(he, she, it) is	íne*	εἶναι
the station	o-stathmós	ὁ σταθμός
Where is the station?	pú-in-o-stathmós?	Ποῦ εἶν' ὁ σταθμός;

Record 1B, beginning.

[there] is	íne	εἶναι
a restaurant	ena-estiatório	ἕνα ἐστιατόριο
Where is there a restaurant?	pú-in-ena-estiatório?	Ποῦ εἶν' ἕνα ἐστιατόριο;
the hotel	to-ksenodhochío	τὸ ξενοδοχεῖο
the toilet	to-méros	τὸ μέρος
you go	páte	πάτε
Where are you going?	pú-páte?	Ποῦ πάτε;
To (the) Salonica.	s-ti-saloníki.	Στὴ Σαλονίκη.
come!	eláte	ἐλᾶτε
together	mazí	μαζί
with me	mazí-mu	μαζί μου
Come with me.	eláte mazí-mu.	'Ελᾶτε μαζί μου.
To the right.	dheksyá.	Δεξιά.
To the left.	aristerá.	'Αριστερά.
<u>Straight</u> ahead.	ísya-brostá.	῍Ισια μπροστά.

*Also '(they) are'.

After you have gone through the *Useful Words and Phrases* once, read the following:

2. Comment on the Aids to Listening

The best way to learn any language is to listen to a native speaker of it, and then copy exactly what he says. That is why we ask you to listen carefully to your Guide (or the speaker on the records) and imitate him as exactly as you can. It would be ideal if you could remember everything he says simply by listening and repeating. However, most of us need to have something on paper to remind us of what we have heard. Now, the Greek script wouldn't help you very much in this respect. Being based, as it is, on the way the language was spelled two thousand years ago, it does not reflect simply and accurately the sounds of the spoken language of the present day. Rather serious mistakes in pronunciation may often arise from the Greek script taken alone. It is for this reason that we use the *Aids to Listening* that you have seen in the foregoing pages. They are simply an attempt to put down systematically on paper the sounds that you hear on the records or that your Guide will probably say. (Later on, in Part III, you will learn to read the regular Greek spelling; pay no attention to it now.) Remember, however, that they are only *aids* to listening. The listening itself is still the most important thing; the printed material is just a reminder.

Three features of this system should be explained at the outset.

1. The Letters. In the *Aids to Listening* we use ordinary English letters and a few extra marks. The letters we use cannot have exactly the same sound values that they have in English, because Greek sounds are more or less different from English sounds. But we do keep them consistent: letters and pairs of letters in the *Aids to Listening* always mean the same Greek sounds.

2. Stress Mark. The *Aids to Listening* mark the loud-stressed vowel in every word or sentence by placing an accent-mark over it. This is highly important, since the meaning of words, in Greek as in English, may be quite different according as the stress falls on one vowel or on another of words that are otherwise similar. In English there is a difference between *cónduct* and *condúct;* and in Greek there is a difference, and a very marked one, between *píno* 'I drink' and *pinó* 'I am hungry'. Notice that Greek words often have no accent when used within a sentence, but are stressed when standing alone; you know instances of the same thing from English, where you have *mister*, but *Mister Jónes*. And don't be surprised if certain little words in Greek, like *íne* 'is', are accented in one sentence and unaccented in another, according to their rôle within a given sentence.

3. Words Run Together. In Greek, words are run together more closely than in English. This is very characteristic of Greek. In the *Aids to Listening* we show this by printing the words with a hyphen between them. This means that these words are run together quite as if they were just one word. Listen to the Guide. It is very important to get used to this way the Greeks have of running their words together, since otherwise one might fail to understand even the most familiar words.

Now go through the *Useful Words and Phrases* again with your book open, following the same procedure as before. Repeat each word and phrase, immediately after hearing it, in a loud, clear voice. Let yourself go and say the phrases right out.

Go through the *Useful Words and Phrases* once more with your book open, but this time, take turns letting each member of your group repeat individually until everybody has taken part. Keep on the alert. If the Guide asks you to repeat, do so with enthusiasm and try to mimic him as best as you can until he is satisfied with your pronunciation. When you have satisfied him, you can be sure that you are speaking understandable Greek. Continue this individual repetition as long as time permits. If you are using only the phonograph records, your Leader will see to it that you repeat and that everyone gets the most out of this individual performance.

3. Check Yourself

Did you go through the *Useful Words and Phrases* at least twice in unison and at least once more individually?

Did you repeat each word and phrase in a loud, clear voice immediately after hearing it?

Did you follow the pronunciation you heard even when it was different from that shown in your book?

Did you keep in mind the meaning of each word and phrase as you heard and spoke the Greek?

If you have failed at any point to carry out the instructions, go over the *Useful Words and Phrases* once again as soon as you can, being careful to follow every step in the procedure outlined.

SECTION B—USEFUL WORDS AND PHRASES (*Cont.*)

Here are other useful words and phrases which you will want to use immediately if you are in Greece. These are being given to you as a "language first aid." **Learn them by heart.**

In working with this material, follow the same procedure that you used with the *Useful Words and Phrases* in Section A. After you have gone through the list once, repeating in unison, read the following *Hints on Pronunciation*. Run through the *Pronunciation Practices*. Then go through the list a second and a third time, as in Section A.

Record 1B, after spiral.

1. Useful Words and Phrases (*Cont.*)
Asking for Things

this *or* that	aftó	αὐτό
What's that?	tí-n-aftó?	Τ' εἶν' αὐτό;
how?	pós	πῶς
you say	léte	λέτε
in Greek	eliniká	ἑλληνικά
How do you say *table* in Greek?	póz-léte table eliniká?	Πῶς λέτε table ἑλληνικά;
you wish	thélete	θέλετε
What do you want?	tí-thélete?	Τί θέλετε;
you have	échete	ἔχετε
cigarettes	sigharéta	σιγαρέτα
Do you have [any] cigarettes?	échete-sigharéta?	Ἔχετε σιγαρέτα;
matches	spírta	σπίρτα
[And] matches, too?	ke-spírta?	Καὶ σπίρτα;

Food

I can	boró	μπορῶ
that I eat	na-fáo	νὰ φάω
Where can I eat?	pú-boró-na-fáo?	Ποῦ μπορῶ νὰ φάω;
the boy	to-pedhí	τὸ παιδί
Waiter!	pedhí!	Παιδί!

I wish	*thélo*	θέλω
that I drink	*na-pyó*	νὰ πιῶ
I want [something] to drink. ('I want that I drink.')	*thélo-na-pyó.*	Θέλω νὰ πιῶ.
I don't want	*dhé-thélo*	δὲ θέλω
water	*neró*	νερό
I don't want water.	*dhé-thélo-neró.*	Δὲ θέλω νερό.
give me!	*dhóste-mu*	δώστε μου
meat	*kréas*	κρέας
with potatoes	*me-patátes*	μὲ πατάτες
Give me meat and potatoes.	*dhóste-mu kréaz-me-patátes.*	Δώστε μου κρέας μὲ πατάτες.

Record 2A, beginning.

A beer.	*mya-bíra.*	Μιὰ μπίρα.
Milk.	*ghála.*	Γάλα.
Wine.	*krasí.*	Κρασί.
the coffee	*o-kafés*	ὁ καφές
good	*kalós*	καλός
The coffee's good.	*o-kafés ine-kalós.*	Ὁ καφὲς εἶναι καλός.
Do you want coffee?	*thélete-kafé?*	Θέλετε καφέ;
Give me a [cup of] coffee.	*dhóste-mu-enan-gafé.*	Δώστε μου ἕναν καφέ.

we have	ékhume	ἔχουμε
we have not	dhén-ékhume	δὲν ἔχουμε
bread	psomí	ψωμί
We haven't [any] bread.	dhén-ékhume-psomí.	Δὲν ἔχουμε ψωμί.

Price

how much?	póso	πόσο
makes	káni	κάνει
How much is it?	póso-káni?	Πόσο κάνει;
fifty	penínda	πενήντα
drachmas	dhrakhmés	δραχμές
Fifty drachmas.*	penínda-dhrakhmés.	Πενήντα δραχμές.

Time

hour	óra	ὥρα
What time is it?	tí-ora-íne?	Τί ὥρα εἶναι;
It's one o'clock.	ine-mía.	Εἶναι μία.
begins	archízi	ἀρχίζει
the movies	o-kinimatóghrafos	ὁ κινηματόγραφος
What time does the show start?	tí-or-archízi-o-kinimatóghrafos?	Τί ὥρ' ἀρχίζει ὁ κινηματόγραφος;
I leave	févgho	φεύγω
the evening	to-vrádhi	τὸ βράδυ
with the train	me-to-tréno	μὲ τὸ τρένο
I leave tonight by train.	févgho to-vrádhi me-to-tréno.	Φεύγω τὸ βράδυ μὲ τὸ τρένο.

*This line not on the record.

we go	páme*	πάμε
at (the) nine	s-tis-enyá	στὶs ἐννιά
to the movies	s-ton-ginimatóghrafo	στὸν κινηματόγραφο
Shall we go to the movies at nine?	páme s-tis-enyá s-ton-ginimatóghrafo?	Πάμε στὶs ἐννιὰ στὸν κινηματόγραφο;

Numbers

one	éna	ἕνα
two	dhío	δύο
three	tría	τρία
four	tésera	τέσσερα
five	pénde	πέντε
six	éksi	ἕξι
seven	eftá	ἐφτά
eight	okhtó	ὀχτώ
nine	enyá	ἐννιά
ten	dhéka	δέκα

*Also 'let's go!'

After you have gone through these *Useful Words and Phrases* once, read the following:

2. Hints on Pronunciation

To the Group Leader: The following section is divided into three parts, and each part is to be taken up separately. First, read through with the group the introductory material and the explanations given in the first part. Then have the Guide read the *Practices* with the group repeating after him, first in unison, and then individually. Don't go on to the next part until everyone has a reasonable control over the items of pronunciation that are being taught. Follow this procedure with each of the three parts.

You will find that the *Practices* are all given on the phonograph records. Between each set of examples there is a clear space of record or *spiral*, so that you can play each set as often as is necessary.

The pronunciation of Greek does not involve any great difficulties. This, of course, does not mean that you can use English sounds in Greek words and expect to be understood. But you will find that many of the sounds are sufficiently similar to your own so that you will have practically no difficulty with them. However, there are a few Greek sounds that are different from anything in English. For that reason it is necessary for you to listen carefully and try hard to imitate your Guide. If you do this and follow the *Hints on Pronunciation* which will be given to you from time to time, you will be able to pronounce Greek so that you can be readily understood.

1. A STRONG ACCENT IS CHARACTERISTIC OF GREEK.

The accent in Greek is of great importance and constitutes one of the main characteristics of the language. In Greek, as in English, we bear down on the accented vowel of a word, stressing it quite hard, that is, forcing out the breath from our lungs with much strength. The accented vowel is pronounced more clearly and with a higher pitch than any unaccented vowel of the same word: listen, for example, to the way your Guide or the speaker on the records pronounces the word *chérete*. For those who sing: the difference between stressed and unstressed vowels is about that of a third or a fifth, that is [musical notation] or [musical notation]. The accented vowels are also longer than the unaccented ones. Thus in *ghála* the accented *á* is longer than the unaccented *a;* in *thélete* the accented *é* is somewhat longer than the unaccented *e*'s; in *archízi* the accented *í* is longer than the unaccented *a* and *i;* in *póso* the accented *ó* is longer than the unaccented *o*. But if the accent falls on the vowel of the last syllable, don't drawl out this vowel: don't make the *-í* longer than the *o* in *psomí*, nor the second *-á* longer than the first *a* in *kalá*.

Record 2A, after spiral.

PRACTICE 1

chérete	good-bye
ghála	milk
thélete	you wish
archízi	begins
póso	how much?
psomí	bread
kalá	well

2. THE GREEK VOWELS.

In the *Aids to Listening* we distinguish five Greek vowel sounds, all of which are found in English, too.

Record 2B, beginning.

Letter	Stands for a sound	PRACTICE 2	
i	close to that of *ee* in *beet* or *i* in *machine*.	*dhespinís*	miss
e	somewhat like that of *e* in *let*.	*léte*	you say
a	like that of *a* in *father*.	*patátes*	potatoes
o	about like that of *o* in *cloth* or *boss*.	*boró*	I can
u	close to that of *ou* in *group* or *u* in *truce*.	*pú*	where?

3. THE GREEK CONSONANTS.

Most of the consonant sounds of Greek are more or less like the ones we have in English. There are only four that are new:

Record 2B, after first spiral.

Letters	How to make the sound	PRACTICE 3	
ch	To get this sound, first whisper a *y*, as in *yes*. Then, holding this *y*, make your whole mouth very tense, and blow hard. Some Americans use this sound for the *h* in a word like *hue*. (Don't say *sh*, and don't say an English *ch* as in *church*.)	*óchi*	no
		échete	you have
kh	When you say the *ck* in a word like *lock* you can feel that your tongue is pressed tightly against the roof of your mouth. If you lower your tongue just enough to let a little air through, you will get the Greek *kh*. We all make this sound in clearing our throats, only we make it a lot more vigorous than the Greek *kh*.	*efkharistó*	thanks
		dhrakhmés	drachmas

gh   when you say the *g* in a word like *garden* you can feel that your tongue is pressed tightly against the roof of your mouth. If you lower your tongue just enough to let a little air through, you will get the Greek *gh*. We all make this sound in gargling, only we make it a lot more vigorous than the Greek *gh*.

sighá	slowly
févgho	I leave

r   Don't ever pronounce this like our American *r*, but make it like the *r* that Scotchmen use in words like *certainly*. Roll the tip of your tongue very fast so that it strikes your palate like an automatic drill. The sound that you get will be the basis of your Greek *r*, but only the basis, because the Greek *r* is usually made with only one tap of the tongue.

neró	water
tría	three

3. Check Yourself

Did you go through the *Useful Words and Phrases* at least twice in unison and at least once more individually?

Did you apply what you learned about the vowel and consonant sounds in *Hints on Pronunciation?*

Did you follow the pronunciation you heard even when it was different from that shown in your book?

Did you keep in mind the meaning of each word and phrase as you heard and spoke the Greek?

If you have failed at any point to carry out the instructions, go over the *Useful Words and Phrases* once again as soon as you can, being careful to follow every step in the procedure outlined.

Section C—Review of Useful Words and Phrases

If your group has time for outside assignments, sections marked *Individual Study* may be done between meetings of the group. Otherwise use them as independent study during a group meeting.

1. Covering the English (Individual Study)

Go back to the *Useful Words and Phrases* in Sections A and B. Cover up the English. Read the Greek aloud. Keep your voice down if you are working with the rest of the group. Follow your Guide's pronunciation as nearly as you can remember, and test yourself to see if you can recall the meaning of each word and phrase. Check the expressions you are not sure about and after you have gone through the whole list, uncover the English and find their meaning. Repeat this procedure at least three times or until you are satisfied that you know every expression.

2. Review of Useful Words and Phrases

To the Group Leader: Read again for your information the numbered suggestions just preceding *Useful Words and Phrases* on page 3. Your Guide has been directed in his manual to pay particular attention to the correct pronunciation of the sounds. He may ask members of the group to repeat words or phrases a good many times in an effort to get a pronunciation that is more nearly correct. See that they listen closely, that they repeat promptly and loud enough so that everyone can hear them, and that they imitate the Guide to the last detail.

Go through the *Useful Words and Phrases* in Sections A and B twice. The first time, have the members of the group repeat individually after the Guide with books open. The second time, have them close their books. The Guide will give each Greek expression twice as before. Let the students take turns giving the English equivalent the first time they hear the Guide speak the Greek and repeating the Greek as usual the second time. This will help them to check on the meaning of all Greek expressions in *Useful Words and Phrases*.

Go back to the *Useful Words and Phrases* in Sections A and B. The first time you go through the list, take turns repeating the Greek after the Guide. Keep your book open, and get all the help you can from the *Aids to Listening*. Pay particular attention to what you have learned about the pronunciation of the vowels and consonants. Make every effort to satisfy your Guide with your pronunciation.

The second time you go through the list, check up on the meaning of the Greek. Keep your books closed and take turns giving the English equivalent the first time you hear the Greek expression and repeating the Greek as usual the second time. If you have any trouble with the English, you should find time for more individual study of the *Useful Words and Phrases*, covering the English and checking up on the meaning when you read the Greek aloud.

Section D—Listening In

1. Listening In

To the Group Leader: The conversations which appear in this section will be read to the group by the Guide or played on the phonograph records. English equivalents are omitted from the *Listening In* material so that students can get practice in understanding spoken Greek which uses the vocabulary they know. Meaning, therefore, is to be emphasized.

The first time you go through the conversations, have the Guide repeat a conversation, if necessary to help clear up the meaning, before you go on to the next conversation. If you have no Guide, lift the needle of the phonograph at the end of each conversation and let the students discuss the meaning of any sentences that are not understood.

Go through the conversations a second time without stopping. Pay about equal attention to pronunciation and meaning.

Finally, assign parts and have the students read the conversations. Give everyone a chance. Suggest that the actors actually take the parts, stand up and move around, sit at a table in the restaurant, stand behind the counter in the store, etc. Keep it moving. Get everyone to speak up! Take a part yourself.

Keep your book closed while the Guide reads the following conversation and repeat after him. If you have no Guide, you should use the phonograph records, repeating the Greek immediately after you hear it. At the end of each conversation take time out to check up on the meaning of what you have heard and said. Ask someone in the group to give you the English equivalent of any expression you do not understand. Almost all the words and the expressions you have had in *Useful Words and Phrases* occur in the following conversations.

Record 2B, after second spiral.

1. Peter Smith, an American businessman, meets a lady whom he knows.

pétros:	kaliméra-sas kiría-khristofóru.	Καλημέρα σας, κυρία Χριστοφόρου.
	tí-kánete?	Τί κάνετε;
i-kiría:	kalá, efkharistó, k-esís?	Καλά, εὐχαριστῶ, κ' ἐσεῖς;
pétros:	kalá, efkharistó.	Καλά, εὐχαριστῶ.
i-kiría:	févgho-s-tis-okhtó me-to-tréno.	Φεύγω στὶς ὀχτὼ μὲ τὸ τρένο.
pétros:	tí-ípate?	Τί εἴπατε;
	dhén-gatálava.	Δὲν κατάλαβα.
	milíte-sighá parakaló.	Μιλεῖτε σιγά, παρακαλῶ.

i-kiría:	févgho-s-tis-okhtó me-to-tréno.	Φεύγω στὶς ὀχτὼ μὲ τὸ τρένο.
	katalávate?	Καταλάβατε;
pétros:	katálava polí-kala.	Κατάλαβα πολὺ καλά.
	pú-páte?	Ποῦ πᾶτε;
i-kiría:	s-ti-saloníki.	Στὴ Σαλονίκη.
pétros:	pú-in-o-stathmós?	Ποῦ εἶν' ὁ σταθμός;
i-kiría:	ine-dheksyá.	Εἶναι δεξιά.
	eláte-mazí-mu.	Ἐλᾶτε μαζί μου.

Record 2B, after third spiral.
2. Peter Smith leaves the lady and meets a gentleman in the station.

pétros:	me-sikhoríte kírie.	Μὲ συχωρεῖτε, κύριε.
	pú-ine-to-méros?	Ποῦ εἶναι τὸ μέρος;
o-kírios:	ísya-brostá.	Ἴσια μπροστά.
pétros:	efkharistó-polí.	Εὐχαριστῶ πολύ.
o-kírios:	parakaló.	Παρακαλῶ.

Record 2B, after fourth spiral.
3. Peter speaks to another gentleman.

pétros:	pú-boro-na-fáo?	Ποῦ μπορῶ νὰ φάω;
o-kírios:	ena-estiatório in-aristerá.	Ἕνα ἑστιατόριο εἶν' ἀριστερά.
pétros:	efkharistó-polí.	Εὐχαριστῶ πολύ.

Record 2B, after fifth spiral.
4. Peter Smith goes into the restaurant and converses with a waiter who knows some English.

to-pedhí:	kaliméra-sas kírie.	Καλημέρα σας, κύριε.
	tí-thélete?	Τί θέλετε;

pétros:	dhóste-mu kréaz-me-patátes.	Δώστε μου κρέας μὲ πατάτες.
	póz-léte bread eliniká?	Πῶς λέτε bread ἑλληνικά;
to-pedhí:	psomí.	Ψωμί.
pétros:	ke-psomí parakaló.	Καὶ ψωμί, παρακαλῶ.
to-pedhí:	thélete-krasí?	Θέλετε κρασί;
pétros:	óchi, dhé-thélo-krasí.	Ὄχι, δὲ θέλω κρασί.
	échete-ghála?	Ἔχετε γάλα;
to-pedhí:	dhén-ekhume-ghála.	Δὲν ἔχουμε γάλα.
	thélete-neró?	Θέλετε νερό;
pétros:	óchi, efkharistó.	Ὄχι, εὐχαριστῶ.
	dhóste-mu mya-bíra.	Δώστε μου μιὰ μπίρα.
to-pedhí:	thélete ke-kafé?	Θέλετε καὶ καφέ;
pétros:	ine-kalós-o-kafés?	Εἶναι καλὸς ὁ καφές;
to-pedhí:	málista kírie, ine-polí-kalós.	Μάλιστα, κύριε, εἶναι πολὺ καλός.
pétros:	kalá, dhóste-mu-enan-gafé.	Καλά, δώστε μου ἕναν καφέ.
	pedhí!*	Παιδί!
	échete-sigharéta ke-spírta?	Ἔχετε σιγαρέτα καὶ σπίρτα;
to-pedhí:	dhén-ékhume-sigharéta.	Δὲν ἔχουμε σιγαρέτα.
pétros:	póso-káni?	Πόσο κάνει;
to-pedhí:	penínda-dhrakhmés.	Πενήντα δραχμές.
	chérete, k-efkharistó.	Χαίρετε, κ' εὐχαριστῶ.

Record 2B, after sixth spiral.
5. After eating, Peter meets a young lady whom he knows.

pétros:	kaliméra-sas dhespinís.	Καλημέρα σας, δεσποινίς.

*On the record *dhóste-mu-enan-gafé pedhí.*

[1–D]   19

i-dhespinís:	*kaliméra-sas.*	Καλημέρα σας.
pétros:	*páme-mazí s-ton-ginimatóghrafo?*	Πάμε μαζί στὸν κινηματόγραφο;
i-dhespinís:	*málista, efkharistó-polí.*	Μάλιστα, εὐχαριστῶ πολύ.
pétros:	*tí-or-archízi-o-kinimatóghrafos?*	Τί ὥρ' ἀρχίζει ὁ κινηματόγραφος;
i-dhespinís:	*archízi s-tis-okhtó.*	Ἀρχίζει στὶς ὀχτώ.

2. Check Yourself

Is there any expression in any of these conversations that you do not understand now? If there is, find the meaning of it or ask other members of your group before you proceed. If no one knows, refer to the *Useful Words and Phrases*.

Go through the conversations once more, following the same plan as before. Imitate carefully and be sure to keep in mind the English equivalent of everything you are saying in Greek.

Finally, go through the conversations again but this time take turns. The Leader will assign parts and the exercise is to continue at least until everyone has had a chance to speak one of the parts. Keep this going as long as you have time. When your turn comes, speak clearly and with enthusiasm. Put yourself in the situation and let yourself go. If the Guide asks you to repeat, do so until he is satisfied with your pronunciation.

SECTION E—CONVERSATION

1. Covering the Greek (Individual Study)

Go back to the *Useful Words and Phrases* in Sections A and B. Cover up the Greek. Read the English silently and test yourself to see if you can speak the Greek for each word and phrase. Check the expressions you are uncertain about and after you have gone through the whole list, uncover the Greek and review them.

Go through the list once more and continue for at least three times or until you can give the Greek readily for all the expressions. To make sure of this, pick out expressions at random and see if you can speak out the Greek quickly. Speak the Greek aloud and try to imitate your Guide's pronunciation as well as you can remember it.

2. Vocabulary Check-Up

To the Group Leader: Go to the *Useful Words and Phrases* in Sections A and B. Read to the group the English equivalent of the Greek expressions. Call on different students, not in any fixed order, asking for the correct Greek for the

English. For instance, say to A, "*póz-lét-eliniká:* Where is the station?" The students are to respond with their books closed. The Guide will indicate by a negative sign whenever he hears a Greek expression that is wrong, or, if there is no Guide, the other members of the group will indicate that they do not agree. Immediately ask someone else to give the expression correctly. Any group member who has difficulty in giving the correct Greek should be told to review the *Useful Words and Phrases* thoroughly before the next meeting of the group. Do not spend any time talking about the *why* of the Greek; stick to the *how*.

There are two precautions which the Leader must observe in all exercises of this sort and in the conversation practice throughout the course. Be sure that everyone understands them. They are as follows:

1. Every Greek expression must be given smoothly and completely before the student's performance can be considered satisfactory. If there is an error in the first attempt, ask the student to give the expression over again in complete form. If he fumbles badly, turn to someone else.
2. Everyone must speak loud enough, so that all can hear. Every student should be encouraged to call out "Louder, please!" if he can't hear. Check on this occasionally by pointing to the student who is listening to someone else's Greek, and ask "What did he say?"

If you do not observe these precautions, much time and effort may be wasted in group meetings.

In this Section you are going to have your first chance to engage in conversation in Greek. This, of course, is the most useful part of the entire Unit, and the part you should do with the greatest amount of pep and realism. Do it half-heartedly and you lose most of the value of the Unit. Do it earnestly and enthusiastically and you will find that you can readily say a great number of things in Greek, fluently and correctly. Read the instructions carefully, get everything you are to do straight in your mind, and then plunge in.

In order to fix in your mind the expressions you will need in the conversation, check yourself on your ability to speak the Greek you have learned. By now you should not have to grope for it. The Leader of the group will ask you to supply in turn the Greek expressions for the English equivalents which he reads from the *Useful Words and Phrases*. If you have done a thorough job of recalling the Greek when you are looking only at the English equivalents, as suggested in Section E, you will have no difficulty in responding promptly and smoothly when you hear the English. Your Guide will let you know if your Greek expressions are not correct. If you have no Guide, the members of the group should be ready to correct faulty expressions.

3. Conversation

To the Group Leader: Read the following directions with the class. Encourage the students to strike out for themselves. Spend all the time you can on free conversation practice in an effort to get to the point where students can speak easily and smoothly with a minimum of *ums* and *ers*.

The Leader will assign parts and will ask you to take turns in pairs, carrying on the following conversations. The two persons who are talking together should stand up and act out their parts, speaking as smoothly and naturally as possible. Make it real and get some fun out of it. The Guide will help you if your Greek is wrong or if your pronunciation is bad. The Leader will prompt you if you are not sure what comes next in your part.

1. Getting Directions

A approaches a stranger, B, and asks him for information.

1. A apologizes for speaking to B and asks him where there is (*a*) a restaurant (*b*) the railroad station or (*c*) a hotel.
2. B gives A directions (*a*) to the right (*b*) to the left or (*c*) straight ahead.
3. A apologizes again, explains that he did not understand, and asks B if he will please speak slowly.
4. B repeats slowly and clearly and asks A if he understood.
5. A says that he did understand and thanks B.
6. B says that A is welcome.
7. A again thanks B and says good-bye.
8. B says good-bye.

2. At a Restaurant

C sits down at a table in a restaurant and is waited on by D.

1. D says (*a*) good morning or (*b*) good evening to C and asks how C is.
2. C says he is well, thanks, and asks after D's health.
3. D is also well and asks what C would like.
4. C orders a meal—meat, potatoes, bread, water, milk, coffee—whatever he would like.
5. After eating, C asks how much it is.
6. D tells C that it is fifty drachmas.
7. D thanks C.
8. C says good-bye to D.
9. D says good-bye to C.

If it is so desired, particularly when the group is too large to give everybody a chance to participate in the conversation, the exercise should be continued for a longer time. It is also a good practice to give people who are having difficulties a second trial.

SECTION F—CONVERSATION (*Cont.*)

To the Group Leader: You can tell from the work that you did on conversation in Section E, whether or not the group needs to spend more time in preparing for successful conversation. If necessary, spend the first part of this Section in individual study, having members of the group say the Greek of the *Useful Words and Phrases* when they have the English expression covered. Check up on their vocabulary as in Section E. Then continue the work with conversation which you started in Section E.

In this Section you are to continue taking part in conversation. If the work didn't go well in Section E, take time to go through the *Useful Words and Phrases* again with the English covered and to give the Greek of the English expressions as your Leader asks for it.

Put everything you can into the conversations. Act your part; don't hesitate to talk for fear of making a mistake. You'll make plenty of mistakes at first, but the important thing is to practice talking. You can't correct an error until you have made it.

Try out your Greek whenever you get a chance. Don't wait for meetings of the group to practice what you have learned. Pair off between meetings and see what you can do with Greek greetings and conversation. When you are alone, run over the list of Greek expressions you know. Review them in your mind. Try saying them. See how much you can improve your pronunciation and control of the language in whatever time you can find between meetings of the group. Make this a regular practice throughout the course.

FINDER LIST

This is a complete alphabetical list of all the words and expressions used in this Unit. The conventional spelling is given in the middle column. This list is for reference only, but you should know all of these before going on to the next Unit.

Abbreviations: *m.* masculine   *s.* singular
                f. feminine   *p.* plural
                n. neuter

A

aftó n.	αὐτό	this; that
archízi	ἀρχίζει	begins; starts
aristerá	ἀριστερά	to the left

B

i bíra	ἡ μπίρα	beer
boró	μπορῶ	I can
brostá see: *ísya-brostá*		

C

chérete	χαίρετε	hello; good-bye

D

dhé see: *dhén*		
dhéka	δέκα	ten
dheksyá	δεξιά	to the right
dhén, dhé	δὲν, δὲ	not
i dhespinís	ἡ δεσποινίς	young lady; miss
dhespinís-khristofóru	δεσποινὶς Χριστοφόρου	Miss Christophorou!
i-dhespinís-khristofóru	ἡ δεσποινὶς Χριστοφόρου	Miss Christophorou
dhío	δύο	two
dhóste	δῶστε	give!
see: *mu*		
dhrakhmés f.p.	δραχμές	drachmas

E

échete	ἔχετε	you have
ékhume	ἔχουμε	we have
efkharistó	εὐχαριστῶ	I thank; thanks
eftá	ἐφτά	seven
ékhume see: *échete*		

éksi	ἕξι	six
eláte	ἐλᾶτε	come!
eliniká	ἑλληνικά	in Greek
éna	ἕνα	one
ena n.	ἕνα	⎫
enan m.	ἕναν	⎬ a
mya f.	μιά	⎭
enan see: *éna*		
enyá	ἐννιά	nine
esís	ἐσεῖς	you
to *estiatório*	τὸ ἐστιατόριο	restaurant

F

fáo		
na-fáo	νὰ φάω	that I eat
févgho	φεύγω	I leave

G

gafé see: *kafés*		
gatálava see: *katálava*		
to *ghála*	τὸ γάλα	milk
ginimatóghrafo see: *kinimatóghrafos*		

I

i see: *o*		
in see: *íne*		
íne, in, n	εἶναι, εἶν'	(he, she, it) is; (they) are; there is

ípate	εἴπατε	you said
isya-brostá	ἴσια μπροστά	straight ahead

K

k see: *ke*		
kafé see: *kafés*		
o *kafés*	ὁ καφές	coffee
kafé, gafé	καφέ	
kalá	καλά	well; all right
polí-kala	πολὺ καλά	very well
kaliméra-sas	καλημέρα σας	good morning; good afternoon
kaliníkhta-sas	καληνύχτα σας	good night
kalispéra-sas	καλησπέρα σας	good evening
kalós m.s.	καλός	good
kánete	κάνετε	you do
káni	κάνει	makes
póso-káni?	πόσο κάνει;	how much is it?
see: *tí*		
káni see: *kánete*		
katálava	κατάλαβα	I understood
dhén-gatálava	δὲν κατάλαβα	I did not understand
katalávate?	καταλάβατε;	did you understand?
katalávate see: *katálava*		
ke, k	καὶ, κ'	and; also; too
khristofóru	Χριστοφόρου	Christophorou (*family name*)

o kinimatóghrafos	ὁ κινηματόγραφος	movies; movie theater
ginimatóghrafo		
i kiría	ἡ κυρία	lady; madam; Mrs.
kiría-khristofóru	κυρία Χριστοφόρου	Mrs. Christophorou!
i-kiría-khristofóru	ἡ κυρία Χριστοφόρου	Mrs. Christophorou
kírie see: kírios		
o kírios	ὁ κύριος	gentleman; Mr.
o-kírios-khristofóru	ὁ κύριος Χριστοφόρου	Mr. Christophorou
kírie	κύριε	sir!
kírie-khristofóru	κύριε Χριστοφόρου	Mr. Christophorou!
to krasí	τὸ κρασί	wine
to kréas, kréaz	τὸ κρέας	meat
kréaz see: kréas		
to ksenodhochío	τὸ ξενοδοχεῖο	hotel

L

léte	λέτε	you say

M

málista	μάλιστα	yes (*polite*)
mazí	μαζί	together
mazí-mu	μαζί μου	with me
me	μὲ	me
me	μὲ	with; by
me-patátes	μὲ πατάτες	with potatoes
me-to-tréno	μὲ τὸ τρένο	by train

to méros	τὸ μέρος	toilet
mía	μία	one o'clock
milíte	μιλεῖτε	speak!
mu	μου	to me
dhóste-mu	δώστε μου	give me!
mazí-mu	μαζί μου	with me
mya see: éna		

N

n see: íne		
na	νὰ	(so) that
né	ναί	yes
to neró	τὸ νερό	water

O

o m.s.	ὁ	
ton m.s.	τὸν	
i f.s.	ἡ	
ti f.s.	τὴ	the
tis f.p.	τὶs	
to n.s.	τὸ	
óchi	ὄχι	no
okhtó	ὀχτώ	eight
or see: óra		
i óra, or	ἡ ὥρα, ὥρ'	hour; time

P

páme	πάμε	we go; let's go
páte	πάτε	you go

parakaló	παρακαλῶ	I beg; please; you are welcome
patátes **f.p.**	πατάτες	potatoes
páte see: *páme*		
to *pedhí*	τὸ παιδί	child; boy; waiter
pedhí!	παιδί!	waiter!
pénde	πέντε	five
penínda	πενήντα	fifty
o *pétros*	ὁ Πέτρος	Peter
polí	πολύ	very; much; very much
see: *kalá*		
pós, póz	πῶs	how?
póso	πόσο	how much?
see: *kánete*		
póz see: *pós*		
to *psomí*	τὸ ψωμί	bread
pú	ποῦ	where?
pyó		
na-pyó	νὰ πιῶ	that I drink

S

s	σ'	to; at
s-ti-saloníki	στὴ Σαλονίκη	to Salonica
s-ton-ginimatóghrafo	στὸν κινηματόγραφο	to the movies
s-tis-enyá	στὶs ἐννιά	at nine
i *saloníki*	ἡ Σαλονίκη	Salonica (*port-city in northern Greece*)
sas	σᾶs	you

[1–F]   29

see: *kaliméra-sas*,
    kalispéra-sas,
    kalinikhta-sas

sighá	σιγά	slowly
sigharéta n.p.	σιγαρέτα	cigarettes
sikhoríte	συχωρεῖτε	you excuse
me-sikhoríte	μὲ συχωρεῖτε	excuse me!
spírta n.p.	σπίρτα	matches
o *stathmós*	ὁ σταθμός	station

T

tésera	τέσσερα	four
thélete see: *thélo*		
thélo	θέλω	I wish; I want
thélete	θέλετε	you wish; you want
tí	τί	what?
tí-kánete?	τί κάνετε;	what are you doing? how are you?
ti see: *o*		
tis see: *o*		
to see: *o*		
ton see: *o*		
to *tréno*	τὸ τρένο	train
tría	τρία	three

V

to *vrádhi*	τὸ βράδυ	evening
to-vrádhi	τὸ βράδυ	in the evening; tonight

UNIT 2

MEETING PEOPLE

Section A—Basic Sentences

To the Group Leader: Adopt the following steps as a standard practice in conducting this course:
1. Before each meeting of the group, be sure to read carefully and get clearly in mind the instructions covering those sections of a Unit which you expect to take up in the group meeting.
2. Before each group meeting, see that the Guide is available with his Ὁδηγίες γιὰ τὸν Ὁδηγό or that phonograph and records are ready.
3. Have the members of the group read together the instructions that precede each piece of work they are to do before they begin it. Let one member of the group read these instructions aloud while the others follow the reading in their books.
4. Take time, following the reading of all instructions, to make sure that everyone understands exactly what he is to do.

In Section A of Unit 2 follow the same procedure as that outlined for *Useful Words and Phrases* of Section A in Unit 1. Go through the *Basic Sentences* once with everyone repeating in unison after the Guide or phonograph record. Then take up the *Hints on Pronunciation* which follow. Come back to the *Basic Sentences* and go through them once more, with repetitions in unison after the Guide. Pay particular attention to those items of pronunciation you have been working on. Finally, go through the *Basic Sentences* a third time with solo repetition. The Guide will call for as many repetitions as may be necessary to get a pronunciation that sounds to him like Greek.

Make everyone speak loudly and clearly. Keep the work moving. Don't let it drag.

Begin this Section by listening, in the manner already outlined in Section A of the preceding Unit, to the *Basic Sentences* which follow. Be sure to keep in mind the meaning of the Greek by reading silently the English equivalent. As you listen to the Greek, keep your eye on the *Aids to Listening*. This will help you imitate accurately the pronunciation you are hearing. Repeat each word and phrase loudly and clearly right after you hear it. As you pronounce the Greek, do so as though you really meant what you are saying. Do not forget that these words and phrases convey a real meaning and it is up to you to say them as though you were actually using them. Go through the sentences in unison and with your book open.

The *Basic Sentences* are set up as conversations so that you may hear and speak the Greek as you would hear and speak it if you were talking with Greek people.

Although numerous characters are introduced in these *Basic Sentences*, it is not important for you to try to keep in mind just who they are or their relationship to one another. You are concerned rather with *what* they say and *how* they say it.

1. Basic Sentences

Record 3A, beginning.

John Cook, an American sailor, accompanied by Mr. and Mrs. Bourboulis and their little boy, meets another couple, Mr. and Mrs. Adamantiou, and their grown-up daughter Phroso, with whom he is already acquainted.

ENGLISH EQUIVALENTS	AIDS TO LISTENING	CONVENTIONAL SPELLING
Mr. A.		
I am	íme	εἶμαι
I'm Mr. Adamantiou.	im-o-kírios-adhamandíu.	Εἶμ' ὁ κύριος 'Αδαμαντίου.
John		
they call me	me-léne	μὲ λένε
My name is Cook.	me-léne-Cook.	Μὲ λένε Cook.
Mr. A.		
you are	íste	εἶστε
friend	fílos	φίλος
of John Kladas	tu-yáni-tu-kladhá	τοῦ Γιάννη τοῦ Κλαδᾶ
You're a friend of John Kladas?	iste-fílos tu-yáni-tu-kladhá?	Εἶστε φίλος τοῦ Γιάννη τοῦ Κλαδᾶ;
John		
of George	tu-yórghu	τοῦ Γιώργου
No, I'm a friend of George [Kladas].	óchi, ime-fílos tu-yórghu.	Ὄχι, εἶμαι φίλος τοῦ Γιώργου.

Mrs. A.		
has	échi	ἔχει
brother	adherfó	ἀδερφό
John Kladas	o-yánis-o-kladhás	ὁ Γιάννης ὁ Κλαδᾶς
Does John Kladas have a brother?	echi-adherfó o-yánis-o-kladhás?	Ἔχει ἀδερφὸ ὁ Γιάννης ὁ Κλαδᾶς;
we know	ksérume	ξέρουμε
Do we know him?	tone-ksérume?	Τόνε ξέρουμε;
Mr. A.		
Of course, George.	né, to-yórgho.	Ναί, τὸ Γιώργο.
knows	kséri	ξέρει
He knows us.	mas-kséri.	Μᾶς ξέρει.
John		
that I present to you	na-sas-parusiáso	νὰ σᾶς παρουσιάσω
Mr.	ton-gírio	τὸν κύριο
Mrs. Bourboulis	tin-giría-burbúli	τὴν κυρία Μπουρμπούλη
May I present (to you) Mr. and Mrs. Bourboulis?	boró-na-sas-parusiáso ton-gírio ke-tin-giría-burbúli?	Μπορῶ νὰ σᾶς παρουσιάσω τὸν κύριο καὶ τὴν κυρία Μπουρμπούλη;
I	eghó	ἐγώ
we are	ímaste	εἴμαστε
friends	fíli	φίλοι
Bourboulis and I are friends.	eghó ky-o-burbúlis imaste-fíli.	Ἐγὼ κι ὁ Μπουρμπούλης εἴμαστε φίλοι.

[2–A]

Mr. A.		
I am very glad	chéro-polí	χαίρω πολύ
my lady!	kiría-mu	κυρία μου
Glad to meet you, madam.	chéro-polí kiría-mu.	Χαίρω πολύ, κυρία μου.
Mrs. A.		
extremely	párapoli.	πάρα πολύ
Delighted:	chéro párapoli.	Χαίρω πάρα πολύ.
a brother	enas-adherfós	ἕνας ἀδερφός
of my father	tu-patéra-mu	τοῦ πατέρα μου
is married	ine-pandreménos	εἶναι παντρεμένος
One of my father's brothers is married to a Bourboulis—	enas-adherfós tu-patéra-mu ine-pandreménos me-mya-burbúli—	Ἕνας ἀδερφὸς τοῦ πατέρα μου εἶναι παντρεμένος μὲ μιὰ Μπουρμπούλη —

Record 3B, beginning.

you know her	tine-ksérete	τήνε ξέρετε
(to) Mary, do you know her?	me-ti-maría, tine-ksérete?	Μὲ τὴ Μαρία, τήνε ξέρετε;
Mr. B.		
I'm very sorry.	lipúme-polí.	Λυποῦμαι πολύ.
I know	kséro	ξέρω
I don't know her.	dhén-dine-kséro.	Δὲν τήνε ξέρω.
Mrs. A.		
this (the) little fellow	aftós-o-mikrós	αὐτὸς ὁ μικρός
who?	pyós	ποιός
And who is this little fellow?	ky-aftós-o-mikrós pyós-íne?	Κι αὐτὸς ὁ μικρὸς ποιὸς εἶναι;

John		
the son	o-yós	ὁ γιός
of Mr. and Mrs.	tu-kiríu ke-tis-kirías	τοῦ κυρίου καὶ τῆς κυρίας
He's the son of Mr. and Mrs. Bourboulis.	in-o-yós tu-kiríu ke-tis-kirías-burbúli.	Εἶν' ὁ γιὸς τοῦ κυρίου καὶ τῆς κυρίας Μπουρμπούλη.
Mr. B.		
like my father	san-dom-batéra-mu	σὰν τὸν πατέρα μου
His name is Peter, like my father.	tone-léne-pétro san-dom-batéra-mu.	Τόνε λένε Πέτρο, σὰν τὸν πατέρα μου.
Mrs. A.		
daughter	kóri	κόρη
Have you a daughter, Mrs. Bourboulis?	échete-kóri kiría-burbúli?	Ἔχετε κόρη, κυρία Μπουρμπούλη;
Mrs. B.		
only	móno	μόνο
the son	to-yó	τὸ γιό
No, I have only one child, my son Peter.	óchi, ékho-éna-pedhí-móno to-yó-mu tom-bétro.	Ὄχι, ἔχω ἕνα παιδὶ μόνο, τὸ γιό μου τὸν Πέτρο.
your daughter	tin-góri-sas	τὴν κόρη σας
And what's your daughter's name?	ke-tin-góri-sas pós-tine-léne?	Καὶ τὴν κόρη σας πῶς τήνε λένε;
Mrs. A.		
Her name is Phroso.	tine-léne-fróso.	Τήνε λένε Φρόσω.
John		
pretty	nóstimo	νόστιμο
girl	korítsi	κορίτσι
She's a pretty girl.	ine-nóstimo-korítsi.	Εἶναι νόστιμο κορίτσι.

[2–A]

Mrs. A.
you	esás	ἐσᾶς
And what's *your* name?	k-esás pó-saz-léne?	Κ' ἐσᾶς, πῶς σᾶς λένε;

John
the name	t-ónoma	τ' ὄνομα
my name	t-onomá-mu	τ' ὄνομά μου
In Greek my name is Giannes.	eliniká t-onomá-mu ine-yánis.	Ἑλληνικά τ' ὄνομά μου εἶναι Γιάννης.

Mrs. A.
the father	o-patéras	ὁ πατέρας
the mother	i-mitéra	ἡ μητέρα
they live	zúne	ζοῦνε
still	akóma	ἀκόμα
Are your father and mother still living?	o-patéra-sas k-i-mitéra-sas zún-akóma?	Ὁ πατέρας σας κ' ἡ μητέρα σας ζοῦν ἀκόμα;

John
Yes, they're [still] living.	málista, zúne.	Μάλιστα, ζοῦνε.

Record 4A, beginning.

sister	adherfí	ἀδερφή
I have a brother and a sister, too.	ékho k-enan-adherfó ke-mya-adherfí.	Ἔχω κ' ἕναν ἀδερφὸ καὶ μιὰ ἀδερφή.

Phroso
who?	pyí	ποιοί
those	aftí	αὐτοί
there	ekí	ἐκεῖ
over there	eki-péra	ἐκεῖ πέρα
Who are those [people] over there?	pyí-n-aftí-eki-péra?	Ποιοὶ εἶν' αὐτοὶ ἐκεῖ πέρα;

Do they know you?	sas-ksérune?	Σᾶς ξέρουνε;

Mr. B.

that (the) lady	aftí-i-kiría	αὐτὴ ἡ κυρία
That man and woman?	aftós-o-kírios ky-aftí-i-kiría?	Αὐτὸς ὁ κύριος κι αὐτὴ ἡ κυρία;
George	o-yórghos	ὁ Γιώργος
with his wife	me-ti-yinéka-tu	μὲ τὴ γυναῖκα του
It's George Christophorou with his wife.	in-o-yórghos-o-khristofóru me-ti-yinéka-tu.	Εἶν' ὁ Γιώργος ὁ Χριστοφόρου μὲ τὴ γυναῖκα του.
I know them very well.	tus-kséro polí-kala.	Τοὺς ξέρω πολὺ καλά.
they have	ékhune	ἔχουνε
children	pedhyá	παιδιά
They have ten children.	ékhune-dhéka-pedhyá.	Ἔχουνε δέκα παιδιά.

Mrs. A.

but it leaves	ma-févyi	μὰ φεύγει
the car	t-aftokínito	τ' αὐτοκίνητο
our car	t-aftokínitó-mas	τ' αὐτοκίνητό μας
Excuse me, but our bus is leaving.	me-sikhoríte, ma-févyi-t-aftokínitó-mas.	Μὲ συχωρεῖτε, μὰ φεύγει τ' αὐτοκίνητό μας.
(Very) glad to have met you.	khárika-polí.	Χάρηκα πολύ.

Mr. B.

gentlemen and ladies	kírii ke-kiríes	κύριοι καὶ κυρίες
Good-bye, everybody!	kírii ke-kiríes, chérete.	Κύριοι καὶ κυρίες, χαίρετε.

Before you go through the *Basic Sentences* a second time, study the following:

2. Hints on Pronunciation

To the Group Leader: The explanations presented in each Section should be read by the group and discussed after the *Practice*. The practice for *Hints on Pronunciation* is in the Guide's Manual and on the phonograph records. Follow the same procedure in working with the practice material that you have followed with the *Basic Sentences*. Go through as many times as may be necessary to give each member of the group reasonable control of the item of pronunciation that is being taught. Have the group repeat after the Guide, first in unison, then individually.

1. THE VOWELS IN COMBINATIONS OF WORDS.

(a) You will have noticed that many Greek words end in a vowel, e.g. *óra* 'hour', *ke* 'and', *to* 'the'. Now let's study these phrases or sentences:

Record 4A, after first spiral.
PRACTICE 1

ti-or-archízi?	What time does it start?
k-esís?	And you?
t-onomá-mu	my name

Notice what has happened to those words mentioned above: *óra* is *ór; ke* and *to* are just the sounds *k*, *t*. As you have seen, *óra* was followed by *archízi*, *ke* by *esís*, *to* by *ónoma*. All these words, then, end with just that vowel with which the following word begins: *óra* ends with *a*, and the following word *archízi* begins with *a*, etc. In easy and rapid speech, when words are run together, two identical vowels are often pronounced as if they were only *one*.

(b) Now let's study the following phrases:

Record 4A, after second spiral.
PRACTICE 2

pyi-n-aftí?	Who are those [people]?
t-aftokínito	the car

Here we have *n* instead of *ine*, and *t* instead of *to;* but the following words do not begin (as in the preceding section) with identical vowels but with a different one, namely with *a*. You will remember that in the *Hints on Pronunciation* in Unit 1 we listed the five vowels of Greek: *i, e, a, o, u*. Now if it happens that of two words which run together the first ends with a vowel different from that with which the second one begins, we often pronounce only one of them. Generally one may say the following: if one of the vowels is *a*, it prevails over any other vowel, that is, over *o* or *u* or *e* or *i*; if it is *o*, it prevails over *u* or *e* or *i*; if it is *u*, it prevails over *e* or *i*; finally, *e* is stronger than *i*.

(c) Now, what we are presenting to you are only hints, not rules, and the pronunciation or omission of vowels in such combinations of words is up to the native speaker. He may or may not pronounce them. Don't argue as to why we pronounce one *i* sound in *tí-n-aftó*, but pronounce two *i* sounds in *tí-ípate*. And don't be surprised if in the *Aids to Listening* you find *pú-ine*, while, after what we have said, you expect *pú-ne*, which is also right. Listen carefully to your Guide or to the phonograph records, and repeat after them.

2. THE SOUND *s* IN COMBINATIONS OF WORDS.

(a) We have just seen what happens to two words which run together in a sentence, and of which the first ends and the second begins with a vowel. Now let's see what happens if a word ending with an *s* runs together with another word. Compare carefully the following words or sentences:

Record 4A, after third spiral.
PRACTICE 3

tis-kirías-khristofóru	of Mrs. Christophorou
o-yós-tu	his son
dhóste-mu-kréas.	Give me some meat.
tus-kséro.	I know them.

tis-kiríaz-burbúli	of Mrs. Bourboulis
o-yóz-mu	my son
kréaz-me-patátes	meat and potatoes
pós-tuz-léne?	What are their names?

The Greek word for 'lady's' is *kirías*, for 'son' *yós*, for 'meat' *kréas*, for 'them' *tus*. The *s* of these words remains intact in the phrases to the left, but becomes *z* in the phrases to the right. The words to the right before which the *s* becomes *z* begin, as you see, with a *b*, an *m*, and an *l*. Whenever in speech two words run together of which the one ends with *s* and the following begins with *b*, *v*, *d*, *dh*, *g*, *gh*, *y*, *m*, *n*, *l*, or *r*, the *s* becomes *z*. In these cases you get the same effect as, for example, in English in the middle of the words *husband*, *cosmetic*, *Desdemona*, and so on. Before all other consonants (except *s*) and before vowels, on the other hand, *s* remains unchanged.

(b) Here are some other expressions you have learned in the *Basic Sentences*:

Record 4A, after fourth spiral.

PRACTICE 4

pós-tine-léne?	What's her name?	*pó-saz-léne?*	What's your name?
o-patéras-tu	his father	*o-patéra-sas*	your father

The Greek word for 'how?' is *pós*, for 'father' *patéras*. You see that in the examples to the right these two words are heard as *pó* and *patéra*. The reason for this is that in these expressions the two words which end with an *s* run together with words which begin with an *s*. Now, Greek has an absolute *horror of long consonants*. If two *s* sounds come into contact through combination of words, one of them is simply lost.

If you are uncertain about any of the points of pronunciation which have been discussed, ask your Guide to repeat the words and phrases with which you are having trouble, and try to improve your pronunciation. Remember that these notes are only approximate and are at best an imperfect description of the sounds.

When you are satisfied that you can pronounce fairly well all the sounds, go through the *Basic Sentences* once more in unison and with your book open. As you repeat after your Guide, keep your eye on the *Aids to Listening*, and note in particular the examples of the sounds discussed. Do not hesitate to ask your Guide to repeat if you are uncertain about any sound.

Finally go through the *Basic Sentences* again, this time taking turns. Keep your book closed, listen carefully to your Guide, and make sure that your pronunciation satisfies him.

3. Check Yourself

Did you go through the *Basic Sentences* at least twice with your book open and then at least once with your book closed?

Did you repeat each word and phrase immediately after hearing it in a loud, clear voice?

Did you follow the pronunciation you heard even if it seemed different from that shown in your book?

Did you keep in mind the meaning of each word and phrase as you heard and spoke the Greek?

If your Guide asked you to repeat, did you do so with enthusiasm and as many times as necessary until he was satisfied with what you were saying?

Section B—Word Study and Review of Basic Sentences

1. Word Study (Individual Study)

If your group has time for outside assignments, do the *Word Study* between meetings of the group. Otherwise make it independent study in the group meeting.

In this Section we take up some of the words and expressions you have just learned and examine them to see how the language is built. First read the words and expressions in each list and make sure that you understand the meaning of the Greek. Then read the comment which follows each list. This should make clear to you just how the words function and how they are put together. If there are any points that are not clear to you, make note of them and ask other members of the group about them. Follow the same procedure with each list and each comment.

COMMENT 1

THE THREE KINDS OF GREEK NOUNS. Look at these words:

o-kírios	the gentleman
i-kiría	the lady
to-ksenodhochío	the hotel

In English we use the little modifying word *the* with all nouns: we say '*the* gentleman', '*the* lady', '*the* hotel'. But we have different words to refer to these nouns: we say *he* if we are referring to a gentleman, we say *she* if we are referring to a lady, and we say *it* if we are referring to a hotel. In Greek we have the same kind of differentiation in the word for 'the' as well: you say *o-kírios* 'the gentleman', *i-kiría* 'the lady', and *to-ksenodhochío* 'the hotel'. From these examples you can see that instead of the plain English *the* (or *definite article*), the Greek has three different words (or forms of the definite article) to put in front of a noun: *o*, *i*, and *to*. The nouns with which *o* is used are called *masculine*, those with which *i* is used are called *feminine*, and those with which *to* is used are called *neuter*, just to have convenient labels for the three kinds of nouns. Now it is easy to understand that a gentleman is a *he* (or male being), a lady a *she* (or female being) and a hotel an *it* (that is, a thing that has no sex), and to use accordingly the corresponding article before each noun. But you will surely have noticed that there are other nouns in Greek which are, without any relation to natural sex, either masculine, or feminine, or neuter, as *o-stathmós* 'the station', *i-óra* 'the hour', *to-tréno* 'the train'. You have probably observed that all nouns entered in the *Finder List* have *o*, *i*, or *to* in front of them. What you will have to do is to remember that the word for 'station' is not *stathmós*, but that it is *o-stathmós*, etc. Always learn new nouns this way.

COMMENT 2

"A" CHILD AND "ONE" CHILD. Look at the following expressions:

enas-adherfós	a brother
mya-bíra	a beer
ena-pedhí	a child

As you see, the nouns are preceded by the words *enas, mya, ena,* respectively. These words correspond to the English *a* (or *indefinite article*). Now we have seen that the definite article appears as *o, i, to* according to the *gender* (masculine, feminine, or neuter) that a noun has. The same holds true with the indefinite article: you say *enas* before a masculine noun, *mya* before a feminine noun, and *ena* before a neuter noun. Now look at these examples you have already heard:

pú-in-ena-estiatório?   *ékho éna-pedhí-móno.*
Where is there a restaurant?   I have only one child.

You see that in the sentence on the left *ena* is unstressed and means 'a', whereas in the sentence on the right *éna* is stressed and means 'one'. In other words, *enas, mya, ena* is the indefinite article 'a', and *énas, myá, éna* is the numeral 'one'.

SUMMARY:

enas-adherfós	a brother	*énas-adherfós*	one brother
mya-bíra	a beer	*myá-bíra*	one beer
ena-pedhí	a child	*éna-pedhí*	one child

The forms given in this lesson are not the total number of forms that Greek has for 'the' or 'a'. More forms will be taken up in the next Unit to complete the picture.

COMMENT 3

SINGULAR AND PLURAL. You have heard forms such as the following:

fílos	friend (male)	*fíli*	friends
kírios	gentleman	*kírii*	gentlemen
kiría	lady	*kiríes*	ladies
pedhí	child	*pedhyá*	children

Like English, Greek has two *numbers:* the *singular* when referring to one object, and the *plural* when referring to more than one.

COMMENT 4

ABOUT VERBS.

(a) Words like 'know', 'want', 'go' are called **verbs**. Notice how they behave in English:

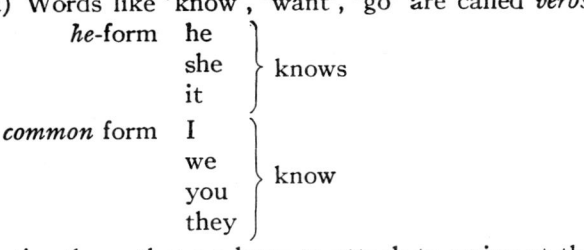

he-form: he, she, it } knows

common form: I, we, you, they } know

Notice the *-s* that we have to attach to arrive at the *he*-form; such a thing is called an *ending*.

Now notice how Greek verbs behave:

ksér*O*	I know
ksér*ETE*	you know
ksér*I*	he, she, it knows
ksér*UME*	we know
ksér*UNE*	they know

As you can see, where English has only two different forms, Greek has five. The differences consist in the endings. They are tacked onto what is called the *stem* of the verb. Thus we have the stem *kser-* plus the endings *-o, -ete, -i, -ume, -une*. When you compare these two verbs, the English one and the Greek one, you see that there is one fundamental difference between the two languages: when we have in English a word like 'know', we have to add 'I' or 'we' or 'you' or 'they' according to what we wish to say. In Greek we generally do not add the Greek equivalents of these words; but we express the same idea by means of endings. For example, the idea of 'I' in 'I know' is expressed in Greek by the ending *-o* in *kséro*; the idea of 'we' in 'we know' is expressed in Greek by the ending *-ume* in *ksérume*.

Many Greek verbs behave like *kséro*, e.g.

thélo	I want	*káno*	I do	*archízo*	I begin
thélete	you want	*kánete*	you do	*archízete*	you begin
théli	he wants	*káni*	he does	*archízi*	he begins
thélume	we want	*kánume*	we do	*archízume*	we begin
thélune	they want	*kánune*	they do	*archízune*	they begin

The stem of *thélo* is, as you see, *thel-*; that of *káno*, *kan-*; that of *archízo*, *archiz-*. The only peculiarities that some of these verbs have are things like the following:

févgho	I leave	*ékho*	I have
févyete	you leave	*échete*	you have
févyi	he leaves	*échi*	he has
févghume	we leave	*ékhume*	we have
févghune	they leave	*ékhune*	they have

Notice that you get *févgho, févghume, févghune* with a *gh*, but *févyete, févyi* with a *y;* and *ékho, ékhume, ékhune* with a *kh*, but *échete, échi* with a *ch*. All verbs whose stems end in *gh* or *kh* do this, that is, they change the *gh* to *y* and the *kh* to *ch* before *e* and *i*.

Now look again at the *first person* (the *I*-form) of the verbs mentioned; it is: *kséro, thélo, káno, archízo, févgho, ékho*. Notice that whether they have two or three (or more) syllables *they always bear the accent on the next to the last syllable.* Notice furthermore that their stems end in a *consonant*. These verbs form a special group in Greek. As we proceed we shall have more of them which behave in the same way.

(b) But there are also other verbs in Greek which bear the accent on the next to the last syllable, with the difference, however, that their stems end in a *vowel*. They behave a little differently from the others. We have had in the *Basic Sentences* a few forms of two of them.

	'go'	'say; call'
you-form	*páTE*	*léTE*
we-form	*páME*	
they-form		*léNE*

The stem of the first verb is *pa-*, that of the second *le-*, and those forms you learned have, as you see, the endings *-te* for the *you*-form, *-me* for the *we*-form, and *-ne* for the *they*-form. The *I*-form ends in *-o* and the *he*-form in *-i* as in the verbs of the type *kséro*. This, then, is the whole set:

páo	I go	*léo*	I say
páte	you go	*léte*	you say
pái	he goes	*léi*	he says
páme	we go	*léme*	we say
páne	they go	*léne*	they say

(c) Not all English verbs behave like 'know'. For instance, the verb 'be' has completely irregular forms: 'am', 'is', 'are'. Notice how the corresponding word behaves in Greek:

íme	I am
íste	you are
íne	he is
ímaste	we are
íne	they are

From now on, all verbs that you are able to handle will be registered in the *Finder List* in the *I*-form (or *first person*). So if you have a word like *kánume*, and you recognize from the ending that it is a *we*-form, but you don't know what it means, you must look it up under *káno*.

2. Covering English and Greek of Word Study

Read aloud several times the examples given you in the *Word Study*. Then cover the English and see if you know the meaning of every item. Repeat the operation until you are sure that you know every expression. As a final test, cover the Greek and see if you can speak out the Greek expressions by simply looking at the English.

3. Review of Basic Sentences

Review the first half of the *Basic Sentences* with your Guide or the phonograph record. Go through them as many times as you can, taking turns repeating the Greek individually. Try it with books closed and see how you get along without the help of the *Aids to Listening*. Always keep in mind the meaning of the Greek you are hearing and speaking. As you go through the *Basic Sentences* be on the lookout for examples of the points in the *Word Study* you have just covered.

SECTION C—REVIEW OF BASIC SENTENCES (*Cont.*)

1. Review of Basic Sentences (*Cont.*)

Review the second half of the *Basic Sentences* with your Guide or the phonograph record. For the detailed procedure to be followed read again the instructions for the review of the first half of the *Basic Sentences*.

2. Covering the English of Basic Sentences (Individual Study)

Here is your chance to find out just how well you have learned the meaning of the Greek expressions you have had up to this point. Go back to the *Basic Sentences* in Section A and cover the English. Read the Greek aloud and see whether you can supply the English equivalents of the words and phrases. Mark those you are not sure about and after reading the list through, uncover the English and look up their meaning. Cover the English again and repeat the procedure until you can go through the entire list giving all the meanings without difficulty.

3. What Would You Say?

For each of the following situations, four Greek sentences are given. All four of the sentences make perfectly good sense and are written in correct Greek, but only one of them fits the situation. Read all four of them out loud and pick out the one that fits the situation. Be sure you know why the other choices are not suitable. At the next meeting of the group you will be asked to say what you have chosen, and you will have a chance to test your answers. Do not write anything down.

1. You meet Mr. Kladas one morning. You say:
   a. *kaliméra-sas dhespinís.*
   b. *kírii, kaliméra-sas.*
   c. *kaliméra-sas kiría-mu.*
   d. *kaliméra-sas kírie-kladhá.*

2. There is a little boy with Mr. Kladas. Indicating the boy, you say to Mr. Kladas:
   a. *aftós-o-mikrós pyós-íne?*
   b. *pyí-in-eki-péra?*
   c. *mas-ksérune?*
   d. *ékho-enan-adherfó.*

3. Mr. Kladas answers:
   a. *ti-yinéka-mu tine-léne-fróso.*
   b. *i-mitéra-mu sas-kséri.*
   c. *aftí-ine-i-kóri-mu.*
   d. *ine-to-pedhí-mu.*

4. You ask the boy's name by saying to Mr. Kladas:
   a. *tí-ora-févyi-to-tréno?*
   b. *ti-yinéka-sas pós-tine-léne?*
   c. *pós-tone-léne to-yó-sas?*
   d. *khárika-polí.*

5. Mr. Kladas answers:
   a. *to-yó-mu tone-léne-pétro.*
   b. *dhén-dine-ksérume.*
   c. *o-yóz-mu ine-pandreménos.*
   d. *boró-na-sas-parusiáso-ti-yinéka-mu?*

6. A lady joins Mr. Kladas and the boy. Mr. Kladas introduces you to the lady by saying:
   a. *aftós-in-o-yóz-mu.*
   b. *ine-i-yinéka-mu.*
   c. *o-kírios ine-fíloz-mu.*
   d. *tone-ksérete ton-adherfó-mu?*

7. He introduces Mrs. Kladas to you by saying:
   a. *aftí-ine-i-yinéka-mu.*
   b. *pyí-in-aftí-eki-péra?*
   c. *im-o-kírios-kladhás.*
   d. *ekho-mya-adherfí.*

8. Mrs. Kladas asks your name by saying:
   a. *iste-pandreménos?*
   b. *pó-saz-léne?*
   c. *échete-kóri kírie-*Cook?
   d. *chéro-polí.*

9. You tell her your name is Cook:
   a. *t-onomá-tu ine*-Cook.
   b. *tone-léne*-Cook.
   c. *t-onomá-mu ine*-Cook.
   d. *imaste-fíli tu*-Cook.

10. Mrs. Kladas asks you if you have any children, saying:
    a. *echi-kóri-o-burbúlis?*
    b. *échete-pedhyá?*
    c. *boró-na-fáo?*
    d. *ékho éna-pedhí-móno.*

11. You tell her that you have a daughter, **saying**:
    a. *óchi kiría-mu, dhén-ekho-pedhyá.*
    b. *málista, ekho-mya-kóri.*
    c. *aftós-ine-o-fíloz-mu.*
    d. *ine-korítsi-akóma.*

12. You tell her your daughter's name:
    a. *to-yó-mu tone-léne-yórgho.*
    b. *tin-góri-mu tine-léne-maría.*
    c. *kalispéra-sas.*
    d. *tus-kséro polí-kala.*

Section D—Listening In

1. What Did You Say?

To the Group Leader: Read the English describing the situations in *What Would You Say?* of Section C, and call on different students, not in any fixed order, to speak the Greek which the situation calls for. Encourage the students to give the Greek, if they can, without reading it from the simplified spelling in their books. Then ask different members of the group to give the meaning in English of the different Greek expressions listed for each situation.

Go back to the last exercise in the preceding Section. The Leader will ask different members of the group to speak the Greek to be used in each of the situations given. Other members of the group will criticize the choices made if they do not agree with them. The Leader will also ask for the English equivalents of all the other expressions offered as choices, taking turns around the group.

2. Word Study Check-Up

To the Group Leader: As a further check on the students' understanding of the *Word Study*, read the English equivalent of the Greek expressions given before each comment under *Word Study*. Call on different students, not in any fixed order, to give the correct Greek for the English. For instance, say to A: "*póz-lét-eliniká:* you want, I want, he wants?" and so on. The Guide will at this point indicate by a negative sign whenever he hears a Greek expression that is wrong. If there is no Guide, the other members of the group will signal that they do not agree. Immediately ask someone else to give the right answer. Any member of the group who has difficulty in giving the correct Greek should be told to review the *Word Study* thoroughly before the next meeting of the group. Do not take time in this exercise to talk about the *why*. Stick to the *how*.

The Leader will ask different members of the group to give the correct Greek for the English equivalents of the expressions you studied in the *Word Study*. If you give the wrong answer, the Guide will let you know by making a negative sign; or, if there is no Guide, the other members of the group will indicate that they think your answer is wrong. The Leader will then immediately call on someone else for the right answer. If you have difficulty in giving the correct Greek, review the *Word Study* thoroughly.

3. Listening In

To the Group Leader: Re-read the note *To the Group Leader* in Section D1 of Unit 1. Follow the same procedure as outlined there. The first time you go through the conversations, check up on the meaning at the end of each conversation. Then go through all of them a second time without stopping. Finally, assign parts and have the students read the conversations. Get them to do a little acting if you can. Encourage them to speak loudly and clearly and to get into the spirit of the situation.

Keep your book closed while the Guide reads the following conversations and repeat after him in unison. If you have no Guide, you should use the phonograph records, repeating the Greek immediately after you hear it. At the end of each conversation take time out to check up on the meaning of any word or phrase about which you are in doubt. Ask some other member of the group to give you the English equivalent or in case no one knows, go back to the *Basic Sentences* of this Unit and make sure that you understand everything before you proceed any further. Go through the conversations a second time, repeating after the Guide individually. Then take parts in the conversations. This exercise contains almost all the new words you have learned in this Unit.

Record 4B, beginning.

1. You introduce yourself to a Greek family.

esís: *me-léne*-Cook.
ime-fílos tu-kiríu-kladhá.
tone-ksérete?

Μὲ λένε Cook.
Εἶμαι φίλος τοῦ κυρίου Κλαδᾶ.
Τόνε ξέρετε;

o-kírios:	tone-kséro polí-kala.	Τόνε ξέρω πολὺ καλά.
	chéro-polí.	Χαίρω πολύ.
i-kiría:	chéro párapoli.	Χαίρω πάρα πολύ.
	aftí-ine-i-kóri-mas i-fróso.	Αὐτὴ εἶναι ἡ κόρη μας, ἡ Φρόσω.
esís:	nóstimo-korítsi i-kóri-sas, polí-nóstimo'	Νόστιμο κορίτσι ἡ κόρη σας, πολὺ νόστιμο!
	chéro-polí dhespinís.	Χαίρω πολύ, δεσποινίς.
to-korítsi:	tí-kánete kírie-Cook?	Τί κάνετε, κύριε Cook;
esís:	polí-kala, efkharistó, k-esís?	Πολὺ καλά, εὐχαριστῶ, κ' ἐσεῖς;
to-korítsi:	kalá, efkharistó.	Καλά, εὐχαριστῶ.

Record 4B, after first spiral.

2. You answer questions about one of your friends.

i-kiría:	ksérete-ton-gírio-burbúli?	Ξέρετε τὸν κύριο Μπουρμπούλη;
esís:	málista kiría-mu, tone-kséro.	Μάλιστα, κυρία μου, τόνε ξέρω.
	ine-fíloz-mu.	Εἶναι φίλος μου.
to-korítsi:	pós-tine-léne ti-yinéka tu-kiríu-burbúli?	Πῶς τήνε λένε τὴ γυναῖκα τοῦ κυρίου Μπουρμπούλη;
esís:	tine-léne-maría.	Τήνε λένε Μαρία.
i-kiría:	echi-pedhyá-o-burbúlis?	Ἔχει παιδιὰ ὁ Μπουρμπούλης;
esís:	echi-éna-yó-móno.	Ἔχει ἕνα γιὸ μόνο.
	tone-léne-pétro.	Τόνε λένε Πέτρο.

Record 4B, after second spiral.

3. A young girl and her mother inquire about you and your family.

i-kiría:	iste-pandreménos kírie-Cook?	Εἶστε παντρεμένος, κύριε Cook;
esís:	óchi, dhén-ime.	Ὄχι, δὲν εἶμαι.
to-korítsi:	o-patéra-sas ke-i-mitéra-sas zún-akóma?	Ὁ πατέρας σας καὶ ἡ μητέρα σας ζοῦν ἀκόμα;

[2–D]

esís:	zúne.	Ζοῦνε.
to-korítsi:	échete-adherfó?	Ἔχετε ἀδερφό;
esís:	ekho-enan-adherfó ke-mya-adherfí.	Ἔχω ἕναν ἀδερφὸ καὶ μιὰ ἀδερφή.
to-korítsi:	ton-adherfó-sas pós-tone-léne?	Τὸν ἀδερφό σας πῶς τόνε λένε;
esís:	tone-léne-yórgho san-dom-batéra-mu.	Τόνε λένε Γιώργο σὰν τὸν πατέρα μου.
	tin-adherfí-mu tine-léne-maría.	Τὴν ἀδερφή μου τήνε λένε Μαρία.
i-kiría:	k-esás pó-saz-léne?	Κ' ἐσᾶς, πῶς σᾶς λένε;
to-korítsi:	tone-léne-yáni.	Τόνε λένε Γιάννη.
	tone-kséro.	Τόνε ξέρω.
	ine-fílos tu-kladhá.	Εἶναι φίλος τοῦ Κλαδᾶ.
esís:	páme-mazí s-ton-ginimatóghrafo?	Πάμε μαζὶ στὸν κινηματόγραφο;
to-korítsi:	málista, s-tis-enyá-to-vrádhi.	Μάλιστα, στὶς ἐννιὰ τὸ βράδυ.

Record 4B, after third spiral.

4. A lady asks about the people you are with.

i-kiría:	aftós-o-mikrós pyós-íne?	Αὐτὸς ὁ μικρὸς ποιὸς εἶναι;
esís:	in-o-yós tu-kladhá.	Εἶν' ὁ γιὸς τοῦ Κλαδᾶ.
i-kiría:	ine-polí-nóstimo-pedhí.	Εἶναι πολὺ νόστιμο παιδί.
	ke-pyós-in-aftós-eki-péra?	Καὶ ποιὸς εἶν' αὐτὸς ἐκεῖ πέρα;
esís:	in-o-yórghos-o-kladhás.	Εἶν' ὁ Γιώργος ὁ Κλαδᾶς.
i-kiría:	ke-pyí-n-aftí-eki-péra?	Καὶ ποιοὶ εἶν' αὐτοὶ ἐκεῖ πέρα;
esís:	ine-fíli-mu.	Εἶναι φίλοι μου.
	boró-na-sas-parusiáso tin-giría-burbúli ke-ton-gírio-khristofóru?	Μπορῶ νὰ σᾶς παρουσιάσω τὴν κυρία Μπουρμπούλη καὶ τὸν κύριο Χριστοφόρου;

[2–D]

i-kiría: chéro-polí.	Χαίρω πολύ.
me-sikhoríte, ma-févyi-t-aftokinitó-mu.	Μὲ συχωρεῖτε, μὰ φεύγει τ' αὐτοκίνητό μου.
kaliníkhta-sas.	Καληνύχτα σας.

Record 4B, after fourth spiral.

5. Adding in Greek.

éna k'éna, dhío.	Ἕνα κ' ἕνα, δύο.
dhío ke-dhío, tésera.	Δύο καὶ δύο, τέσσερα.
tría ke-tría, éksi.	Τρία καὶ τρία, ἕξι.
tésera ke-tésera, okhtó.	Τέσσερα καὶ τέσσερα, ὀχτώ.
pénde ke-pénde, dhéka.	Πέντε καὶ πέντε, δέκα.
okhtó k'éna, enyá.	Ὀχτὼ κ' ἕνα, ἐννιά.
tría k'eftá, dhéka.	Τρία κ' ἐφτά, δέκα.

Is there any word or phrase in this conversation that you do not understand now? If there is, be sure to find out its meaning by asking members of your group or looking it up in the *Basic Sentences*.

Go through the conversations again, following the same plan as before. Imitate carefully and keep in mind the meaning of everything you are saying in Greek.

Finally, go through the conversations a third time.

Take turns speaking the parts and continue until everybody has had a chance to speak at least one of the parts. Keep this exercise going as long as you have time. Get the most out of this individual performance and when your turn comes, speak clearly and with feeling. The Guide will correct any errors he hears by asking you to repeat. Make every effort to satisfy him with your pronunciation.

Section E—Conversation

1. Covering the Greek of Basic Sentences (Individual Study)

Go back to the *Basic Sentences* of this Unit. Cover up the Greek. Read the English silently and test yourself to see how many words and phrases you can say in Greek. Check the words you are uncertain about and after you have gone through the whole list, uncover the Greek and review them. Go through the list once more and continue for at least three times or until you can give the Greek readily for all the expressions. This test is hard, but if you succeed in saying the Greek for all the sentences by merely looking at the English, you are doing well indeed. To make sure of this, after you are certain you know the material, pick out expressions at random and see if you can still speak the Greek quickly. As you practice, you must always speak the Greek aloud and try to imitate the pronunciation of your Guide as well as you can recall it.

2. Vocabulary Check-Up

To the Group Leader: Go to the *Basic Sentences*. Read to the group the English equivalents of the Greek expressions. Call on different students, not in any fixed order, asking for the correct Greek for the English. This check-up is to be conducted in the same way as the *Vocabulary Check-Up* of Section E2 of Unit 1. If you have any question about the proper procedure, review the note *To the Group Leader* in that Section. Remember not to spend any time talking about the *why* of the Greek; stick to the *how*.

In this Section you are going to have your second chance to engage in conversation in Greek. Remember that this is the most useful part of your study. Therefore, you should make the greatest effort to do this part as well as you possibly can. Get perfectly clear what you are to do and then plunge into it with enthusiasm.

Before you begin the conversation, check yourself on your ability to speak the Greek you have learned up to this point. As in the *Vocabulary Check-Up* of Unit 1, the Leader of the Group will ask you to supply in turn the Greek expressions for the English equivalents which he reads from the *Basic Sentences*. Figure out how to say the Greek for each English phrase or sentence whether it is your turn to speak or not. Only in this way can you get the most value out of the *Check-Up*. If there is much of the Greek which you don't know, review the *Basic Sentences* at the first opportunity outside of the group meeting.

3. Conversation

To the Group Leader: This Section represents the real purpose of the entire Unit. The course is intended to teach you to speak Greek and to understand it when you hear it spoken. Follow the instructions and give all the time you can to free conversation practice. Any members of the group who have special difficulty recalling the Greek words and phrases they need to express a meaning should be told to do more work with the *Useful Words and Phrases* and *Basic Sentences*. They need, in particular, more practice in covering the Greek and recalling it when they read the English. Practice in getting the meaning of the *Listening In* records will also help. Arrangements should be made for students to play and listen to the records whenever they can between meetings of the group.

Then turn to the outlined conversations which follow. Assign parts and ask the students to act them out. Vary the situations and suggest to the students that they vary the Greek slightly as they gain confidence in their speaking. Remember to keep the speaking loud enough so that everyone can hear. See that everyone is listening and trying to understand the Greek that is being spoken.

The Leader will assign parts and will ask you to reproduce the conversational situations which follow. Act your part. Don't be afraid to vary the conversation if you are sure of your Greek and use the Greek you have learned in Unit 1 as well as that of Unit 2. Continue this practice until everyone can speak any part of the conversations even though slight changes in the situations are introduced.

I. *You meet your friend Mr. Kladas on the street.*
  1. You say how do you do.
  2. He says very well, thank you, and asks how you are.
  3. After replying that you are fine you ask where his wife is.
  4. He says that she is leaving tonight by train.
  5. You ask where she is going.
  6. He says to Salonica, and adds that his father and mother live over there. Then he suggests going together to the movies.
  7. You say that you are extremely sorry, but your bus is leaving.
  8. He asks where you are going.
  9. You counter by asking *him* whether he knows Mr. Adamantiou.
  10. He says that he knows him well, and adds that Mr. Adamantiou has a daughter and that she is a very pretty girl.

II. *At the house of the Adamantious you are presented to various people.*
  1. You ask Mrs. Adamantiou who that man there is.
  2. She says that it is Mr. Bourboulis.
  3. You ask whether it is George Bourboulis.
  4. No, she says, it is Peter Bourboulis, and adds that he is married to a Christophorou.
  5. You reply that you do not know her.
  6. She asks whether she may introduce Mr. Bourboulis to you.
  7. You say that you are glad to meet Mr. Bourboulis.
  8. Mr. Bourboulis says that he knows your brother and that they are friends.
  9. You ask him whether he has any children.
  10. He tells you that he has only one son, and that John is his name.

Throw yourself into these conversations. Do the best you can with pronunciation and with the Greek, but don't worry too much about mistakes. Think more of acting your part and speaking smoothly and as though you must mean what you are saying. The Guide will help you correct your errors. If you can do this work well, it means that you are actually conversing in Greek, and that is your chief aim in this course.

Section F—Conversation (*Cont.*)

Read again the instructions given in Section F of the preceding Unit. Then continue the conversations which you started in Section E of this Unit (2).

Take every opportunity between now and the next meeting of the group to try out your Greek on other members of the group or on native speakers around you. Carry on conversations with them whenever you get a chance. Ask questions. At this stage of the game, don't try to use phrases or sentences which are different from those you have learned thus far in this course.

FINDER LIST

This is a complete alphabetical list of all the words and expressions used in this Unit which are in any way new or unusual. The conventional spelling is given in the middle column. From now on we shall not repeat words which have been drilled sufficiently in previous Units. This list is for reference only, but you should know all these before going on to the next Unit.

A

adhamandíu	Ἀδαμαντίου	Adamantiou (*family name*)
i adherfí	ἡ ἀδερφή	sister
adherfó see: *adherfós*		
o adherfós	ὁ ἀδερφός	brother
adherfó	ἀδερφό	
aftí see: *aftós*		
to aftokínito	τὸ αὐτοκίνητο	car; bus
t-aftokinitó-mas	τ' αὐτοκίνητό μας	our car

aftós m.s.	αὐτός	this; that
aftí f.s.	αὐτή	this; that
aftí m.p.	αὐτοί	these; those
akóma	ἀκόμα	still

B

batéra see: *patéras*
bétro see: *pétros*
boró

boró-na-sas-parusiáso	μπορῶ νὰ σᾶς παρουσιάσω	may I present to you . . . ?
burbúli see: *burbúlis*		
burbúlis	Μπουρμπούλης	Bourboulis (*family name*)
burbúli	Μπουρμπούλη	Bourboulis; Bourboulis's

C

chéro

chéro-polí	χαίρω πολύ	glad to meet you
chéro párapoli	χαίρω πάρα πολύ	delighted

D

dine see: *eghó*
dom see: *o*

E

eghó	ἐγώ	I
tone	τόνε	him
tine, dine	τήνε	her
mas	μᾶς	us
esás	ἐσᾶς	you

sas, saz	σᾶς	you; to you
tus m.	τοὺς	them
ékho	ἔχω	I have
ekí	ἐκεῖ	there
eki-péra	ἐκεῖ πέρα	over there
enas	ἔνας	a
esás see: eghó		

F

fíli see: fílos		
o fílos, filoz	ὁ φίλος	friend
fíli	φίλοι	friends
fíloz see: fílos		
i fróso	ἡ Φρόσω	Phroso (*first name; endearing for* Euphrosyne)

G

giría see: kiría
gírio see: kírios
góri see: kóri

I

ím see: íme

íme, ím	εἶμαι, εἶμ'	I am

K

ke, ky	καί, κι	and; also
khárika		
khárika-polí	χάρηκα πολύ	glad to have met you
i kiría	ἡ κυρία	Mrs.

giría	τῆς κυρίας	of Mrs.
tis-kirías, tis-kiríaz	κυρία μου	madam
kiría-mu	κυρία Μπουρμπούλη	Mrs. Bourboulis!
kiría-burbúli	κυρίες	ladies!
kiríes		
kirías see: *kiría*		
kiríaz see: *kiría*		
kiríes see: *kiría*		
kírii see: *kírios*		
o *kírios*	ὁ κύριος	Mr.
gírio		
tu-kiríu	τοῦ κυρίου	of Mr.
kírii	κύριοι	gentlemen!
kiríu see: *kírios*		
kladhá see: *kladhás*		
kladhás	Κλαδᾶς	Kladas (*family name*)
kladhá	Κλαδᾶ	Kladas; Kladas's
i *kóri*	ἡ κόρη	daughter
kóri, góri	κόρη	
to *korítsi*	τὸ κορίτσι	girl
kséro	ξέρω	I know
ky see: *ke*		

L

léo	λέω	I say; I call
me-léne . . .	μὲ λένε . . .	my name is . . .
lipúme	λυποῦμαι	I am sorry

M

ma	μὰ	but
maría	Μαρία	Mary
mas see: *eghó*		
mas see: *mu*		
me see: *pandreménos*		
o mikrós	ὁ μικρός	little fellow
i mitéra	ἡ μητέρα	mother
móno	μόνο	only
mu	μου	my
tu	του	his
mas	μας	our
sas	σας	your

N

nóstimo n.s.	νόστιμο	pretty

O

o	ὁ	the
ton, tom, dom, to m.s.	τὸν, τὸ	the
tu m.s.	τοῦ	of the
tin f.s.	τὴν	the
tis f.s.	τῆς	of the
to, t n.s.	τὸ, τ'	the
to ónoma	τὸ ὄνομα	name
t-onomá-mu	τ' ὄνομά μου	my name

P

pandreménos   παντρεμένος   married
    pandreménos me   παντρεμένος μὲ   married to

párapoli   πάρα πολύ   extremely
    see: chéro

parusiáso see: boró

patéra see: patéras

o patéras   ὁ πατέρας   father
    patéra, batéra   πατέρα
    tu-patéra   τοῦ πατέρα   of the father

to pedhí   τὸ παιδί   child
    pedhyá   παιδιά   children

péra see: ekí

pétro see: pétros

o pétros   ὁ Πέτρος   Peter
    pétro, bétro   Πέτρο

pó see: pós

polí see: chéro; khárika

pós, pó   πῶς   how?

pyí see: pyós

pyós m.s.   ποιός   who?
    pyí m.p.   ποιοί

S

san   σὰν   like
    san-dom-batéra-mu   σὰν τὸν πατέρα μου   like my father

sas see: *eghó*
sas see: *mu*
saz see: *eghó*

T

t see: *o*
tin see: *o*
tine see: *eghó*
tis see: *o*
to see: *o*
tom see: *o*
tone see: *eghó*
tu see: *mu*
tu see: *o*
tus see: *eghó*

Y

yáni see: *yánis*

o *yánis*	ὁ Γιάννης	John
yáni	Γιάννη	
tu-yáni	τοῦ Γιάννη	John's
i *yinéka*	ἡ γυναῖκα	woman; wife

yó see: *yós*
yórgho see: *yórghos*

o *yórghos*	ὁ Γιώργος	George
yórgho	Γιώργο	
tu-yórghu	τοῦ Γιώργου	George's

yórghu see: *yórghos*

yós, yoz	ὁ γιός	son
yó	γιό	
yóz see: yós		

Z

zún see: zúne
zúne, zún   ζοῦνε, ζοῦν   they live

UNIT 3

WHAT'S YOUR TRADE?

Section A—Basic Sentences

To the Group Leader: Read carefully the note to the Leader in Section A of Unit 2. Then go through the *Basic Sentences* once, and take up the *Hints on Pronunciation*. Go through the *Basic Sentences* at least twice more individually, paying especial attention to pronunciation.

Go through the *Basic Sentences*, in unison, in the same way you did for Section A of the preceding Unit. Be sure to put plenty of life into your repetition of the sentences. After you have gone through the *Basic Sentences* once in unison and have done the *Hints on Pronunciation*, come back to the *Basic Sentences*. Pay particular attention to the points of pronunciation you have just been working on and go through the sentences at least twice more individually.

1. Basic Sentences

Record 5A, beginning.

John Cook is in civilian clothes and meets Nick Roilos in a café.

ENGLISH EQUIVALENTS	AIDS TO LISTENING	CONVENTIONAL SPELLING
Nick		
my friend	fíle-mu	φίλε μου
Good evening, my friend.	kalispéra-sas fíle-mu.	Καλησπέρα σας, φίλε μου.
[an] American	amerikanós	Ἀμερικανός
is it not so?	dhén-in-étsi?	δὲν εἶν' ἔτσι;
You're an American, aren't you?	ist-amerikanós, dhén-in-étsi?	Εἶστ' Ἀμερικανός, δὲν εἶν' ἔτσι;
work	dhulyá	δουλειά
What work do you do?	tí-dhulyá-kánete?	Τί δουλειὰ κάνετε;

you work	ergházeste	ἐργάζεστε
in the city	s-tim-bóli	στὴν πόλι
or in the country	í-s-tin-eksochí	ἢ στὴν ἐξοχή
Where do you work, in the city or in the country?	pú-ergházeste, s-tim-bóli í-s-tin-eksochí?	Ποῦ ἐργάζεστε, στὴν πόλι ἢ στὴν ἐξοχή;
you labor	dhulévete	δουλεύετε
on farm	se-khtíma	σὲ χτῆμα
or in factory	í-se-erghostásio	ἢ σὲ ἐργοστάσιο
Do you work on a farm or in a factory?	dhulévete se-khtíma í-se-erghostásio?	Δουλεύετε σὲ χτῆμα ἢ σὲ ἐργοστάσιο;

John

No, my boy.	óchi pedhí-mu.	Ὄχι, παιδί μου.
neither farmer	míte-yeorghós	μήτε γεωργὸς
nor worker	mít-erghátis	μήτ' ἐργάτης
I'm (not) neither a farmer nor a factory worker.	dhén-ime míte-yeorghós mít-ergháti-s-erghostásio.	Δὲν εἶμαι μήτε γεωργὸς μήτ' ἐργάτης σ' ἐργοστάσιο.

Nick

we	emís	ἐμεῖς
farms	khtímata	χτήματα
We have farms.	emís ékhume-khtímata.	Ἐμεῖς ἔχουμε χτήματα.
my children	ta-pedhyá-mu	τὰ παιδιά μου
we work	erghazómaste	ἐργαζόμαστε
My children and I work hard.	eghó ke-ta-pedhyá-mu erghazómaste-polí.	Ἐγὼ καὶ τὰ παιδιά μου ἐργαζόμαστε πολύ.

[3–A]

John

they call them	ta-léne	τὰ λένε
What are your children's names?	pós-ta-léne ta-pedhyá-sas?	Πῶς τὰ λένε τὰ παιδιά σας;

Nick

Their names are Spyros, Metsos, and Pope.	ta-léne spíro mítso ke-pópi.	Τὰ λένε Σπύρο, Μήτσο καὶ Πόπη

John

on ship	se-vapóri	σὲ βαπόρι
I'm on a ship.	eghó-ime se-vapóri.	Ἐγὼ εἶμαι σὲ βαπόρι.

Nick

[So] you're a sailor!	iste-náftis!	Εἶστε ναύτης!
Isn't there a Nick Aravantinos on your ship, too?	dhén-ine k-enaz-níkos-aravandinós s-to-vapóri-sas?	Δὲν εἶναι κ' ἕνας Νίκος Ἀραβαντινὸς στὸ βαπόρι σας;

John

Yes.	málista.	Μάλιστα.

Record 5B, beginning.

Nick

of my boy	tu-pedhyú-mu	τοῦ παιδιοῦ μου
He's a friend of my son Spyros.	ine-fílos tu-pedhyú-mu tu-spíru.	Εἶναι φίλος τοῦ παιδιοῦ μου τοῦ Σπύρου.

John

He's a good fellow.	ine-kaló-pedhí.	Εἶναι καλὸ παιδί.

Nick

He works very hard.	erghádzete párapolí.	Ἐργάζεται πάρα πολύ.

[3–A]

John
I work hard, too.	k-eghó ergházome-polí.	Κ' ἐγὼ ἐργάζομαι πολύ.
such is life ('these things the life has')	aftá-echi-i-zoí	αὐτὰ ἔχει ἡ ζωή
Such is a sailor's life, Nick.	aftá níko, echi-i-zoí-tu-náfti.	Αὐτά, Νίκο, ἔχει ἡ ζωὴ τοῦ ναύτη.

Nick
I know (it), I know (it).	to-kséro to-kséro.	Τὸ ξέρω, τὸ ξέρω.
of a friend of mine	enos-fílu-mu	ἑνὸς φίλου μου
is soldier	ine-stratyótis	εἶναι στρατιώτης
The son of a friend of mine is a soldier.	o-yós enos-fílu-mu ine-stratyótis.	Ὁ γιὸς ἑνὸς φίλου μου εἶναι στρατιώτης.

John
in (the) Athens	s-tin-athína	στὴν 'Αθήνα
Is he in Athens?	ine-s-tin-athína?	Εἶναι στὴν 'Αθήνα;

Nick
I cannot that I tell you	dhém-boró-na-sas-pó	δὲν μπορῶ νὰ σᾶς πῶ
I can't tell you where he is.	dhém-boró-na-sas-pó pu-íne.	Δὲν μπορῶ νὰ σᾶς πῶ ποῦ εἶναι.

John
a lot	ena-soró	ἕνα σωρὸ
friends	fílus	φίλους
who work	pu-ergházonde	ποὺ ἐργάζονται
I have a lot of friends who work in Athens.	ékho ena-soró-fílus pu-ergházonde s-tin-athína.	Ἔχω ἕνα σωρὸ φίλους ποὺ ἐργάζονται στὴν 'Αθήνα.

[3–A]

one of my friends is teacher One of my friends is a teacher.	énas-ap-tus-fíluz-mu ine-dháskalos énas-ap-tus-fíluz-mu ine-dháskalos.	ἕνας ἀπ' τοὺς φίλους μου εἶναι δάσκαλος Ἕνας ἀπ' τοὺς φίλους μου εἶναι δάσκαλος.
is [college-] student His son is a student.	ine-fititís o-yós-tu ine-fititís.	εἶναι φοιτητής Ὁ γιός του εἶναι φοιτητής.
reads books He reads a lot of books.	dhyavázi vivlía dhyavázi ena-soro-vivlía.	διαβάζει βιβλία Διαβάζει ἕνα σωρὸ βιβλία.

Nick

of a sister of mine is [college-] student The daughter of a sister of mine is a student, too.	myas-adherfíz-mu ine-fitítria k-i-kóri myas-adherfíz-mu ine-fitítria.	μιᾶς ἀδερφῆς μου εἶναι φοιτήτρια Κ' ἡ κόρη μιᾶς ἀδερφῆς μου εἶναι φοιτήτρια.
stays with her mother She lives with her mother.	méni me-ti-mitéra-tis méni-me-ti-mitéra-tis.	μένει μὲ τὴ μητέρα της Μένει μὲ τὴ μητέρα της.

Record 6A, beginning.

John

another is employee in office Another friend of mine is an employee in an office.	enas-álos in-ipálilos se-ghrafío enas-áloz-mu-fílos ine-ipálilo-se-ghrafío.	ἕνας ἄλλος εἶν' ὑπάλληλος σὲ γραφεῖο Ἕνας ἄλλος μου φίλος εἶναι ὑπάλληλος σὲ γραφεῖο.

is doctor	ine-yatrós	εἶναι γιατρός
His brother is a doctor.	o-adherfós-tu ine-yatrós.	Ὁ ἀδερφός του εἶναι γιατρός.
their sisters	i-adherfés-tus	οἱ ἀδερφές τους
good girls	kalá-korítsya	καλὰ κορίτσια
Their sisters are very nice girls.	i-adherfés-tus ine-polí-kala-korítsya.	Οἱ ἀδερφές τους εἶναι πολὺ καλὰ κορίτσια.
I know them	tis-kséro	τὶς ξέρω
their sisters	tis-adherfés-tus	τὶς ἀδερφές τους
I know their sisters.	tis-kséro tis-adherfés-tus.	Τὶς ξέρω τὶς ἀδερφές τους.

Nick

What can I treat you to? ('What can I that I offer you?')	tí-boró-na-sas-prosféro?	Τί μπορῶ νὰ σᾶς προσφέρω;
Do you want a beer?	thélete-mya-bíra?	Θέλετε μιὰ μπίρα;

John

Yes, thanks a lot.	málista, efkharistó-polí.	Μάλιστα, εὐχαριστῶ πολύ.

Before you go through the *Basic Sentences* a second time study the following:

2. Hints on Pronunciation

1. VOWEL QUALITY OF *i, e, o*.

Remember that the Greek vowel *i* always has the sound of the *i* in *machine* or *police* (never the sound of the *i* in *finish*), even in unstressed syllables. What will perhaps be harder for you to bear in mind, because it is foreign to our speech habits, is that in Greek the *e* is always pronounced like the *e* in *let*, *sell* (never like the *e* of *café*, *fiancée*), and that the *o* is always pronounced like the *o* of *cloth*, *boss* (never like the *o* of *solo*, *piano*), even when the *e* or *o* comes at the end of a word.

Record 6A, after first spiral.
PRACTICE 1

(a)	*dhespinís*	miss	(b)	*ksérete*	you know	(c)	*eghó*	I
	fílos	friend		*dhulévete*	you work		*kóri*	daughter
	lipúme	I'm sorry		*kafés*	coffee		*thélo*	I want
	yinéka	woman; wife		*kírie*	sir; Mr.		*korítsi*	girl

2. THE SOUND *n* IN COMBINATIONS OF WORDS.

(a) Before vowels.

ton-adherfó-mu tone-léne-yórgho.   My brother's name is George.
tin-adherfí-mu tine-léne-maría.   My sister's name is Mary.
echi-énan-adherfó.   He has one brother.
dhén-ekhume-ghála.   We have no milk.

The very common words *ton* 'the', *tin* 'the', *énan* 'one', *enan* 'a', *dhén* 'not' (and a few more ending in *n*), when running together with other words which begin with a vowel, keep their final *n*.

(b) Before *f, v, th, dh, s, z, ch, kh, gh, l, r, m, n, y.*

échi-éna-yó-móno to-dháskalo.   He has only one son, the teacher.
ke-ti-mitéra-sas maría-tine-léne?   [And] your mother's name is Mary, too?
dhé-thélo-krasí.   I don't want wine.

You see from these examples that the same little words *ton, tin, énan, dhén* before the words *dháskalo, mitéra, yó, thélo*, respectively, are pronounced *to, ti, éna, dhé*. In word combinations the final *n* disappears before the consonants *f, v, th, dh, s, z, ch, kh, gh, l, r, m, n, y.* To make it easier to remember, notice that these are all sounds you can produce without interruption as long as you have any breath.

(c) Before *k, g, t, d.*

boró-na-sas-parusiáso ton-gírio ke-tin-giría-burbúli?   May I present (to you) Mr. and Mrs. Bourboulis?
dhóste-mu-enan-gafé.   Give me a [cup of] coffee.

dhén-gatálava.
san-don-adherfó-mu

Here we again have the words *ton, tin, enan, dhén* plus the little word *san* 'like' in combination with words such as *kírio, kiría, kafé, katálava, ton.* As you see, the final *n* does not disappear. Before *k, g, t, d* final *n*

(d) Before *p, b.*
ékho éna-pedhí-móno to-yó-mu tom-bétro.
ménete-s-tim-bóli í-s-tin-eksochí?
tom-batéra-tu tone-léne-pétro.
dhém-boró-na-sas-pó.

Here you have *ton, tin, dhén* in combination with words such as *pétro, patéra, póli, boró.* As you see, the final *n* of *ton, tin, dhén* has become *m*, and the im-

I didn't understand.
like my brother
does not disappear. Notice, however, that the *k* and *t* sounds with which the following words begin become *g* and *d*, respectively.

I have only one child, my son Peter.
Do you live in the city or in the country?
His father's name is Peter.
I can't tell you.
mediately following *p* of *pétro, patéra,* and *póli* has changed to *b*. Before *p, b* final *n* becomes *m*; the immediately following *p* changes to *b*.

Record 6A, after second spiral.
PRACTICE 2

(a) *ton-adherfó*
   tin-adherfí
   enan-adherfó
   dhén-ékhume

(b) *to-dháskalo*
   ti-mitéra
   ena-yó
   dhé-thélo

(c) *ton-gírio*
   tin-giría
   enan-gafé
   dhén-gatálava

(d) *tom-bétro*
   tim-bóli
   enam-batéra
   dhém-boró

Don't be surprised, however, if you hear pronunciations like *ti-giría, sa-do-batéra-mu, dhé-boró.* The consonant groups *ng, nd, mb,* whether in combinations of words or within a word, are often reduced to *g, d, b* in the speech of many Greeks.

Now listen to the way your Guide (or the speaker on the records) says these sounds. Repeat each word or phrase right after him, imitating him as well as you can.

Now go through the *Basic Sentences* once more individually, and with your book open. As you repeat after your Guide, keep your eyes on the *Aids to Listening* and note in particular the examples of the sounds discussed. Again do not hesitate to ask your Guide to repeat if you are uncertain about any sound.

Finally, go through the *Basic Sentences* at least once again individually. Keep your book closed, listen carefully to your Guide and make sure that your pronunciation satisfies him.

3. Check Yourself

Are you always careful to pronounce the Greek vowels in the right way?

Do you pronounce the *i* like the *i* in *machine*, the *e* like the *e* in *let*, and the *o* like the *o* in *boss*?

Are you paying enough attention to the way consonants change when words are run together? If you do this smoothly and easily you will get a real Greek "accent".

Never forget that you must always say *ton-Gírio, dhén-Dine-thélo, tom-Batéra-mu*.

SECTION B—WORD STUDY AND REVIEW OF BASIC SENTENCES

1. Word Study (Individual Study)

As in Section B1 of Unit 2, read the words and expressions in each list and make sure that you understand the meaning of the Greek. Then read the comments which follow each list. When you have finished the *Word Study* ask other members of the group about points which are not clear to you.

COMMENT 1

THE DEFINITE ARTICLE. You already know that instead of the plain English 'the' (or definite article) Greek uses three different words, one before masculine nouns, one before feminine nouns, and one before neuter nouns. In Unit 2 you found that nouns have two sets of forms, singular and plural. So does the Greek word for 'the'. The following examples show you how these three words are used. You will recognize some of the examples as coming directly from the *Basic Sentences;* the others have been made up from the material you have already had.

Form 1

(a) singular
masculine: *o-stathmós ine-dheksyá.* — The station is to the right.
feminine: *i-kóri myas-adherfís-mu ine-fitítria.* — The daughter of a sister of mine is a student.
neuter: *to-tréno févyi-s-tis-pénde.* — The train leaves at five.

(b) plural
masculine: *i-fíli tu-kladhá ergházonde se-ghrafío.* — The friends of Kladas work in an office.
feminine: *i-adherfés tu-burbúli ine-polí-kalá-korítsya.* — Bourboulis's sisters ('The sisters of Bourboulis') are very nice girls.
neuter: *ta-korítsya ménune s-tin-eksochí.* — The girls live in the country.

Notice that you get this Form when you ask 'who (or what) is?' or 'who (or what) does?'

Form 2

(a) singular
masculine: *thélo-na-pyó-ton-gafé-mu.* — I want to drink my coffee.
feminine: *boró-na-sas-parusiáso-tin-giría-burbúli?* — May I present (to you) Mrs. Bourboulis?
neuter: *thélo-na-fáo-to-kréas.* — I want to eat the meat.

(b) plural
masculine: *kséro-tus-fílus tu-kladhá.* — I know the friends of Kladas.
feminine: *tis-kséro tis-adherfés-tus.* — I know their sisters.
neuter: *dhóste-mu ta-spírta.* — Give me the matches.

Notice when you get Form 2. You get it first of all after verbs like 'know', 'give', 'present', 'call', 'eat', 'drink', etc. This Form answers the question 'whom (or what)?': 'whom do I know?' 'whom may I present?' or 'what do I want to eat?' etc.

[3–B]

You will remember these examples:

s-ton-ginimatóghrafo	to the movies
me-to-tréno	by train
énas-ap-tus-fílus	one of the friends
san-dom-batéra-mu	like my father

You see that you get Form 2 also after the little words *se* or *s* meaning 'to', 'in', 'on', 'at', *me* meaning 'with', 'by', and *apo*, *ap* meaning 'from', 'of', all of which indicate some kind of relation and are called prepositions. You get it furthermore after the word *san* 'like', if the noun that follows is accompanied by the definite article.

Form 3

singular
masculine: *o-adherfós tu-patéra-mu ine-pandreménos.*   Father's brother ('The brother of my father') is married.

feminine: *in-o-yós tis-kiríaz-burbúli.*   He's Mrs. Bourboulis's son ('the son of Mrs. Bourboulis').

neuter: *o-fílos tu-pedhyú*   the boy's friend ('the friend of the boy')

Notice when you get Form 3. In the English sentence "Father's brother is married," the function of the word 'father's' is to distinguish this brother from all other brothers. By the use of the word 'father's' the other word 'brother' is restricted in its application. As you see from the English of the examples above, Form 3 is the equivalent of an English noun in the possessive form or the equivalent of a noun preceded by our preposition 'of'. This Form is used in answering the questions 'whose?' 'of whom?' 'of what?'

We omit Form 3 of the plural, which isn't used very much; for the most part it is replaced by the preposition *ap* with Form 2, as in the phrase *énas-ap-tus-fílus* for 'one of the friends'.

These different Forms are called *cases;* Form 1 we shall call the *subject* case, Form 2 the *object* case, and Form 3 the *restrictive* case, just to have convenient labels for them.

SUMMARY: the definite article

	singular			plural		
	m.	f.	n.	m.	f.	n.
subject	o	i	to	i	i	ta
object	ton	tin	to	tus	tis	ta
restrictive	tu	tis	tu			

COMMENT 2

THE INDEFINITE ARTICLE. In the second Unit we spoke of the *indefinite article*, which corresponds to English 'a, an' and you saw that in Form 1 (the subject case) Greek uses *enas* before masculine nouns, *mya* before feminine nouns, and *ena* before neuter nouns. Here are some examples which show the use of the indefinite article in Form 2 (the object case) and in Form 3 (the restrictive case).

object case
m. *dhóste-mu-enan-gafé.* — Give me a [cup of] coffee.
f. *thélete-mya-bíra?* — Do you want a beer?
n. *s-ena-erghostásio* — in a factory

restrictive case
m. *o-yós enos-fílu* — a friend's son ('the son of a friend')
f. *i-kóri myas-adherfís* — a sister's daughter ('the daughter of a sister')
n. *o-fílos enos-pedhyú* — a child's friend ('the friend of a child')

SUMMARY: the indefinite article

	m.	f.	n.
subject	enas	mya	ena
object	enan	mya	ena
restrictive	enos	myas	enos

COMMENT 3

ABOUT NOUNS. You have seen from Unit 2 that Greek nouns have two sets of forms, singular and plural. Now you have surely noticed that you have not always the same form of a noun throughout the whole singular or throughout the whole plural. This is true in English, too.

(a) In Greek you have:
subj. *i-mitéra-tu ergházete se-ghrafío.*
obj. *kséro-ti-mitéra-tu.*
address *mitéra!*
rest. *o-adherfós tiz-mitéras-tu dhulévi s-erghostásio.*

And in English you have:
His mother works in an office.
I know his mother.
Mother!
His mother's brother works in a factory.

These are feminine nouns and you see that there is no difference between Greek and English: the feminine nouns have in the subject case and in the object case (and, whenever it may be used, in the case of address) the same form (*mitéra* in Greek, 'mother' in English); and in order to get the restrictive case, you simply add an *s* to the subject-object form (*mitéras* in Greek, 'mother's' in English). All* feminine nouns in Greek end in the subject-object form with one of the five vowels of Greek, that is, -*i*, -*e*, -*a*, -*o*, -*u*, and in the restrictive case with a vowel plus *s*, that is, with -*is*, -*es*, -*as*, -*os*, -*us*, respectively.

(b) Now look at these examples of masculine nouns:
subj. *o-yánis ergházete se-ghrafío.*
obj. *kséro-to-yáni.*
address *yáni!*
rest. *o-adherfós tu-yáni dhulévi s-erghostásio.*

John works in an office.
I know John.
John!
John's brother works in a factory.

You see that there is a marked difference between masculine and feminine nouns. The masculine nouns (with one exception to be discussed below) have the same form for the object case and the restrictive case (and, whenever it may be used, the case of address), but a different form for the subject case; the subject case

i-dhespinís (with the object case *dhespinídha*) is an exception. Though it is the established word for the title 'Miss', it is a word of the upper classes and townspeople.

always ends in one of the five vowels plus *s*, that is, in *-is*, *-es*, *-as*, *-os*, *-us*. In order to get the object-restrictive (address) form, you simply take away the final *s* from the subject case.

SUMMARY:

	masculine		feminine
subj.	*yánis*	subj.-obj. (address)	*mitéra*
obj.-rest. (address)	*yáni*	rest.	*mitéras*

(c) The **nouns in *-os*** show a few peculiarities. Look first at this example:

o-yós tu-fílu-mu ine-stratyótis. My friend's son ('The son of my friend') is a soldier.

The form *tu-fílu* shows you that the nouns in *-os* have a special ending for the restrictive case, namely *-u*. So you get *tu-adherfú* 'of the brother', *tu-yú* 'of the son', *tu-yórghu* 'of George', etc.

But note carefully these examples:

subj.	o-kírios	rest.	tu-kiríu
	o-dháskalos		tu-dhaskálu
	o-ipálilos		tu-ipalílu
	o-kinimatóghrafos		tu-kinimatoghráfu

You see, those masculine nouns in *-os* which have the stress on the second from the last syllable shift the accent to the next to the last syllable in the restrictive case of the singular.

Now you remember the phrases *kírie* 'Mr!' and *fíle-mu* 'my friend!' which are in the case of address. You have just learned that the case of address (whenever you need it) is identical with the object case (address) form, you simply take away the final *s* from the subject case.

Thus you say: *kiría-mu* 'madam', *patéra* 'father!', and you address your friends *mítsos*, *níkos*, *pétros*, *spíros*, *yórghos* as *mítso*, *níko*, *pétro*, *spíro*, *yórgho*. But *kírie* and *fíle* differ from this pattern. Almost all the *-os* nouns which are not first names have in the case of address the ending *-e*.

SUMMARY: nouns in *-os*

	'friend'	'Mr.'	'Nick'
subj.	*o-fílos*	*o-kírios*	*o-níkos*
obj.	*to-fílo*	*ton-gírio*	*to-níko*
rest.	*tu-fílu*	*tu-kiríu*	*tu-níku*
address	*fíle*	*kírie*	*níko*

Since you have now learned how to handle Greek masculine and feminine nouns in the singular, we shall not hereafter register in the *Finder List* the object and restrictive cases and the form of address of those nouns, but only the subject case, from which you can easily derive the other forms.

[3–B]

COMMENT 4

A VERB IN -me. In Unit 2 we spoke about verbs like *kséro*. In this Unit you have met some more verbs that behave in the same way. They are *dhyavázo* 'I read', *dhulévo* 'I labor', *méno* 'I stay; I live'.

But you have also found in this Unit a verb that behaves very differently from the former ones. In *ergházome* 'I work' *erghaz-* is the stem to which the following endings are attached:

I-form	-ome	ergház*OME*
you-form	-este	ergház*ESTE*
he-, *she*-, *it*-form	-ete	ergház*ETE*
we-form	-ómaste	erghaz*ÓMASTE*
they-form	-onde	ergház*ONDE*

Notice that in the *we*-form the accent shifts from the stem, where it is in all the other forms, to the *o* of the ending.

From now on, verbs that are to be handled like *ergházome* will be registered in the *Finder Lists* in the *I*-form only.

COMMENT 5

HOW TO ASK QUESTIONS, AND HOW TO SAY 'YES' OR 'NO'. Now let's see how you ask questions in Greek and how you give either an affirmative or a negative answer to questions.

QUESTION:	AFFIRMATIVE ANSWER:	NEGATIVE ANSWER:
echi-adherfó?	*né.*	*óchi.*
Has he a brother?	Yes.	No.
échete-kóri?	*málista.*	*óchi, dhén-ekho-kóri.*
Have you a daughter?	Yes.	No, I have no daughter.
iste-pandreménos?	*né, íme.*	*óchi, dhén-ime.*
Are you married?	Yes, I am.	No, I'm not.
o-patéra-sas k-i-mitéra-sas zún-akóma?	*zúne.*	*óchi, dhé-zúne.*
Are your father and mother still living?	Yes. ('They are living.')	No. ('No, they're not living.')

For 'yes' you say *né*, or more politely *málista*. For plain 'no' you say *óchi*. For 'not' you say *dhén*, which you place before the verb: *dhén-ime* 'I am not', *dhén-ekho-kóri* 'I have no daughter.' ('I have not a daughter.')

Very often you repeat the most essential word of the question asked: *zúne* 'They are living.' When we say in English 'can I?', we know that it is a question and not the same as 'I can', because we put 'I' after the verb. But in Greek, as you know, we don't ordinarily use the equivalents for 'I', 'you', 'he', etc. with the verb. Therefore the difference between *boró* 'I can' and *boró?* 'can I?' consists only in the higher pitch with which you pronounce the accented vowel when you ask a question. Greek has nothing to match our phrases like 'do you want?' or 'I don't want'; it says simply 'you want?' *thélete?* or 'I want not' *dhé-thélo*. Notice finally that for English 'where are you going?' Greek says simply 'where go you?' *pú-páte?*

Read aloud several times all the examples given in this Section on *Word Study*. Then cover the English and see if you know the meaning of every item. Repeat this operation until you are sure that you know every expression. As a final test, cover the Greek and see if you can say the Greek expression simply by looking at the English.

Before you go on to the next section, turn back to the *Basic Sentences* and look for examples of the things that have just been explained to you. Examine the forms of the nouns. Ask yourself why this or that noun stands in the subject case, or the object case, or the restrictive case. Have you mastered the special set of forms of the masculine nouns in *-os*, which are so frequent in Greek? Can you tell whether a noun is masculine, feminine, or neuter by looking at the word for 'a' or 'the' which accompanies the noun? If the *Basic Sentences* don't show you what kind of a word a noun is, be sure to look it up in the *Finder List*. Remember that you have to have this information on every noun; if you don't, you can't use it.

2. Covering English and Greek of Word Study (Individual Study)

Before you leave the *Word Study*, cover the English equivalents in each list and make sure that you know the meaning of every Greek expression. Then cover the Greek and see if you can say each Greek expression when you are looking only at the English.

3. Review of Basic Sentences

Review the first half of the *Basic Sentences*. Repeat individually with books closed. Work always to perfect your pronunciation; keep the meaning in mind; and observe examples of the points in the *Word Study* you have just covered.

Section C—Review of Basic Sentences (*Cont.*)

1. Review of Basic Sentences (*Cont.*)

Review the second half of the *Basic Sentences.* Follow the procedure suggested above.

2. Covering the English of Basic Sentences (Individual Study)

Go back to the *Basic Sentences* in Section A, cover the English and test yourself by reading the Greek, just as you did in Section C of the previous Unit. If you are not sure about the meaning of any words or phrases when you have finished reading the *Basic Sentences* aloud, uncover the English and look up their meaning. Keep this up until you know all the meanings completely.

3. What Would You Say? (Individual Study)

In the following exercise you have certain situations presented for which you are to choose the correct expression in Greek. Read the situation, repeat aloud all the solutions for each situation, and then indicate for the next class meeting the answer which you consider the most appropriate.

1. You are at a friend's house one evening. Two gentlemen, John Cook and Nick Roilos, call. Your friend greets them, saying:
   a. *kaliméra-sas.*
   b. *kalispéra-sas.*
   c. *kaliníkhta-sas.*
   d. *ti-kánete?*

2. He then introduces them to you:
   a. *boró-na-sas-parusiáso ton-gírio-*Cook *ke-ton-gírio-roiló?*
   b. *aftí-ine-i-yinéka-mu.*
   c. *aftós-in-o-yóz-mu o-spíros.*

3. Mr. Roilos is a farmer, so your friend says:
   a. *o-kírioz-roilós ine-stratyótis.*
   b. *o-kírioz-roilós ine-náftis.*
   c. *o-kírioz-roilós echi-khtíma.*
   d. *o-kírioz-roilós ine-ipálilo-se-ghrafío.*

4. He tells you where Mr. Roilos works, saying:
   a. *o-fíloz-mu-o-roilós dhulévi s-to-khtíma-tu.*
   b. *o-fíloz-mu-o-roilós ine-se-vapóri.*
   c. *o-fíloz-mu-o-roilós dhulévi s-erghostásio.*
   d. *o-fíloz-mu-o-roilós ergházete se-ghrafío.*

5. You ask about Mr. Cook's work:
    a. *o-álos-kírios pyós-íne?*
    b. *o-álos-kírios tí-dhulyá-káni?*
    c. *pyós-in-o-kírios-*Cook?
    d. *pós-ta-léne ta-pedhyá-tis?*

6. The friend answers:
    a. *aftós-in-o-kírios-*Cook?
    b. *o-kírios-*Cook *ine-náftis.*
    c. *méni s-tin-eksochí.*

7. Mr. Roilos offers this information about Mr. Cook:
    a. *o-fíloz-mu ine-se-vapóri.*
    b. *to-fílo-mu tone-léne-aravandinó.*
    c. *méni me-tis-adherfés-tu s-tin-athína.*
    d. *ine-fitítria.*

8. Mr. Cook asks you about your trade, saying:
    a. *échete-pedhyá?*
    b. *ist-amerikanós, dhén-in-étsi?*
    c. *iste-dháskalos í-yatrós?*

9. You reply to his question:
    a. *dhén-ime míte-dháskalos míte-yatrós.*
    b. *o-patéras-tu méni se-ksenodhochío.*
    c. *tis-ksérume tis-adherfés-tus.*

10. You tell him that you are a student:
    a. *im-erghátis.*
    b. *ime-fititís.*
    c. *ime-yeorghós.*

Section D—Listening In

1. What Did You Say?

To the Group Leader: Follow the same procedure as for Section D of Unit 2. Call on different students, not in any fixed order, to give their answers in Greek for the exercise *What Would You Say?* in Section C3 of this Unit. Encourage them to give the answers directly and not from the books, if possible. Then check on the students' knowledge of the meaning in English of the different expressions in Greek.

Go back to the last exercises in the preceding Section. The Leader will call for your answers in Greek for the exercises. If you can, give the correct answers without reading from the book. Other members of the group will criticize the choice made if they disagree. The Leader will then call for the English equivalents of all the expressions in the exercises.

2. Word-Study Check-Up

To the Group Leader: Follow the same procedure as for this part of Section D of Unit 2. Call on various students for the correct Greek for the English equivalents of the expressions given in the *Word Study*. Make sure that all the students have learned the material thoroughly.

Go back to the *Word Study* in Section B. The Leader will ask different members of the group to give the correct Greek for the English equivalents of the expressions you went over in the *Word Study*. Be sure you are able to give the correct form without having to read it from the book. If you have any difficulty, review the *Word Study* thoroughly.

3. Listening In

To the Group Leader: Follow the same procedure as for *Listening In* in Section D3 of Unit 2. Check up on meaning at the end of each conversation on the first time through; then, after the second time through, assign parts and have the students read the conversations.

Keep your book closed while the Guide reads the following conversations, or while they are played on the phonograph, and repeat the Greek immediately after hearing it. At the end of each conversation, check up on the meaning of any word or phrase about which you are in doubt, either by asking some other member of the group or by going back to the *Basic Sentences* if no one knows.

Go through the conversations again, with your books open, being sure to imitate carefully and to keep in mind the meaning of everything you are saying. Then take turns speaking the parts. Make the conversations real. Say your part as though you meant it.

Record 6A, after third spiral.

1. Nick introduces himself to John.

níkos:	kalispéra-sas.	Καλησπέρα σας.
yánis:	kalispéra-sas.	Καλησπέρα σας.
níkos:	t-onomá-mu ine-roilós.	Τ' ὄνομά μου εἶναι Ροϊλός.
yánis:	chéro-polí.	Χαίρω πολύ.

níkos:	k-esás pó-saz-léne?	Κ' ἐσᾶς, πῶς σᾶς λένε;
yánis:	me-léne-Cook.	Μὲ λένε Cook
níkos:	chéro párapoli.	Χαίρω πάρα πολύ.

Record 6A, after fourth spiral.

2. John invites Nick to have a drink with him.

yánis:	eláte-mazí-mu.	Ἐλᾶτε μαζί μου.
	tí-boró-na-sas-prosféro?	Τί μπορῶ νὰ σᾶς προσφέρω;
	thélete mya-bíra i-enan-gafé?	Θέλετε μιὰ μπίρα ἢ ἕναν καφέ;
níkos:	enan-gafé parakaló.	Ἕναν καφέ, παρακαλῶ.

Record 6B, beginning.

yánis:	pedhí!	Παιδί!
	échete-bíra?	Ἔχετε μπίρα;
to-pedhí:	málista.	Μάλιστα.
yánis:	enan-gafé ke-mya-bíra parakaló.	Ἕναν καφὲ καὶ μιὰ μπίρα, παρακαλῶ.

Record 6B, after first spiral.

3. John and Nick speak about their work and that of their friends.

níkos:	pú-ménete? s-tim-bóli i-s-tin-eksochí?	Ποῦ μένετε; Στὴν πόλι ἢ στὴν ἐξοχή;
	tí-dhulyá-kánete?	Τί δουλειὰ κάνετε;
	pú-ergházeste?	Ποῦ ἐργάζεστε;
yánis:	ime-náftis.	Εἶμαι ναύτης.
	dhulévo se-vapóri.	Δουλεύω σὲ βαπόρι.

[3–D]

níkos:	ékho-ena-fílo pu-ine-náftis.	Ἔχω ἕνα φίλο ποὺ εἶναι ναύτης.
	tone-léne aravandinó.	Τόνε λένε 'Αραβαντινό.
	tone-ksérete?	Τόνε ξέρετε;
yánis:	to-níko-ton-aravandinó?	Τὸ Νίκο τὸν 'Αραβαντινό;
	tone-kséro.	Τόνε ξέρω.
	dhulévume-mazí.	Δουλεύουμε μαζί.
	ine-fíloz-mu.	Εἶναι φίλος μου.
	ine-polí-kalo-pedhí.	Εἶναι πολὺ καλὸ παιδί.
	échete-fílu-s-tin-athína?	Ἔχετε φίλους στὴν 'Αθήνα;
níkos:	né, ékho-ena-soro-fílu-s-tin-athína.	Ναί, ἔχω ἕνα σωρὸ φίλους στὴν 'Αθήνα.
	énas-ap-tus-fíluz-mu ine-ipálilo-se-ghrafío.	Ἕνας ἀπ' τοὺς φίλους μου εἶναι ὑπάλληλος σὲ γραφεῖο.
	ke-i-adherfés-tu ergházonde se-ghrafío.	Καὶ οἱ ἀδερφές του ἐργάζονται σὲ γραφεῖο.
	o-adherfós-tu ine-stratyótis.	Ὁ ἀδερφός του εἶναι στρατιώτης.
yánis:	to-pedhí enos-fílu-mu in-ergháti-s-erghostásio.	Τὸ παιδὶ ἑνὸς φίλου μου εἶν' ἐργάτης σ' ἐργοστάσιο.
	ke-i-yinéka-tu dhulévi s-erghostásio.	Καὶ ἡ γυναῖκα του δουλεύει σ' ἐργοστάσιο.
	i-adherfí-tu ine-fitítria.	Ἡ ἀδερφή του εἶναι φοιτήτρια.
	dhyavázi ena-soro-vivlía.	Διαβάζει ἕνα σωρὸ βιβλία.

Record 6B, after second spiral.

4. John and Nick speak about their families.

yánis:	iste-pandreménos?	Εἶστε παντρεμένος;
níkos:	né, íme.	Ναί, εἶμαι.
	ime-yeorghós.	Εἶμαι γεωργός.
	i-yinéka-mu-i-maría méni-s-to-khtíma-mas.	Ἡ γυναῖκα μου ἡ Μαρία μένει στὸ χτῆμα μας.
	dhulévi párapoli.	Δουλεύει πάρα πολύ.

yánis:	échete-pedhyá?	Ἔχετε παιδιά;
níkos:	né, ékho tría: to-spíro to-mítso ke-tim-bópi.	Ναί, ἔχω, τρία: τὸ Σπύρο, τὸ Μήτσο καὶ τὴν Πόπη.
	k-esís? iste-pandreménos?	Κ' ἐσεῖς; Εἶστε παντρεμένος;
yánis:	óchi, dhén-ime.	Ὄχι, δὲν εἶμαι.
	dhén-ekho míte-yinéka míte-pedhyá.	Δὲν ἔχω μήτε γυναῖκα μήτε παιδιά.
níkos:	aftá-echi-i-zoí-tu-náfti.	Αὐτὰ ἔχει ἡ ζωὴ τοῦ ναύτη.

Record 6B, after third spiral.

5. John has to leave.

yánis:	me-sikhoríte.	Μὲ συχωρεῖτε.
	tí-ora-íne?	Τί ὥρα εἶναι;
níkos:	in-eftá.	Εἶν' ἐφτά.
yánis:	tí-ípate! in-eftá?	Τί εἴπατε! Εἶν' ἐφτά;
	s-tis-okhtó févyi-to-tréno-mu.	Στὶς ὀχτὼ φεύγει τὸ τρένο μου.
	pú-in-o-stathmós?	Ποῦ εἶν' ὁ 'σταθμός;
níkos:	ksérete pu-méni-o-yatrós-o-kladhás?	Ξέρετε ποῦ μένει ὁ γιατρὸς ὁ Κλαδᾶς;
yánis:	óchi, dhén-gzéro.	Ὄχι, δὲν ξέρω.
níkos:	ksérete pu-íne-to-ksenodhochío tu-mítsu tu-khristofóru?	Ξέρετε ποῦ εἶναι τὸ ξενοδοχεῖο τοῦ Μήτσου τοῦ Χριστοφόρου;
yánis:	óchi, dhén-gzéro.	Ὄχι, δὲν ξέρω.
níkos:	ksérete pu-íne-to-estiatório tu-spíru tu-burbúli?	Ξέρετε ποῦ εἶναι τὸ ἐστιατόριο τοῦ Σπύρου τοῦ Μπουρμπούλη;
yánis:	né, to-kséro, in-aristerá.	Ναί, τὸ ξέρω· εἶν' ἀριστερά.
níkos:	polí-kala.	Πολὺ καλά.
	ekí-pu-íne-to-estiatório ke-to-ksenodhochío íne-ky-o-stathmós.	Ἐκεῖ ποὺ εἶναι τὸ ἐστιατόριο καὶ τὸ ξενοδοχεῖο εἶναι κι ὁ σταθμός.

yánis:	sas-efkharistó-polí.	Σᾶς εὐχαριστῶ πολύ.
níkos:	parakaló.	Παρακαλῶ.
yánis:	chérete.	Χαίρετε.
níkos:	kalinikhta-sas.	Καληνύχτα σας.

Section E—Conversation

1. Covering the Greek of Basic Sentences (Individual Study)

Just as you did in Section E of Unit 2, go back to the *Basic Sentences* of this Unit, cover up the Greek and test yourself to see how many words and phrases you can say in Greek when you are looking only at the English.

2. Vocabulary Check-Up

To the Group Leader: As in Unit 2, go around the class calling on various students and asking them: *"póz-lét-eliniká . . .?"* for the English equivalents in the *Basic Sentences*, with their books closed. If any student does not answer in a reasonable time, do not allow hemming and hawing; call on another student. Make sure that every student speaks loud enough so that all can hear. Do not allow any mumbling. Any student who cannot give satisfactory answers needs more review of the *Basic Sentences*.

As you did in Unit 2, supply the Greek expressions for the English equivalents in the *Basic Sentences*, when the Leader calls on you. Give your answers in a loud, clear voice, so that everyone can hear you.

3. Conversation

To the Group Leader: Follow the same procedure as for Section E3 of Unit 2. Have the students converse, first following closely the model of the conversations outlined below and then changing the situation slightly.

As you did in the Conversation in Section E3 of Unit 2, first go through the conversations outlined below, taking turns. As soon as you can speak the parts smoothly, pass to acting them out in front of the group; keep this up until you can do it easily and smoothly.

I. *You discuss jobs with a Greek acquaintance of yours.*

1. You ask him what his job is.
2. He tells you he is a sailor.
3. You ask him what the name of his ship is.
4. He says that it is named *Pope* like his sister. He asks what work you do.
5. You tell him that you are a teacher.
6. He mentions that he has a friend who is a teacher in Salonica, and adds that another friend of his is a doctor, and a very good one, too.
7. You inquire what his friend's name is and where he lives.
8. He says that his name is Aravantinos, but he cannot tell you where he lives. His sister knows (it). Let's go together to her office, he suggests.
9. No, you say, you can't. You are going to the factory of a friend of yours. Fifty girls work over there and one (man) worker only.
10. A lot of girls, he replies, and only one boy—such is life!

II. *You talk to a Greek college girl.*

1. She announces that she is a student.
2. You ask her whether she works hard.
3. She assures you that she does, and that she reads a lot of books.
4. You say that you and your friends read a lot of books, too; but neither your brother, who is a soldier, nor your father, who is an employee in an office, read much.
5. You ask her whether she lives in Athens or in Salonica.
6. She says that she is staying with her sister in Athens; her father and mother live out in the country—they have farms there.
7. You ask her if she knows Mr. Hill. He is a student and lives in Athens.
8. She counters by asking you if he is an American.
9. You say yes, and add that he is a very nice fellow.
10. No, she says, I am sorry, but I don't know him.

After you have practiced these conversations until you can do them easily and smoothly, change the situations somewhat and introduce more material from previous units. Use your imagination in thinking up various combinations of situations. For example, when you introduce yourself to a Greek, you can discover that you have a common friend in Chicago, or some such place. The Greek asks how the common friend is, then invites you to a restaurant. In the restaurant he and asks you what you want, orders the meal, and then pays for it. Or a friend you meet can ask you about your parents—where they're living now and how they are.

SECTION F—CONVERSATION (*Cont.*)

Continue the conversations started in Section E. If necessary to make the conversations smoother and more successful, review parts 1 and 2 of Section E.

FINDER LIST

This *Finder List* has all the new words and expressions used in this Unit. (The conventional spelling is given in the middle column.) These as well as those of the previous two Units, are words and expressions which by this time you should know quite well.

Abbreviations:
- *m.* masculine
- *f.* feminine
- *n.* neuter
- *subj.* subject
- *obj.* object
- *rest.* restrictive
- *s.* singular
- *p.* plural

A

adherfés f.p.	ἀδερφές	sisters
aftá n.p.	αὐτά	these *or* those things
álos m.s., subj.	ἄλλος	other; another
enas-álos	ἕνας ἄλλος	another
o amerikanós	ὁ Ἀμερικανός	the American
ap	ἀπ'	of
aravandinós	Ἀραβαντινός	Aravantinos (*family name*)
i athína	ἡ Ἀθήνα	Athens

B

bóli see: póli

D

o dháskalos	ὁ δάσκαλος	teacher
dhém see: dhén		
dhén, dhém	δὲν	not
dhulévo	δουλεύω	I labor; I work
i dhulyá	ἡ δουλειά	work; job
dhyavázo	διαβάζω	I read

E

eghó		
emís	ἐμεῖς	we
tis f.	τὶς	them
to	τὸ	it
ta n.	τὰ	them
i eksochí	ἡ ἐξοχή	country(side)
emís see: eghó		
énas m., subj.	ἔνας	one
enas		
nos m. and n.	ἐνὸς	of a
myas f.	μιᾶς	of a
enos see: enas		
o erghátis	ὁ ἐργάτης	worker
ergházome	ἐργάζομαι	I work
to erghostásio	τὸ ἐργοστάσιο	factory
étsi	ἔτσι	so
dhén-in-étsi?	δὲν εἶν' ἔτσι;	is it not so?

[3–F]

F

o fílos	ὁ φίλος	friend
fílus p., obj.	φίλους	
fílus see: *fílos*		
o fititís	ὁ φοιτητής	(college) student (male)
i fitítria	ἡ φοιτήτρια	(college) student (female)

G

to ghrafío	τὸ γραφεῖο	office
gzéro see: *kséro*		

I

í	ἤ	or
i see: *o*		
o ipálilos	ὁ ὑπάλληλος	employee

K

kalá see: *kalós*		
kaló see: *kalós*		
kalós	καλός	good
kaló n.s.	καλό	
kalá n.p.	καλά	
to khtíma	τὸ χτῆμα	farm; estate
khtímata p.	χτήματα	
korítsya n.p.	κορίτσια	girls
kséro	ξέρω	I know
dhén-gzéro	δὲν ξέρω	I don't know

M

méno	μένω	I stay; I live
míte...míte	μήτε...μήτε	neither...nor
o mítsos	ὁ Μήτσος	Metsos (*first name; endearing for* Demetrius)

mu
    tis   της   her
    tus   τους   their

myas see: *enas*

N

o náftis	ὁ ναύτης	sailor
o níkos	ὁ Νίκος	Nick

O

o	ὁ	the
i m.p., subj.	οἱ	
tus m.p., obj.	τοὺς	
tim f.s., obj.	τὴν	
i f.p., subj.	οἱ	
tu n.s., rest.	τοῦ	
ta n.p., subj.-obj.	τὰ	

P

to pedhí		
tu-pedhyú	τοῦ παιδιοῦ	of the boy
pedhyú see: *pedhí*		
pó		
na-pó	νὰ πῶ	that I tell

[3–F]

i póli	ἡ πόλι	city; town
bóli		
i pópi	Πόπη	Pope (*first name; endearing for* Penelope)
prosféro		
na-prosféro	νὰ προσφέρω	that I offer
pu	ποὺ	where; who; which; that

R

roilós	Ροϊλός	Roilos (*family name*)

S

s see: *se*

se, s (*s* always before the definite article)	σὲ, σ'	to; in; on; at
soró		
ena-soró	ἕνα σωρὸ	a lot (of)
o *spíros*	ὁ Σπύρος	Spyros (*first name; endearing for* Spyridon)
o *stratyótis*	ὁ στρατιώτης	soldier

T

ta see: *eghó*
ta see: *o*
tim see: *o*
tis see: *eghó*
tis see: *mu*
to see: *eghó*
tu see: *o*
tus see: *o*
tus see: *mu*

V

to vapóri	τὸ βαπόρι	(steam)ship
vivlía n.p.	βιβλία	books

Y

o yatrós	ὁ γιατρός	doctor
o yeorghós	ὁ γεωργός	farmer

Z

i zoí	ἡ ζωή	life; living

UNIT 4

WHERE ARE YOU FROM?

Section A—Basic Sentences

To the Group Leader: From this point on you will need special instructions only when new sections or procedures are introduced in the learning units. With other sections, simply follow the procedures which have been recommended in the first three Units and the instructions provided for the group at the beginning of the sections.

Go through the *Basic Sentences* in unison. Then work on the *Hints on Pronunciation* and after that go through the *Basic Sentences* at least twice more individually.

1. Basic Sentences

Record 7A, beginning.

Peter Smith, the American businessman, and John Cook, the sailor, speak with Nick Roilos about the places they are from and where they have lived.

——— ENGLISH EQUIVALENTS ———	——— AIDS TO LISTENING ———	——— CONVENTIONAL SPELLING ———
Nick		
tell me, please	dhe-mu-léte	δὲ μοῦ λέτε
from what place?	apo-pyó-méros	ἀπὸ ποιὸ μέρος
Tell me, won't you, Mr. Smith, what part of the United States are *you* from?	dhe-mu-léte kírie-Smith, esís apo-pyó-méros-tis-amerikís íste?	Δὲ μοῦ λέτε, κύριε Smith, ἐσεῖς, ἀπὸ ποιὸ μέρος τῆς ᾽Αμερικῆς εἶστε;
Peter		
I'm from San Francisco.	im-ap-to-sanfrandzísko.	Εἶμ' ἀπ' τὸ Σὰν Φραντζίσκο.

[4–A]

Nick

a big city	megháli-póli	μεγάλη πόλι
one says	léi	λέει
They say San Francisco's a big city.	ine-megháli-póli-léi to-sanfrandzísko.	Εἶναι μεγάλη πόλι, λέει, τὸ Σὰν Φραντζίσκο.

Peter

Yes, and a very beautiful one.	né, ke-polí-oréa.	Ναί, καὶ πολὺ ὡραία.

Nick

relatives	singenís	συγγενεῖς
Do you have relatives over there?	échete-singenís-eki-péra?	Ἔχετε συγγενεῖς ἐκεῖ πέρα;

Peter

two uncles	dhyó-thíus	δυὸ θείους
three aunts	trís-thyádhes	τρεῖς θειάδες
Yes, I have two uncles and three aunts.	né, ekho-dhyó-thíus ke-trís-thyádhes.	Ναί, ἔχω δυὸ θείους καὶ τρεῖς θειάδες.

John

you were	ísaste	εἴσαστε
always	pánda	πάντα
Have you always been in San Francisco?	ísaste-pánda-s-to-sanfrandzísko?	Ἤσαστε πάντα στὸ Σὰν Φραντζίσκο;

Peter

before the war	prín-ap-tom-bólemo	πρὶν ἀπ' τὸν πόλεμο
I was living	émena	ἔμενα
No, before the war I used to live in New York.	óchi, prín-ap-tom-bólemo émena-s-ti-néa-yórki.	Ὄχι, πρὶν ἀπ' τὸν πόλεμο ἔμενα στὴ Νέα Ὑόρκη.

John

she was living	émene	ἔμενε
she, too	ky-aftí	κι αὐτή
My brother's daughter used to live there, too.	i-kóri-t-adherfú-mu émene-ky-aftí-ekí.	Ἡ κόρη τ' ἀδερφοῦ μου ἔμενε κι αὐτὴ ἐκεῖ.
she was	ítane	ἤτανε
in the Red Cross	s-ton-erithró-stavró	στὸν Ἐρυθρὸ Σταυρὸ
She was in the Red Cross.	ítane s-ton-erithró-stavró.	Ἤτανε στὸν Ἐρυθρὸ Σταυρό.
the man	o-ándras	ὁ ἄντρας
is an aviator	in-aeropóros	εἶν' ἀεροπόρος
Her husband's an aviator.	o-ándras-tis in-aeropóros.	Ὁ ἄντρας της εἶν' ἀεροπόρος.

Peter

afterwards	ístera	ὕστερα
I was	ímuna	ἤμουνα
in Italy	s-tin-italía	στὴν Ἰταλία
Later I was in Italy.	ístera imuna-s-tin-italía.	Ὕστερα ἤμουνα στὴν Ἰταλία.
a little Italian	ligha-italiká	λίγα ἰταλικά
I know a little Italian.	kséro-ligha-italiká.	Ξέρω λίγα ἰταλικά.

Record 7B, beginning.

John

I'm from Chicago.	eghó-ime-ap-to-sikágho.	Ἐγὼ εἶμαι ἀπ' τὸ Σικάγο.
the parents	i-ghonís	οἱ γονεῖς
they were living	ménane	μένανε
My parents have always lived there.	i-ghoníz-mu ménane-pánda-ki.	Οἱ γονεῖς μου μένανε πάντα 'κεῖ.

the grandfather	o-papús	ὁ παπποῦς
[a] Greek	romyós	Ρωμιός
My grandfather was a Greek.	o-papúz-mu itane-romyós.	Ὁ παπποῦς μου ἦτανε Ρωμιός.

Peter

now I understand	tóra-katalavéno	τώρα καταλαβαίνω
why	yatí	γιατί
you speak	milíte	μιλεῖτε
so well	tóso-kalá	τόσο καλά
Now I understand why you speak Greek so well.	tóra-katalavéno yatí-milíte tóso-kalá-eliniká.	Τώρα καταλαβαίνω γιατί μιλεῖτε τόσο καλά ἑλληνικά.

Nick

like me	san-g-eména	σὰν κ' ἐμένα
Yes, you speak Greek like me.	né, milít-eliniká san-g-eména.	Ναί, μιλεῖτ' ἑλληνικὰ σὰν κ' ἐμένα.

John

I don't speak	dhé-miló	δὲ μιλῶ
No, I don't speak it so [very] well.	óchi, dhén-da-miló tóso-kalá.	Ὄχι, δὲν τὰ μιλῶ τόσο καλά.
when	otan	ὅταν
I knew	íksera	ἤξερα
When I was a boy, I knew it well.	otan-ímuna-pedhí tá-ksera-kalá.	Ὅταν ἤμουνα παιδί, τά 'ξερα καλά.
[at] our home	spíti-mas	σπίτι μας
you see	vlépete	βλέπετε
we speak	milúme	μιλοῦμε

[4–A]

English	angliká	ἀγγλικά
more than	pyó-polí-apo	πιὸ πολὺ ἀπὸ
At home, you see, we speak English rather than Greek.	spíti-mas vlépete milúme-angliká pyó-polí-apo-eliniká.	Σπίτι μας, βλέπετε, μιλοῦμε ἀγγλικὰ πιὸ πολὺ ἀπὸ ἑλληνικά.

Peter

from Patras	ap-tim-bátra	ἀπ' τὴν Πάτρα
from another part	apo-álo-méros	ἀπὸ ἄλλο μέρος
of Greece	tis-eládhas	τῆς Ἑλλάδας
What about *you*, are you from Patras or from another part of Greece?	k-esís ist-ap-tim-bátra í-apo-álo-méros tis-eládhas?	Κ' ἐσεῖς, εἶστ' ἀπ' τὴν Πάτρα ἢ ἀπὸ ἄλλο μέρος τῆς Ἑλλάδας;

John

you were living	ménate	μένατε
near to	kondá-se	κοντὰ σὲ
Have you always lived near Patras?	ménate-pánda kondá-s-tim-bátra?	Μένατε πάντα κοντὰ στὴν Πάτρα;

Nick

| we were living before | méname-prín | μέναμε πρὶν |
| No, we lived at Salonica before. | óchi; méname-prín s-ti-saloníki. | Ὄχι, μέναμε πρὶν στὴ Σαλονίκη. |

Record 8A, beginning.

I had	íkha	εἶχα
a house	ena-spíti	ἕνα σπίτι
I had a house there.	íkha-ena-spíti-ekí.	Εἶχα ἕνα σπίτι ἐκεῖ.

John
far	makriá	μακρειά
here	edhó	ἐδώ
How far is it from here to Salonica?	póso-makriá-ine-apo-dhó-s-ti-saloníki?	Πόσο μακρειὰ εἶναι ἀπὸ 'δὼ στὴ Σαλονίκη;

Nick
It's five hundred kilometers.	ine-pendakósya-chilyómetra.	Εἶναι πεντακόσια χιλιόμετρα.

Peter
how many miles?	pósa-mílya	πόσα μίλια
How many miles is five hundred kilometers?	pendakósya-chilyómetra pósa-mílya-ine?	Πεντακόσια χιλιόμετρα πόσα μίλια εἶναι;

John
Three hundred miles.	trakósya-mílya.	Τρακόσια μίλια.

Peter
you would like	tha-thélate	θὰ θέλατε
that you go	na-páte	νὰ πάτε
with us	m-emás	μ' ἐμᾶς
Would you like to go along with us to Salonica?	tha-thélate-na-páte mazí-m-emás-s-ti-saloníki?	Θὰ θέλατε νὰ πάτε μαζὶ μ' ἐμᾶς στὴ Σαλονίκη;

Nick
I would like	thá-thela	θά 'θελα
that I go	na-páo	νὰ πάω
Yes, I'd like to go.	né, thá-thela-na-páo.	Ναί, θά 'θελα νὰ πάω.

[4–A]

Before you go through the *Basic Sentences* a second time, study the following:

2. Hints on Pronunciation

SHIFT OF ACCENT IN NOUNS. You have probably noticed certain little one-syllable or two-syllable words with no accent of their own, and have seen that some of them lean for support on the word that follows, while others lean on the word that precedes. Words which lean on the preceding word are, for example, *mu* 'my', *sas* 'your', *tu* 'his; its', *tis* 'her', *mas* 'our', and *tus* 'their'. Now if any one of the set just mentioned happens to stand right after a word that ordinarily has the accent on the second from the last syllable, this accent shifts to the last syllable.

You say:

   t-aftokínito 'the car'

But you say:

   t-aftokinitó-mas 'our car'

Some other words you know which are accented on the second from the last syllable are: *o-dháskalos* 'the teacher', *to-erghostásio* 'the factory', *to-estiatório* 'the restaurant', *o-ipálilos* 'the employee', *ta-khtímata* 'the farms', *t-ónoma* 'the name', *o-pólemos* 'the war'. Try saying these in combination with the little words for 'my', 'your', etc.

Record 8A, after first spiral.   PRACTICE

to-erghostásio	*to-erghostasió-mu*	*o-dháskalos*	*to-pedhí me-to-dhaskaló-tu*
o-ipálilos	*o-ipaliló-sas*	*o-pólemos*	*o-polemóz-mas*
t-aftokínito	*aftós ke-t-aftokinitó-tu*	*ta-khtímata*	*ta-khtimatá-tus*
t-ónoma	*t-onomá-tis*		

3. Check Yourself

Are you taking every opportunity to practice your Greek by talking with other members of the group or with Greek-speaking people whom you may meet?

SECTION B—WORD STUDY AND REVIEW OF BASIC SENTENCES

1. Word Study (Individual Study)

Work through the following as recommended in the previous Units.

COMMENT 1

PERSONAL SUBSTITUTES. In a sentence like "John had promised Mary the book three weeks ago, but he didn't give it to her until today," the word 'he' stands for 'John', 'her' for 'Mary', and 'it' for 'book'. These shor words 'he', 'her', and 'it' are a few of the many words that are substituted for nouns and are, therefore, called *pronouns*. There are several kinds of these pronouns, and the kind we are studying now ('I', 'me', 'you', 'he', 'him', etc.) are called, just to have a convenient label, *personal pronouns*.

(a) SUBJECT PRONOUNS. As you have heard, our English words 'I', 'we', 'he', 'they', etc., are normally not expressed in Greek: they are contained in the ending of the verb.

Now look at the following sentences, almost all of which you have already heard:

eghó ke-ta-pedhyá-mu erghazómaste-polí.	My children and I work hard.
emís ékhume-khtímata.	*We* (in contrast to *you*) have farms.
tí-kánete?—kalá, efkharistó, k-esís?	How are you?—Well, thank you, and *you?*
aftós k-i-yinéka-tu ítan-ap-ti-saloníki.	He and his wife were from Salonica.
i-kóri-t-adherfú-mu émene-ky-aftí-ekí.	My brother's daughter, (she) too, used to live there.
i-adherfé-sas ménune-ky-aftés-ekí-péra?	Do your sisters live over there, (they) too?

You have noticed that in these examples the substitutes *eghó* 'I', *emís* 'we', *esís* 'you', *aftós* 'he', *aftí* 'she', *aftés* 'they' (which are always the *subject* of the sentence) are strongly stressed or particularly singled out: 'I and my children'; 'we (in contrast to *you*)'; 'and you'; 'he and his wife', etc. This means that in Greek subject pronouns are expressed if they are stressed. The words for 'he', 'she', 'it', 'they' deserve a special remark. The example *ky-aftí* 'she, too' reminds you, no doubt, of the word *aftí* 'this' which you learned earlier. Indeed, Greek uses the same word for 'he' and 'this', 'she' and 'this', 'they' and 'these', etc. This identity may explain to you the fact that in Greek one uses the subject pronouns if one definitely insists or distinguishes.

(b) OBJECT PRONOUNS.

'me' *me-sikhoríte.*	Excuse me.

Now compare these examples:

o-níkos dhén-íksere-to-fílo-mu tom-bétro ma-íkser-eména.	Nick didn't know my friend Peter, but he knew me.
eláte s-eména.	Come to me.
milít-eliniká san-g-eména.	You speak Greek like me.

[4–B] 99

You see that for English 'me' Greek uses two forms *me* and *eména*. Notice that *me* is unstressed, whereas *eména* bears an accent. If you do not stress 'me' you use in Greek *me*; if you stress or particularly single out 'me' you use in Greek *eména*. You also use the stressed form of the pronouns after almost all the prepositions (e.g. the preposition *se* 'to' in *s-eména* 'to me'), or after *san-ge* 'like' (e.g. *san-g-eména* 'like me').

'us' Unstressed form:
    mas-kséri.   He knows us.
  Stressed form:
    mazí-m-emás   along with us

English 'us' is in Greek *mas* when unstressed, and *emás* when stressed.

'you' Unstressed form:
    sas-efkharistó-polí.   Thank you very much.
  Stressed form:
    k-esás pó-saz-léne?   And what's *your* name? ('And you, how do they call you?')

English 'you' is in Greek *sas* when unstressed, and *esás* when stressed.

'him' *tone-léne-yáni.*   His name is John. ('They call him John.')
The Greek word for 'him' is *tone*.*

'her' *tine-léne-maría.*   Her name is Mary. ('They call her Mary.')
The Greek word for 'her' is *tine*.**

'it' *dhém-boró-na-sas-to-pó.*   I can't tell you. ('I can't tell it to you.')
The Greek word for 'it' is *to*.

'them' m. *tus-kséro polí-kala.*   I know them very well.
The Greek word for masculine 'them' is *tus*.

---

*For *tone* many Greeks use *ton*. **For *tine* many Greeks use *tin*.

'them' f.   *tis-kséro tis-adherfés-tus.*   I know (them) their sisters.

The Greek word for feminine 'them' is *tis*.

'them' n.   *pós-ta-léne ta-pedhyá-sas?*   What are your children's names?
('How do they call them, your children?')

The Greek word for neuter 'them' is *ta*.

In our examples all the unstressed forms *me, mas, sas*, etc., and a few of the stressed forms stand in some relation to the verb: they are the goal or the *object* of the verb, and since they are pronouns, we call them *object pronouns*.

One difference between English and Greek should be kept in mind: when we say in English 'he' or 'him', we refer to a male; when we say 'she' or 'her', we refer to a female; and things are referred to by 'it'. This is a distinction according to sex. In Greek, however, the distinction is a grammatical one: we refer with a masculine pronoun to a masculine noun, with a feminine pronoun to a feminine noun, and with a neuter pronoun to a neuter noun.

Observe that in English we have only one form 'they' and one form 'them' to refer to male or female beings or to things. In Greek, however, we have three words for 'they', one masculine, one feminine, one neuter, and similarly three words for 'them'.

Now let's sum up what you have learned in this Comment about the *personal pronouns* (the list of which is, however, not yet complete):

Subject pronouns

eghó	I
emís	we
esís	you
aftós	he
aftí	she
aftó	it
aftí	they *m.*
aftés	they *f.*
aftá	they *n.*

Object pronouns

me, eména	me
mas, emás	us
sas, esás	you
tone	him
tine	her
to	it
tus	them *m.*
tis	them *f.*
ta	them *n.*

COMMENT 2

HOW TO EXPRESS 'MY', 'YOUR', 'HIS', ETC., IN GREEK. You have heard most of these phrases before:

t-onomá-mu	my name
to-vapóri-sas	your ship
o-yós-tu	his son
i-mitéra-tis	her mother
to-pedhí me-ti-mitéra-tu	the child with its mother
t-aftokinitó-mas	our car
i-adherfés-tus	their sisters

These substitutes express possession. They are unstressed and are placed after the noun. They are used according to gender, not according to sex. This set is complete.

SUMMARY:

mu	my	tu	its
sas	your	mas	our
tu	his	tus	their
tis	her		

COMMENT 3

VERBS WITH THE ACCENT ON THE LAST SYLLABLE. In Unit 2 you learned such verbs as *kséro*, *thélo*, *káno*, all of which bear the accent on the next to the last syllable in the *I*-form. But you must surely have noticed other verbs like *boró* 'I can', *efkharistó* 'I thank', *miló* 'I speak', and *parakaló* 'I beg', all of which bear the accent on the last syllable.

Here is a complete table of *miló*:

		Endings:
I speak	milÓ	-ó
you speak	milÍTE	-íte
he speaks	milÍ	-í
we speak	milÚME	-úme
they speak	milÚNE	-úne

You see that besides the difference in accent this set contains only one new form: the *you*-form (or *second person*) ends in *-íte* (instead of *-ete* as in *kséretе*). You say *milíte* 'you speak', *boríte* 'you can', *efkharistíte* 'you thank', *parakalíte* 'you beg'.

One other verb that behaves like *miló* is the short word *zó* 'I live'. You know from the *Basic Sentences* the *they*-form, which is *zúne* 'they live'. Here is the whole set:

zó	I live
zíte	you live
zí	he lives
zúme	we live
zúne	they live

COMMENT 4

'I WAS LIVING'.

(a) THE FORMS. In Unit 3 you had the verb *meno* 'I stay; I live'. Now in the *Basic Sentences* you have had the following phrases:

émena-s-ti-néa-yórki.	I used to live in New York.
ménate-pánda kondá-s-tim-bátra?	Have you always lived near Patras?
émene-ky-aftí-ekí.	She, too, used to live there.
méname-prín s-ti-saloníki.	We lived at Salonica before.
i-ghoníz-mu ménane-pánda-ki.	My parents have always lived there.

All the above sentences refer to the past: "*I used to live* in New York," "*We lived* at Salonica before," etc. You notice that this is a new tense that you are learning. We shall call it the *imperfective past*. First let's look at the forms:

	Endings:
émenA	-a
ménATE	-ate
émenE	-e
ménAME	-ame
ménANE	-ane

I was living; I used to live
you were living; you used to live
he was living; he used to live
we were living; we used to live
they were living; they used to live

You see how the imperfective past of *méno* is formed: to the stem *men-* you have to add the endings *-a*, *-ate*, *-e*, *-ame*, *-ane*. Furthermore you always put the accent on the second from the last syllable: *ménate*, *méname*, *ménane*. Where this is not possible (because there are not sufficient syllables), you have to attach an *é-* at the beginning, on which you put the stress: *I*-form: *émena*; *he*-form: *émene*. This *é-* placed in front of a verb is very characteristic of Greek. At first, perhaps, it may appear strange to you; but fairly soon its use will be quite natural to you. In this way you get the imperfective past of practically all the verbs which in the *-o* form are accented on the next to the last syllable and whose stem ends in a consonant. The following verbs behave like *méno*:

févgho	I leave	*éfevgha*	I was leaving; I used to leave
káno	I do	*ékana*	I was doing; I used to do
vlépo	I see	*évlepa*	I was seeing; I used to see

Of course, verbs whose stems have more than one syllable do not need the *é-* in the *I*-form (first person) or in the *he*-form (third person). Here are some verbs of this kind:

archízo	I begin	*árchiza*	I was beginning; I used to begin
dhulévo	I work	*dhúleva*	I was working; I used to work
dhyavázo	I read	*dhyávaza*	I was reading; I used to read
katalavéno	I understand	*katalávena*	I used to understand

(b) THE MEANING. Now to find out the use of this tense, the *imperfective past*, study carefully the sentences given above, and the following ones:

otan-ímuna-pedhí émena s-to-sikágho.
otan-ímuna-pedhí dhúleva-se-khtíma.
to-vapóri éfevye-pánda s-tis-okhtó-to-vrádhi ap-tim-bátra.

When I was a child, I used to live in Chicago.
When I was a child, I used to work on a farm.
The ship always left Patras at eight o'clock in the evening.

You see from these examples that the *imperfective past* emphasizes the fact that a given action or condition lasted over a certain length of time ("My parents have always lived there"), or was a regular habit ("I used to live in New York"), or was repeated ("The ship always left Patras at eight o'clock in the evening"), or was taking place at the same time something else occurred ("When I was a child, I used to work on a farm"). In English we have no such tense, but we use other forms instead, like 'I was living', 'I used to live', 'I always lived', etc.

(c) SOME SPECIAL (BUT VERY FREQUENT) FORMS.

otan-ímuna-pedhí   When I was a child,
íksera-kalá-eliniká.   I knew Greek well.

You see that the imperfective past *íksera* is a little different from the corresponding form of the other verbs (like *méno*, *káno*, etc.) whose stems have only one syllable. You say *émena*, *émene*, but *íksera*, *íksere*, with *í-* instead of *é-*. The verb *thélo* also behaves like *kséro*. You say *íthela* 'I wanted', *íthele* 'he wanted'.

And *ékho* 'I have' behaves somewhat differently, too. You have heard in the *Basic Sentences*:

ikha-ena-spíti-ekí.   I had a house there.

The imperfective past of *ékho* is *íkha*, with stressed *í-* in all the forms:

íkha	I	
íkhate	you	
íche	he	} had
íkhame	we	
íkhane	they	

Notice that you get *íkha*, *íkhate*, *íkhame*, and *íkhane* with a *kh*, but *íche* with a *ch*. This change of the *kh* to *ch* before *e* is not unfamiliar to you. You have had it already in the second person *échete* 'you have'. And finally, you will remember that the *gh* of *févgho* 'I leave' changes to *y* before *e: févyete* 'you leave'; now, we have the same change in the *he*-form of the imperfective past: *éfevye* 'he was leaving; he used to leave'.

(d) 'I WAS'. In this Unit you have also met the past of *íme* 'I am'. Here is a table of all the forms:

ímuna	I was; I have been
ísaste	you were; you have been
ítane	he was; he has been
ímaste	we were; we have been
ítane	they were; they have been

You say *ítane* for 'he was' *and* 'they were', and *ímaste* for 'we are' *and* 'we were'.

2. Covering English and Greek of Word Study (Individual Study)

Review this *Word Study* by reading aloud all of the Greek expressions. Then cover the English and make sure that you know the meaning of every item. Finally, cover the Greek and see if you can say each Greek expression when you are looking only at the English.

3. Review of Basic Sentences

With Guide or records, review the first half of the *Basic Sentences* for better pronunciation, meaning, and examples of points in the *Word Study*.

Section C—Review of Basic Sentences (*Cont.*)

1. Review of Basic Sentences (*Cont.*)

Review the second half of the *Basic Sentences*.

2. Covering the English of Basic Sentences (Individual Study)

Go back to the *Basic Sentences* in Section A, and read them aloud covering up the English. Note any words or phrases you are not sure about, and when you have finished reading the *Basic Sentences*, uncover the English and look up the meaning of what you did not get. Keep this up until you know all the meanings completely.

3. What Would You Say? (Individual Study)

I. Read aloud each of the following and then pick out the expression you think most suitable:

1. Two young men meet one morning. One is an American and the other is a Greek. The American greets the Greek, saying:
   a. *ime-romyós.*
   b. *kalispéra-sas kiría-mu.*
   c. *kaliméra-sas.*
   d. *efkharistó yatré-mu.*

2. After the Greek returns the greeting, the American asks where he is from, saying:
   a. *pó-saz-léne?*
   b. *tí-dhulyá-kánete?*
   c. *i-thyá-sas méni-s-tin-italía?*
   d. *apo-pú-iste?*
   e. *eláte-s-to-khtíma-mu.*

3. The Greek replies:
   a. *imun-aeropóros.*
   b. *iste-pandreménos?*
   c. *im-ap-tin-athína.*
   d. *otan-émena s-to-sanfrandzísko ikha-k-ekí-ena-estiatório.*

4. The Greek then asks the American where he is from, and the latter replies:
   a. *i-thyá-mu itane-mazí-m-emá-s-tin-eládha.*
   b. *enas-thíoz-mu méni-kondá-s-tim-bátra.*
   c. *otan-imaste-pedhyá i-ghoníz-mu ménane-s-to-sikágho.*
   d. *im-ap-ti-néa-yórki.*
   e. *ístera imuna-s-to-sikágho.*

5. The American tells where his father is from:
   a. *o-papús-tis ky-o-patéras-tis itane-ky-aftí
      ap-ti-néa-yórki.*
   b. *o-patéraz-mu in-ap-to-sanfrandzísko.*
   c. *i-adherfí-tu-patéra-mu ine-s-ton-erithró-stavró.*
   d. *i-thyá-mu méni-s-tin-italía.*
   e. *o-mítsos íksere-móno-eména.*

6. The American says that his mother is from Chicago:
   a. *otan-ísaste-s-tin-amerikí ménate-s-to-sikágho?*
   b. *ekho-singení-s-to-sikágho.*
   c. *i-mitéra-mu in-ap-to-sikágho.*
   d. *i-mitéra-sas émene-s-to-sikágho
      prin-ap-tom-bólemo?*
   e. *milún-eliniká pyó-polí-apo-angliká s-to-sikágho?*

7. The Greek asks him if his parents speak Greek:
   a. *dhé-miló-eliniká.*
   b. *spíti-mas milúm-eliniká.*
   c. *i-singení-sas póz-milún-eliniká?*
   d. *i-ghoní-sas milún-eliniká?*
   e. *o-ándras tis-thyáz-mu-tiz-marías
      milí-ligha-eliniká.*

8. He says that he speaks Italian:
   a. *miló-eliniká ky-angliká.*
   b. *milí-ky-aftí-ligha-italiká?*
   c. *eghó-miló-italiká.*
   d. *aftóz-dhé-milí tóso-kalá-italiká.*

9. The Greek asks if he has any brothers and sisters:
   a. *échete-thyádhes?*
   b. *i-ghoní-sas zún-akóma?*
   c. *ékhune-thíus?*
   d. *echet-adherfó-i-adherfí?*

10. The American answers:
    a. *ekho-ena-thío pu-méni-s-ti-salonikí.*
    b. *o-ándras-tis-adherfíz-mu in-aeropóros.*
    c. *ekho-enan-adherfó ke-trís-adherfés.*
    d. *méno-mazí-me-ton-adherfó-mu.*

11. The Greek says that it is three hundred miles from Athens to Salonica:
    a. *ap-to-spíti-pu-méname, s-ti-salonikí
       itane-dhéka-chilyómetra.*
    b. *póso-makriá-ine-ap-tin-athína-s-ti-salonikí?*
    c. *ine-trakósya-mílya ap-tin-athína-s-ti-salonikí.*
    d. *páme-s-tin-athína k-ístera s-ti-salonikí.*
    e. *tha-thélate-na-páte-s-ti-salonikí?*

II. The following sections are made up of sentences from a conversation between an American, John, and a Greek, Nick, only the sentences are not given in the order in which they should be spoken. Restore the conversation to a natural order, each person giving only one sentence each time.

1. Nick greets John. John asks how Nick is. Nick says that he is well and inquires about John's health. John says that he is fine.
   a. *polí-kala, efkharistó.*
   b. *kaliméra-sas.*
   c. *kalá, efkharistó, k-esís?*
   d. *tí-kánete?*

2. Nick asks if John isn't American. John explains that he is, and answers Nick's question about the part of the United States he is from.
   a. *im-ap-to-sikágho.*
   b. *né, ím-amerikanós.*
   c. *ist-amerikanós, dhén-in-étsi?*
   d. *apo-pyó-méros-tis-amerikís íste?*

3. Nick asks John about his parents.
   a. *óchi, ménune-s-to-sikágho.*
   b. *i-ghoní-sas zún-akóma?*
   c. *óchi, in-amerikanós.*
   d. *ménune-s-ti-néa-yórki-i-ghoní-sas?*
   e. *né, zúne.*
   f. *ine-romyós-o-patéra-sas?*

4. Nick and John discuss the languages they speak, don't speak, or would like to speak; Nick makes the first remark.
   a. *óchi, dhé-miló.*
   b. *milít-angliká?*
   c. *milíte-italiká?*
   d. *óchi, ma-thá-thela-na-ta-miló.*
   e. *né, lígha, k-esís?*

5. John asks Nick where he was born, and then the conversation is about Salonica.
   a. *im-ap-ti-saloníki.*
   b. *páme-mazí-s-ti-saloníki?*
   c. *in-oréa-póli-léi.*
   d. *apo-pú-íste?*
   e. *né, páme.*

Section D—Listening In

1. What Did You Say?

Give your answers for the last exercise in the preceding Section, when the Leader calls for them. Do it without reading from the book, if possible. Other members of the group will criticize your choice if they disagree with it. Then give the English equivalents of all the expressions in the exercise.

2. Word Study Check-Up

Give the correct Greek for each English expression in the *Word Study*, without having to read it from the book. If you cannot do this easily, it means you need to put in more work on the *Word Study*. The Group Leader will give the English and call on different members of the group for the Greek.

3. Listening In

With your book closed, listen to the following conversations as read by the Guide or phonograph record.

Record 8A, after second spiral.

1. Nick and John tell each other where they are from.

Repeat the Greek immediately after hearing it. After the first repetition of each conversation, check up on the meaning of anything you do not understand, by asking someone else or by going back to the *Basic Sentences* if no one knows.

Go through the conversations again with books open, following the same plan as before, imitating carefully and keeping in mind the meaning of everything you say. Finally, take parts and carry on the conversation.

níkos:	apo-pyó-méros-tis-amerikís íste?	Ἀπὸ ποιὸ μέρος τῆς Ἀμερικῆς εἶστε;
yánis:	im-ap-to-sikágho.	Εἶμ' ἀπ' τὸ Σικάγο.
	k-esís apo-pyó-méros-tis-eládhas íste?	Κ' ἐσεῖς, ἀπὸ ποιὸ μέρος τῆς Ἑλλάδας εἶστε;
níkos:	im-ap-ti-saloníki.	Εἶμ' ἀπ' τὴ Σαλονίκη.
	otan-ímuna-pedhí émena-ekí.	Ὅταν ἤμουνα παιδί, ἔμενα ἐκεῖ.
	dhe-mu-léte, ménete-s-to-sikágho?	Δὲ μοῦ λέτε, μένετε στὸ Σικάγο;
yánis:	óchi, méno-s-ti-néa-yórki.	Ὄχι, μένω στὴ Νέα Ὑόρκη.
	k-esís ménet-edhó-s-tin-athína?	Κ' ἐσεῖς, μένετ' ἐδῶ στὴν Ἀθήνα;
níkos:	óchi, méno-s-to-khtíma-mu kondá-s-tim-bátra.	Ὄχι, μένω στὸ χτῆμα μου, κοντὰ στὴν Πάτρα.

Record 8B, beginning.

2. They speak about languages.

níkos:	i-fíli-sa-s-to-sikágho milúne-ky-aftí-kalá-eliniká?	Οἱ φίλοι σας στὸ Σικάγο, μιλοῦνε κι αὐτοὶ καλὰ ἑλληνικά;

[4–D] 109

yánis:	né, kśerune-ligha-eliniká.
	ma-dhé-milúne-kalá.
níkos:	esíz-milíte polí-kala-eliniká.
yánis:	ma-dhé-miló tóso-kalá san-g-esás.
níkos:	né, milít-eliniká san-g-eména.
yánis:	i-mitéra-mu aftí-kśeri-kalá-eliniká.
	o-papúz-mu vlépete itane-romyós.
níkos:	tóra-katalavéno yatí-milít-eliniká.
	kśerete-italiká?
yánis:	né, kśero-k-italiká.
níkos:	zúne-s-tin-italía-i-ghoní-sas?
yánis:	óchi, zúne-s-tin-amerikí.

Ναί, ξέρουνε λίγα ἑλληνικά.
Μὰ δὲ μιλοῦνε καλά.
Ἐσεῖς μιλεῖτε πολὺ καλὰ ἑλληνικά.
Μὰ δὲ μιλῶ τόσο καλὰ σὰν κ' ἐσᾶς.
Ναί, μιλεῖτ' ἑλληνικὰ σὰν κ' ἐμένα.
Ἡ μητέρα μου, αὐτὴ ξέρει καλὰ ἑλληνικά.
Ὁ παππούς μου, βλέπετε, ἤτανε Ρωμιός.
Τώρα καταλαβαίνω γιατί μιλεῖτ' ἑλληνικά.
Ξέρετε ἰταλικά;
Ναί, ξέρω κ' ἰταλικά.
Ζοῦνε στὴν Ἰταλία οἱ γονεῖς σας;
Ὄχι, ζοῦνε στὴν Ἀμερική.

Record 8B, after first spiral.

3. Nick and John speak about their relatives.

níkos:	echete-singení-s-to-sikágho?
yánis:	né, ekho-ena-soro-singenís-eki-péra.
	ekho-trís-thíus ke-pénde-thyádhes.
níkos:	echet-adherfó-i-adherfí?*
yánis:	né, ekho-enan-adherfó ke-mya-adherfí.
níkos:	o-adherfó-sas ine-pandreménos?
yánis:	né, íne.
níkos:	echi-pedhyá-o-adherfó-sas?

Ἔχετε συγγενεῖς στὸ Σικάγο;
Ναί, ἔχω ἕνα σωρὸ συγγενεῖς ἐκεῖ πέρα.
Ἔχω τρεῖς θείους καὶ πέντε θειάδες.
Ἔχετ' ἀδερφὸ ἢ ἀδερφή;
Ναί, ἔχω ἕναν ἀδερφὸ καὶ μιὰ ἀδερφή.
Ὁ ἀδερφός·σας εἶναι παντρεμένος;
Ναί, εἶναι.
Ἔχει παιδιὰ ὁ ἀδερφός σας;

*On the record adhelfó and adhelfí, which may also be heard.

yánis: *né, échi.*
k-i-adherfí-mu-echi-pedhyá.
níkos: *pósa-pedhyá-ékhune?*
yánis: *o-adherfóz-mu echi-dhyó-korítsya,*
ke-i-adherfí-mu echi-ena-yó.
níkos: *íste-o-thíos-tus o-yánis!*
yánis: *né, im-o-thíos-tus o-yánis.*
níkos: *tí-dhulyá-káni-o-ándras-tis-adherfí-sas?*
yánis: *in-aeropóros.*
ine-s-tin-italía-tóra.
i-yinéka-t-adherfú-mu ine-s-ton-erithró-stavró.

Ναί, ἔχει.
Κ' ἡ ἀδερφή μου ἔχει παιδιά.
Πόσα παιδιὰ ἔχουνε;
Ὁ ἀδερφός μου ἔχει δυὸ κορίτσια, καὶ ἡ ἀδερφή μου ἔχει ἕνα γιό.
Εἶστε ὁ θεῖος τους ὁ Γιάννης!
Ναί, εἶμ' ὁ θεῖος τους ὁ Γιάννης.
Τί δουλειὰ κάνει ὁ ἄντρας τῆς ἀδερφῆς σας;
Εἶν' ἀεροπόρος.
Εἶναι στὴν Ἰταλία τώρα.
Ἡ γυναῖκα τ' ἀδερφοῦ μου εἶναι στὸν Ἐρυθρὸ Σταυρό.

Record 8B, after second spiral.

4. Nick and John speak about Salonica.

yánis: *mya-thyá-mu méni-s-ti-saloníki.*
póso-makriá-ine ap-tin-athína-s-ti-saloníki?
níkos: *ine-pendakósya-chilyómetra í trakósya-mílya*
apo-dhó-s-ti-saloníki.
oréa-póli-i-saloníki ke-meghâli!
yánis: *thá-thela-na-páo ma-dhém-boró-na-páo-tóra.*
níkos: *páme pedhí-mu tóra-s-ton-ginimatóghrafo,*
k-ístera páme-mazí-me-tom-bétro s-to-
khtíma-mu.*

Μιὰ θειά μου μένει στὴ Σαλονίκη.
Πόσο μακρειὰ εἶναι ἀπ' τὴν Ἀθήνα στὴ Σαλονίκη;
Εἶναι πεντακόσια χιλιόμετρα ἢ τρακόσια μίλια ἀπὸ 'δῶ στὴ Σαλονίκη.
Ὡραία πόλι ἡ Σαλονίκη καὶ μεγάλη!
Θά 'θελα νὰ πάω, μὰ δὲν μπορῶ νὰ πάω τώρα.
Πάμε, παιδί μου, τώρα στὸν κινηματόγραφο, κ' ὕστερα πάμε μαζὶ μὲ τὸν Πέτρο στὸ χτῆμα μου.

---

*On the record *tu.*

Section E—Conversation

1. Covering the Greek of Basic Sentences (Individual Study)

Cover the Greek of the *Basic Sentences* and practice saying the Greek equivalents of the English expressions.

2. Vocabulary Check-Up

As in previous Units, the Group Leader will call on various members of the group to give the Greek expressions which correspond to the English in the *Basic Sentences*.

3. Conversation

Work through the following outlined conversation, taking parts. Act it out in front of the group; keep this up until you can express yourself easily and smoothly. When the outlined conversation goes well, then change the situation somewhat. You now have more material which you can work into additional conversations. Invent topics as you did for the previous Units.

You and a new acquaintance of yours in Greece exchange information about your respective families.

1. He asks you whether you are an American.
2. You say yes, you are from America.
3. He says he has a good many relatives in America and that they live in New York or near New York.
4. He asks what part of America you are from.
5. You answer that now your parents live in Chicago, but that you used to live in San Francisco before.
6. You tell him that your father and mother are from Greece, and that your grandfather still lives there, in Patras.
7. In surprise he asks what you said, whether you said your grandfather was (is) still living.
8. You reply that it is true, he is still living.
9. He asks whether you would like to go to your grandfather's house.
10. You assure him that you would, and you inquire how far it is from here.
11. He says that it is five hundred kilometers; reminiscing, he remarks that before the war he had a friend who had a farm there.
12. You say that you have a good many relatives here—three uncles and six aunts.
13. He asks you whether you know where they live.

14. You answer that you know only where your Uncle John and your Aunt Mary and their children live.
15. He comments that you speak Greek very well.
16. You explain that your parents and your brother and sister speak Greek at home, but you say, "We don't speak it like you here in Greece."
17. He says he knows why: you always speak English rather than Greek.

SECTION F—CONVERSATION (*Cont.*)

Continue the conversation started in Section E, with a review of parts 1 and 2 of the Section if necessary.

FINDER LIST

A

o aerópóros	ὁ ἀεροπόρος	aviator
aftí see: *aftós*		
aftós	αὐτός	he
aftí	αὐτή	she
aftí m.	αὐτοί	they
álo n.	ἄλλο	other; another
i ameriki	ἡ 'Αμερική	America; U. S. A.
o ándras	ὁ ἄντρας	man; husband
angliká n.p.	ἀγγλικά	English (language)
apo, ap (*ap* is used before the definite article) see: *prín, pyó*	ἀπό, ἀπ'	from; of; than

B

bátra see: *pátra*
bólemo see: *pólemos*

C

chilyómetra n.p.	χιλιόμετρα	kilometers (*1 kilometer* = ⅝ *of a mile*)

D

da see: *ta*

dhío	δύο	two
dhyó (before nouns)	δυό	

dhó see: *edhó*
dhyó see: *dhío*

E

edhó, dhó	ἐδώ, 'δώ	here
ekí, kí	ἐκεῖ, 'κεῖ	there
i eládha	ἡ Ἑλλάδα	Greece
eliniká n.p.	ἑλληνικά	Greek (language)
emás	ἐμᾶς	us
eména	ἐμένα	me
o erithró-stavrós	ὁ Ἐρυθρὸς Σταυρός	Red Cross

G

g see: *ke*

ghonís m.p.	γονεῖς	parents

I

íksera	ἤξερα	I knew
tá-ksera	τά 'ξερα	I knew them
ístera	ὕστερα	afterwards
i italía	ἡ Ἰταλία	Italy
italiká n.p.	ἰταλικά	Italian (language)

íthela	ἤθελα	I wanted
thá-thela	θά 'θελα	I would like
tha-thélate	θὰ θέλατε	you would like

K

katalavéno   καταλαβαίνω   I understand
ke, ge, g   καὶ, κ'   and; also; too
   see: *san*
kí see: *ekí*
kondá-se   κοντὰ σὲ   near to
   kondá-s-tim-bátra   κοντὰ στὴν Πάτρα   near Patras
ksera see: *íksera*

L

léo   λέω   I say
   dhe-mu-léte   δὲ μοῦ λέτε   tell me, please
   léi   λέει   one says
lígha n.p.   λίγα   few
   ligha-italiká   λίγα ἰταλικά   a little Italian

M

makriá   μακρειά   far
mazí   μαζί   together
   mazí-me   μαζὶ μὲ   together with
   mazí-m-emás   μαζὶ μ' ἐμᾶς   along with us
megháli f.s.   μεγάλη   large; big

to méros	τὸ μέρος	place; part
miló	μιλῶ	I speak
na-miló	νὰ μιλῶ	that I speak
mílya n.p.	μίλια	miles

N

i néa-yórki	ἡ Νέα Ὑόρκη	New York

O

oréa f.s.	ὡραία	beautiful
otan	ὅταν	when

P

pánda	πάντα	always
páo	πάω	I go
na-páo	νὰ πάω	that I go
na-páte	νὰ πάτε	that you go
o papús	ὁ παπποῦς	grandfather
i pátra	ἡ Πάτρα	Patras (*seaport in western Greece*)
bátra		
pendakósya n.p.	πεντακόσια	five hundred
o pólemos	ὁ πόλεμος	war
bólemo		
pósa see: *póso*		
póso	πόσο	how much?
pósa n.p.	πόσα	how many?

prín	πρίν	before; previously
prín-apo	πρὶν ἀπὸ	before
prín-ap-tom-bólemo	πρὶν ἀπ' τὸν πόλεμο	before the war
pyó n.s.	ποιό	what?
pyó	πιό	more
pyó-polí	πιὸ πολύ	more
pyó . . . apo	πιὸ . . . ἀπὸ	more . . . than

R

o romyós	ὁ Ρωμιὸς	the Greek

S

san	σὰν	like
san-g-eména	σὰν κ' ἐμένα	like me
san-g-esás	σὰν κ' ἐσᾶς	like you
see: *tóso*		
to sanfrandzísko	τὸ Σὰν Φραντζίσκο	San Francisco
to sikágho	τὸ Σικάγο	Chicago
o singenís	ὁ συγγενής	relative
singenís p.	συγγενεῖς	
to spíti	τὸ σπίτι	house
spíti	σπίτι	at home
spíti-mas	σπίτι μας	at our home
stavrós see: *erithró-stavrós*		

T

ta, da n.	τὰ	them
tha see: *íthela*		
thela see: *íthela*		
thélate see: *íthela*		

o thíos	ὁ θεῖος	uncle
thíus p., obj.	θείους	
thíus see: thíos		
i thyá	ἡ θειά	aunt
thyádhes p.	θειάδες	
tóra	τώρα	now
tóso	τόσο	so; so much
tóso-kalá	τόσο καλά	so well
tóso ... san	τόσο ... σὰν	so ... as; as ... as
trakósya n.p.	τρακόσια	three hundred
tría	τρία	three
trís m. and f.	τρεῖς	
tría n.	τρία	
trís see: tría		

V

vlépo	βλέπω	I see

Y

yatí	γιατί	why?
o yatrós	ὁ γιατρός	doctor
yatré-mu	γιατρέ μου	doctor˙

118   [4–F]

UNIT 5

LET'S TALK ABOUT THE WEATHER

Section A—Basic Sentences

Go once through the *Basic Sentences* in unison, then *Hints on Pronunciation*, and then go twice more through the *Basic Sentences* individually.

1. Basic Sentences

Record 9A, beginning.

John Cook and Peter Smith have spent the night at Nick Roilos's farm. They wake up in the morning.

―― ENGLISH EQUIVALENTS ――   ―― AIDS TO LISTENING ――   ――CONVENTIONAL SPELLING――

John
Nick! — níko! — Νίκο!
Nick
I'm coming. — érkhome. — Ἔρχομαι.
Peter
what weather — tí-kerós — τί καιρός
How's the weather? — tí-keros-íne? — Τί καιρὸς εἶναι;
Nick
The weather's fine. ('It's fine weather.') — ine-kalós-kerós. — Εἶναι καλὸς καιρός.
John
sun — ílyos — ἥλιος
The sun's shining. — ine-ílyos. — Εἶναι ἥλιος.

[5–A]   119

Peter

in California	s-tin-galifórnya	στὴν Καλιφόρνια
three hundred	trakósyes	τρακόσιες
sixty	eksínda	ἑξήντα
five days of sún	pénde méres ílyo	πέντε μέρες ἥλιο
per year	to-khróno	τὸ χρόνο
In California we have three hundred [and] sixty-five days of sunshine a year.	s-tin-galifórnya ékhume trakósyes eksínda pénde méres ílyo to-khróno.	Στὴν Καλιφόρνια ἔχουμε τρακόσιες ἑξήντα πέντε μέρες ἥλιο τὸ χρόνο.

John

years	khrónya	χρόνια
every four years	káthe-tésera-khrónya	κάθε τέσσερα χρόνια
And every four years three hundred [and] sixty-six.	ke-káthe-tésera-khrónya trakósyes-eksinda-éksi.	Καὶ κάθε τέσσερα χρόνια τρακόσιες ἑξήντα ἕξι.

Peter

without	khorís	χωρίς
the jokes	t-astía	τ' ἀστεῖα
No joking!	khorís-t-astía!	Χωρὶς τ' ἀστεῖα!

John

bad	.kakós	κακός
in the winter	to-chimóna	τὸ χειμῶνα
Is the weather bad here in winter?	ine-kakós-o-kerós edhó-to-chimóna?	Εἶναι κακὸς ὁ καιρὸς ἐδὼ τὸ χειμῶνα;

Nick

not so very	óchi-ke-tóso	ὄχι καὶ τόσο
Not so very bad.	óchi-ke-tóso-kakós.	Ὄχι καὶ τόσο κακός.

the cold	to-krío	τὸ κρύο
It's cold. ('It makes cold.')	káni-krío.	Κάνει κρύο.
heavy	varí	βαρύ
But we don't have a hard winter.	ma-dhén-ékhume-varí-chimóna.	Μὰ δὲν ἔχουμε βαρὺ χειμῶνα.
this year	efétos	ἐφέτος
frosts	paghonyés	παγωνιές
This year we had [a lot of] frost.	efétos íkhame-paghonyés.	Ἐφέτος εἴχαμε παγωνιές.
the nights	i-níkhtes	οἱ νύχτες
cold	kríes	κρύες
Our nights were cold.	i-níkhtez-mas ítane-kríes.	Οἱ νύχτες μας ἤτανε κρύες.
it was snowing	chyónize	χιόνιζε
up	páno	πάνω
in the mountains	s-ta-vuná	στὰ βουνά
And it snowed up in the mountains.	ke-chyónize páno-s-ta-vuná.	Καὶ χιόνιζε πάνω στὰ βουνά.

Record 9B, beginning.

John

the snow	to-chyóni	τὸ χιόνι
But your snow here in Patras is like water.	ma-to-chyóni-sas edhó-s-tim-bátra ine sa-neró.	Μὰ τὸ χιόνι σας ἐδῶ στὴν Πάτρα εἶναι σὰ νερό.

Nick

You want ice?	págho-thélete?	Πάγο θέλετε;
go!	piyénete	πηγαίνετε
Go to Macedonia.	piyénete-s-ti-makedhonía.	Πηγαίνετε στὴ Μακεδονία.

[5–A] 121

They have *real* winters there. ('Their winter there is hard.')	o-chimónas-tus-ekí-ine-varís.	Ὁ χειμῶνας τους ἐκεῖ εἶναι βαρύς
in our region*	s-ta-méri-mas	στὰ μέρη μας
a little	ligháki	λιγάκι
humidity	ighrasía	ὑγρασία
Here in these parts we have only a little humidity.	edhó-s-ta-méri-mas ékhume-móno-lighák-ighrasía.	Ἐδῶ στὰ μέρη μας ἔχουμε μόνο λιγάκ' ὑγρασία.

John

hot winds	zestí-aéridhes	ζεστοὶ ἀέριδες
they bring	férnune	φέρνουνε
rains	vrochés	βροχές
Yes, these ('the') hot winds of yours bring rain.	né, i-zestí-sas-aéridhes férnune-vrochés.	Ναί, οἱ ζεστοί σας ἀέριδες φέρνουν βροχές.

Nick

it rains	vréchi	βρέχει
But it doesn't rain so very much.	ma-dhé-vréchi ke-tóso-polí.	Μὰ δὲ βρέχει καὶ τόσο πολύ.
the roads	i-dhrómi	οἱ δρόμοι
are dry	ine-steghní	εἶναι στεγνοί
And our roads are dry.	k-i-dhrómi-mas ine-steghní.	Κ' οἱ δρόμοι μας εἶναι στεγνοί.

Peter

it makes heat	káni-zésti	κάνει ζέστη
in the summer	to-kalokéri	τὸ καλοκαίρι
Is it hot here in summer?	káni-zésti-edhó-to-kalokéri?	Κάνει ζέστη ἐδῶ τὸ καλοκαίρι;

*On the record 'regions'.

Nick
sometimes	kápote	κάποτε
sufficient	arketí	ἀρκετή
Yes, sometimes it's pretty hot.	né, káni-kápote-arketí-zésti.	Ναί, κάνει κάποτε ἀρκετή ζέστη.

Peter
fine climate	oréo-klíma	ὡραῖο κλίμα
Does Greece have a good climate?	echi-oréo-klíma-i-eládha?	Ἔχει ὡραῖο κλίμα ἡ Ἑλλάδα;

Nick
Our winter is beautiful.	o-chimónaz-mas in-oréos.	Ὁ χειμῶνας μας εἶν' ὡραῖος.
as in America	sá-s-tin-amerikí	σὰ στὴν Ἀμερική
Our summer is just like in America.	to-kalokéri-mas ine-sá-s-tin-amerikí.	Τὸ καλοκαίρι μας εἶναι σὰ στὴν Ἀμερική.

John
about	páno-káto	πάνω κάτω
More or less like Chicago's.	páno-káto sa-s-to-sikágho.	Πάνω κάτω σὰ στὸ Σικάγο.

Record 10A, beginning.

Nick
down	káto	κάτω
at the sea	s-ti-thálasa	στὴ θάλασσα
there is ('it has') wind	echi-aéra	ἔχει ἀέρα
But down by the sea it's windy.	ma-káto-s-ti-thálasa echi-aéra.	Μὰ κάτω στὴ θάλασσα ἔχει ἀέρα.
small	mikrí	μικρή
You see, Greece is small.	i-eládha-vlépete ine-mikrí.	Ἡ Ἑλλάδα, βλέπετε, εἶναι μικρή.

[5–A]

It has mountains and sea.	echi-vuná ke-thálasa.	Ἔχει βουνὰ καὶ θάλασσα.
coolness	dhrosyá	δροσιά
And there it's always cool in the evening.	k-ekí-ine-pánda-dhrosyá-to-vrádhi.	Κ' ἐκεῖ εἶναι πάντα δροσιὰ τὸ βράδυ.

John

But come now, boys.	ma-eláte-tóra pedhyá.	Μὰ ἐλᾶτε τώρα, παιδιά.
It's time.	ine-kerós.	Εἶναι καιρός.

Before you go through the *Basic Sentences* a second time, study the following:

2. Hints on Pronunciation

Consider again the sounds *kh*, *ch*, *gh*, and *y*.

Of these four sounds you know well the *y* sound, which is just like *y* in English *yes*. The other three sounds we discussed in Unit 1. All verbs and nouns whose stems end in *kh* or *gh* change the *kh* into *ch*, and the *gh* into *y*, whenever the ending that follows begins with an *i* or an *e*.

Record 10A, after first spiral.
PRACTICE

Our examples are: *ékho* 'I have', *íkha* 'I had', *érkhome* 'I come', *févgho* 'I leave', *éfevgha* 'I was leaving', *o-yeorghós* 'the farmer'.

	kh	ch	gh	y
I-form	ékho		févgho	
you-form		échete		févyete
he-form		échi		févyi
we-form	ékhume		févghume	
they-form	ékhune		févghune	

I-form	*íkha*		*éfevgha*	
you-form	*íkhate*		*févghate*	
he-form		*íche*		*éfevye*
we-form	*íkhame*		*févghame*	
they-form	*íkhane*		*févghane*	

I-form	*érkhome*	
you-form		*ércheste*
he-form		*érchete*
we-form	*erkhómaste*	
they-form	*érkhonde*	

subj. sing.	*o-yeorghós*	
subj. plur.		*i-yeoryí*

You have probably noticed by this time that the sounds *kh* and *gh* appear only before the vowels *a* (*íkha* and *éfevgha*), *o* (*ékho* and *févgho*), *u* (*ékhume* and *févghume*) and consonants (*khrónos*, *khtíma* and *steghnós*, *ghrafío*). On the other hand, the sound *ch* appears only before *e* (*échete*), *i* (*échi*), and *y* (*chyóni*).

Now go twice through the *Basic Sentences* individually, once with book open and once with book closed.

Section B—Word Study and Review of Basic Sentences

1. Word Study (Individual Study)

COMMENT 1

The neuter noun. Do you still remember the forms of the neuter article? They are:

	sing.	plur.
subj.-obj.	*to*	*ta*
rest.	*tu*	

You have seen that there is only one form for both the subject and the object case, and one for the restrictive case. That makes it very easy. Now the same is true also of the neuter noun. There are only two forms to remember: (1) the subject-object (and when-

[5–B]

ever it occurs) -address form; (2) the restrictive form. From the first Unit on you have learned many neuter nouns, most of which end in *-o*, or *-i*, or *-a*. Let's look at them.

(a) First, THE NEUTER NOUNS IN *-o*. You have had a lot of them; they are very easy. They behave just like the neuter article. Let's pick out just two of them: *to-ghrafío* 'the office', and *to-neró* 'the water'.

	sing.	subj.-obj.	*to-ghrafío*	*to-neró*	Endings: *-o* or *-ó*
		rest.	*tu-ghrafíu*	*tu-nerú*	*-u* or *-ú*
	plur.	subj.-obj.	*ta-ghrafía*	*ta-nerá*	*-a* or *-á*

You have had certain others of this kind, but only in the plural, e.g. *ta-chilyómetra* 'the kilometers', *ta-sigharéta* 'the cigarettes', *ta-spírta* 'the matches', *ta-vivlía* 'the books', *ta-vuná* 'the mountains'. The singular is: *to-chilyómetro, to-sigharéto, to-spírto, to-vivlío, to-vunó*. The restrictive case of such nouns as *aftokínito* 'car', which bear the accent on the second from the last syllable, is *aftokínitu*. You may hear some Greeks saying *aftokinítu*, with a shift of accent. The thing you have to do is to follow your Guide or the phonograph records and to repeat after them.

(b) Next, THE NEUTER NOUNS IN *-i*. The neuter nouns in *-i* have the stress either on the last syllable, as *to-krasí* 'the wine', *to-psomí* 'the bread', or on the next to the last syllable, as *to-korítsi* 'the girl', *to-spíti* 'the house'.

Now look at these sentences:
ékhune-dhéka-pedhyá. — They have ten children.
ine-polí-kalá-korítsya. — They are very nice girls.

Here *pedhyá, korítsya* are in the plural. You see that the plural of these neuter nouns is formed by substituting *-yá* for *-í*, and *-ya* for *-i*. Some other neuter words you have heard with the plural in *-ya* are: *ta-khrónya* 'the years', *ta-mílya* 'the miles'. The singular of *ta-mílya* is *to-míli* 'the mile'.

Here is another sentence you know:
ine-fílos tu-pedhyú-mu. — He is a friend of my boy's.

The word *pedhyú* is in the restrictive case. The restrictive case of these neuter nouns is formed by substituting *-yú* for *-í*. You say not only *tu-pedhyú* 'of the boy', but also *tu-korítsyu* 'of the girl', shifting the accent to the last syllable.

Here is a table of all the forms:

	neuters in *-i*	Endings:	neuters in *-i*	Endings:
sing. subj.-obj.	*to-pedhí*	*-i*	*to-korítsi*	*-i*
rest.	*tu-pedhyú*	*-yú*	*tu-korítsyú*	*-yú*
plur. subj.-obj.	*ta-pedhyá*	*-yá*	*ta-korítsya*	*-ya*

(c) Finally, THE NEUTER NOUNS IN *-a*. You know the following: *to-ghála* 'the milk', *to-khtíma* 'the farm', *to-klíma* 'the climate', *t-ónoma* 'the name'. All the neuter nouns in *-a* (except *ghála*) have an *m* before the *-a*. They behave a little differently from the other neuter nouns.

Look carefully at the following sentences:

i-yinéka-mu-i-maría méni-s-to-khtíma-mas.   My wife Mary lives at our farm.
emís ékhume-khtímata.   We have farms.

To form the plural of these neuters in *-a* you just have to add *-ta* to the singular form. You say *ta-khtímata, ta-klímata, ta-onómata*. The noun *ónoma* is a word stressed on the second from the last syllable. Since Greek does not like to stress a word farther back than on the second from the last syllable, and since we add one syllable to form the plural, namely *-ta*, the accent must be shifted one syllable nearer to the end, so that it remains on the second from the last syllable.

COMMENT 2

THE PLURAL OF THE MASCULINE AND FEMININE NOUNS. In Unit 3 you learned the singular of the masculine and feminine nouns. Now let's see how they behave in the plural.

(a) THE PLURAL OF MASCULINE NOUNS IN *-os*. Let's first remember the forms of the masculine article in the plural. They are:

subj. *i*
obj. *tus*

Now let's look at the following sentences:

i-dhrómi-mas ine-steghní.   Our roads are dry.
kírii, kaliméra-sás.   Good morning, gentlemen.
ekho-trís-thíus.   I have three uncles.

The nouns *dhrómi, kírii, thíus* are in the plural. You see that the plural endings of the nouns in *-os* correspond to the plural forms of the masculine article. In the plural the masculine nouns in *-os* have the subject case and (whenever it occurs) the form of address in *-i*, and the object case in *-us*.

Here are a few things which should be remembered.

(1) Look at the following sentences:

ime-yeorghós.	I am a farmer.
dhóste-ta-khtímata s-tuz-yeorghús.	Give the farms to the farmers.
imaste-yeoryí.	We are farmers.

You say *yeorghós, yeorghús* with *gh* before *o* or *u*, but *yeoryí* with *y* before *i*. We just discussed this problem in the *Hints on Pronunciation*.

(2) Study carefully the following sentences:

trís-ipálili ergházonde s-to-ghrafío-tu.	Three employees work in his office.
echi-trís-ipalílus.	He has three employees.

The word *ipálilos* belongs to those masculine nouns in *-os* which have the accent on the second from the last syllable. As you may remember, these masculines shift the accent to the next to the last syllable in the restrictive case of the singular. They do so also in the object case of the plural. You say *i-ipálili* 'the employees', *i-dháskali* 'the teachers', but *tus-ipalílus, tuz-dhaskálus*.

(b) THE PLURALS IN *-es* AND *-dhes*. The following sentences have either occurred among the *Basic Sentences* or are made up from the material already presented:

I.
i-adherfí:	*kséro-tis-adherfés-tus.*	I know their sisters.
o-stratyótis:	*févghune-i-stratyótes.*	The soldiers are leaving.
i-kiría:	*kírii ke-kiríes, chérete.*	Goodbye, everybody. ('Gentlemen and ladies, goodbye.')

II.
o-kafés:	*dhóste-mu dhyó-kafédhes.*	Give me two coffees.
i-thyá:	*ekho-trís-thyádhes.*	I have three aunts.

In these sentences you find examples of masculine and feminine nouns with either the ending -es (Group I) or the ending -dhes (Group II). This, in short, is what you need to know about the plural: 1. Almost all masculine and feminine nouns (with the exception of the masculine nouns in -os), if used in the plural, end either in -es (or -és), which *replaces* the final vowel of the object case of the singular, or in -dhes, which *is added* to the object case of the singular. 2. Subject case, object case, and case of address are alike, so that only one plural form has to be learned. 3. There is no shift of accent in the plural. The main trouble comes in learning which nouns form their plural in -es (or -és), and which nouns form their plural in -dhes. The following remarks may help you in this.

I. The plural in -es (or -és).

1. Almost always with feminine nouns in -i (or -í).

Examples: *kóres* 'daughters', *zéstes* 'heat waves', and *adherfés* 'sisters', *dhrakhmés* 'drachmas', *vrochés* 'rains', *zoés* 'lives'.*

2. Almost always with feminine nouns in -a (or -á).

Examples: *bíres* 'beers', *fitítries* 'students', *kiríes* 'ladies', *méres* 'days', *mitéres* 'mothers', *níkhtes* 'nights', *óres* 'hours', *patátes* 'potatoes', *yinékes* 'women; wives', and *dhulyés* 'jobs', *paghonyés* 'frosts'.

*Note that for *póli* 'city' the plural is *pólis*.

3. Very often with masculine nouns in -is (or -ís).

Examples: *erghátes* 'workers', *náftes* 'sailors', *stratyótes* 'soldiers', and *fitités* 'students'.

4. Almost always with masculine nouns in -as.

Examples: *ándres* 'men; husbands', *chimónes* 'winters', *patéres* 'fathers'.

II. The plural in -dhes.

1. Sometimes with feminine nouns in -á.

Example: *thyádhes* 'aunts'.

2. Very often with masculine nouns in -is (or -ís).

Examples: *bakálidhes* 'grocers' (sing. *bakális*), and *kafedzídhes* 'coffee-house keepers' (sing. *kafedzís*).

3. Always with masculine nouns in -és, -ás, -ús.

Examples: *kafédhes* 'coffees', *psomádhes* 'bakers' (sing. *psomás*), *papúdhes* 'grandfathers'.

For your convenience the plural form of a noun will always be given in the *Finder List*, if there could be any doubt about its formation or if it is a form that you would not expect, e.g. *aéridhes* 'winds' (sing. *aéras*). In any case, don't be worried if you hear Greeks using a different plural form from what you expected. The thing you have to do now is to follow your Guide or the phonograph records and to repeat after them.

By now you have a fairly good knowledge of the patterns of the Greek nouns. Here is a summary of what you have learned up to now.

(a) Masculine nouns

sing. subj.	-is	-es	-as	-us	-os
obj.					-o
add.	-i	-e	-a	-u	-e or -o
rest.					-u
plur. subj.-add.	-es or	-edhes	-es or	-udhes	-i
obj.	-idhes		-adhes		-us

(b) Feminine nouns

sing. subj.-obj.-add.	-i	-a	-o
rest.	-is	-as	-os
plur. subj.-obj.-add.	-es	-es or -adhes	

(c) Neuter nouns

sing. subj.-obj.-add.	-i	-a	-o
rest.	-yu		-u
plur. subj.-obj.-add.	-ya	-ata	-a

COMMENT 3

GREEK ADJECTIVES. Words like 'good', 'bad', 'warm', 'cold' that describe nouns are called *adjectives*. In English we have only one form of an adjective: we say

o-kalós-kerós	the good weather
i-kalí-bíra	the good beer
to-kaló-ksenodhochío	the good hotel

'a *good* father', 'a *good* mother', '*good* fathers', '*good* mothers'. Greek adjectives, however, behave in a different way. Study carefully the following expressions:

o-kerós ine-kalós.	The weather is good.
i-bíra ine-kalí.	The beer is good.
to-ksenodhochío ine-kaló.	The hotel is good.

You see that our adjective 'good', if describing a noun with the article *o* (a *masculine* noun), is *kalós*; if describing a noun with the article *i* (a *feminine* noun), is *kalí*; and if describing a noun with the article *to* (a *neuter* noun), is *kaló*. In other words, just as Greek nouns or the Greek articles have three different genders, so Greek adjectives have three genders, too; and if you wish to describe a noun by using an adjective, you must always see that both your adjective and your noun have the same gender. Thus, in our examples, *bíra* 'beer' is feminine, and so we use the feminine form of the adjective, namely *kalí*. We say, in such a case, that the adjective *agrees* with its noun.

Now look at the following examples:

(a) masculine

sing.	subj.	*o-dhrómos ine-steghnós.*	The road is dry.
	obj.	*dhén-ekhune-steghnó-dhrómo.*	They have no dry road.
plur.	subj.	*i-dhrómi ine-steghní.*	The roads are dry.
	obj.	*ekhune-steghnúz-dhrómus.*	They have dry roads.

(b) feminine

sing.	subj.	*i-adherfí-tu ine-nóstimi.*	His sister is pretty.
	obj.	*echi-nóstimi-adherfí.*	He has a pretty sister.
plur.	subj.	*i-adherfés-tu ine-nóstimes.*	His sisters are pretty.
	obj.	*echi-nóstimes-adherfés.*	He has pretty sisters.

(c) neuter

sing.	subj.	*to-pedhí-tus ine-mikró.*	Their child is small.
	obj.	*ekhune-mikró-pedhí.*	They have a small child.
plur.	subj.	*ta-pedhyá-tus ine-mikrá.*	Their children are small.
	obj.	*ekhune-mikrá-pedhyá.*	They have small children.

You see that nouns and adjectives agree also in case and number. The endings of these adjectives do not offer any difficulty: *kalós* and *steghnós*, masculine adjectives in *-os*, are treated like the masculine nouns in *-os*, e.g. *fílos*; *kalí* and *nóstimi*, feminine adjectives in *-i*, are treated like the feminine nouns in *-i*, e.g. *adherfí*;

kaló and *mikró*, neuter adjectives in *-o*, are treated like the neuter nouns in *-o*, e.g. *neró*. Generally, if you have an adjective ending in *-os* in the masculine (like *kalós*), the feminine ends in *-i*, and the neuter in *-o*.

SUMMARY: adjectives in *-os*, *-i*, *-o*

	masc.	fem.	neut.
sing. subj.	*kalós*	} *kalí*	} *kaló*
obj.	*kaló*		
add.	*kalé*		
rest.	*kalú*	*kalís*	*kalú*
plur. subj.-add.	*kalí*	} *kalés*	} *kalá*
obj.	*kalús*		

Now look at these examples:
i-néa-yórki in-oréa-póli.
i-yinéka-tu ine-plúsya.

New York is a beautiful city.
His wife is rich.

Here we have three adjectives: *néos* 'new; young', *oréos* 'beautiful', and *plúsyos* 'rich'. All appear in the feminine: *néa*, *oréa*, and *plúsya*. You see that the feminine singular ending of an adjective is *-a* (instead of *-i*) when the sound before the masculine ending *-os* is a vowel or *y*. The feminine adjectives in *-a*, like *kría*, *néa*, *oréa*, behave like the feminine nouns in *-a*, e.g. *kiría*, that is:

sing. subj.-obj.-add.	*oréa*	plur. subj.-obj.-add.	*orées*
rest.	*oréas*		

In all other forms these adjectives are treated like *kalós*.

Remember: 1. that the plural of the feminine adjectives in *-i* or *-a* is always in *-es*, never in *-dhes*; 2. that throughout all the cases the accent remains on the same syllable, e.g. *nóstimos*, *nóstimu*, *nóstimi*, *nóstimus*; 3. that in general the Greek adjective, like the English adjective, is placed before the noun.

From now on in the *Finder Lists* we will give for every adjective the three different endings that it has in the subject case of the singular.

2. Covering English and Greek of Word Study (Individual Study)

Check yourself on your knowledge of the *Word Study* by covering first the English, then the Greek, and making sure you know everything thoroughly.

3. Review of Basic Sentences

With the Guide or records, review the first half of the *Basic Sentences* as in previous Units.

SECTION C—REVIEW OF BASIC SENTENCES (*Cont.*)

1. Review of Basic Sentences (*Cont.*)

Review the second half of the *Basic Sentences*.

2. Covering the English of Basic Sentences (Individual Study)

Go through the *Basic Sentences* covering up the English and reading aloud the Greek. Check up on anything you do not know, until you are sure of everything.

3. What Would You Say? (Individual Study)

I. Read aloud all the following, and pick out the expression you think most suitable:

1. You wake up in the morning and ask your roommate what the weather is like:
   a. *tí-ora-íne?*
   b. *ine-kerós?*
   c. *tí-keros-íne?*
   d. *échete-keró?*

2. He answers that the weather is fine:
   a. *tí-dhulyá-káni?*
   b. *ine-kalós-kerós.*
   c. *ine-kakós-kerós.*
   d. *ékho-keró.*

3. You say that the section of the country where you are is too hot and damp:
   a. *o-kerós-edhó ine-polí-kríos ma-oréos.*
   b. *edhó-s-ta-méri-mas dhén-gáni míte-zésti míte-krío.*
   c. *ekhume-zésti-edhó k-ighrasía.*
   d. *o-aéras-edhó ine-zestós.*

4. He says that we are not having a bad winter:
   a. *káni-krío to-chimóna?*
   b. *o-kerós-efétos dhén-ítane-kakós.*
   c. *o-chimónaz-mas dhén-ine-varís.*
   d. *ine-dhrosyá-edhó to-kalokéri?*

II. Here are two sets of words: the numbered set is a list of nouns, some preceded by articles, some not; the lettered set is made up of descriptive adjectives. Make as many combinations as you can, but see that they do not conflict either with the demands of gender and number, or with common sense.

1. *mya —— yinéka*	a. *kakós*	9. *mya —— bíra*	i. *mikrí*
2. *ghála*	b. *kría*	10. *o —— ándras*	j. *zestó*
3. *o —— kafés*	c. *kalí*	11. *korítsya*	k. *kaló*
4. *kiríes*	d. *oréos*	12. *neró*	l. *megháles*
5. *o —— kerós*	e. *kakó*	13. *patátes*	m. *kakí*
6. *pedhyá*	f. *megháli*	14. *enas —— chimónas*	n. *kríos*
7. *dhrómi*	g. *krío*	15. *adherfés*	o. *oréa*
8. *klíma*	h. *kalés*	16. *mya —— méra*	p. *zestós*

III. Do the same in the following exercise as in the one above. The numbered set is made up of articles followed by descriptive adjectives; the lettered set is composed of nouns.

1. *enas-kalós*	a. *níkhta*	6. *i-megháles*	f. *ksenodhochío*
2. *mya-kalí*	b. *fílos*	7. *i-zestí*	g. *kafédhes*
3. *ena-kaló*	c. *astío*	8. *i-kríi*	h. *aeropóros*
4. *mya-kría*	d. *korítsya*	9. *i-oréa*	i. *aéridhes*
5. *ta-nóstima*	e. *adherfí*	10. *i-mikrí*	j. *pólis*

IV. In the following columns read aloud the Greek expressions, then match the English with the Greek, making sure that you can say promptly the Greek equivalents of the English sentences.

1. It's a little windy.
2. It doesn't rain very much.
3. How's the weather?
4. The sun is shining.
5. This year we didn't have a bad winter.
6. It's snowing up in the mountains.
7. Sometimes it's cool in the evening.
8. Our roads are dry.
9. Our climate is good.
10. In which part of America do they always have beautiful weather?

a. *tí-keros-íne?*
b. *ine-ílyos.*
c. *efétos dhén-íkhame-varí-chimóna.*
d. *páno-s-ta-vuná chyonízi.*
e. *to-klíma-mas ine-kaló.*
f. *echi-lígho-aéra.*
g. *i-dhrómi-mas ine-steghní.*
h. *dhé-vréchi-polí.*
i. *kápote ine-dhrosyá-to-vrádhi.*
j. *se-pyó-méros-tis-amerikís ekhune-pánda-oréo-keró?*

Section D—Listening In

1. What Did You Say?

Give your answers in Greek for each of the exercises in the preceding section, when the Leader calls for them. Then, as the Leader calls for them, give the English equivalents of all the expressions in the exercise.

2. Word Study Check-Up

As you have done in the previous Units, go back to the *Word Study* and give the correct Greek for each English expression, without having to read it from the book. The Leader or one of the members of the group should read the English.

3. Listening In

With your book closed, listen to the following conversations as read by the Guide or phonograph record. Repeat the Greek immediately after hearing it. After the first repetition of each conversation, check up on the meaning of anything you do not understand, by asking someone else or by going back to the *Basic Sentences* if no one knows. Repeat each conversation, if necessary; then take parts and carry on the conversation.

Record 10A, after second spiral.

1. Peter is talking to Nick's children about the weather. Nick joins the group and tells a joke.

pétros:	tí-keros-íne?	Τί καιρὸς εἶναι;
mítsos:	ine-kakós-kerós.	Εἶναι κακὸς καιρός.
spíros:	óchi, dhén-ine-ke-tóso-kakós.	Ὄχι, δὲν εἶναι καὶ τόσο κακός.
	páme-s-ton-ginimatóghrafo.	Πάμε στὸν κινηματόγραφο.
mítsos:	ma-pedhí-mu, dhém-borúme-na-páme.	Μά, παιδί μου, δὲν μποροῦμε νὰ πάμε.
	vréchi k-echi-aéra.	Βρέχει κ' ἔχει ἀέρα.
pópi:	né, vréchi-ligháki k-echi-polí-aéra.	Ναί, βρέχει λιγάκι κ' ἔχει πολὺ ἀέρα.
mítsos:	efétos ikhame-varí-chimóna.	Ἐφέτος εἴχαμε βαρὺ χειμῶνα.
spíros:	ma-tóra érchete-to-kalokéri.	Μὰ τώρα ἔρχεται τὸ καλοκαίρι.
níkos:	kalispéra-sas, tí-kánete?	Καλησπέρα σας, τί κάνετε;
pétros:	kalá, efkharistó.	Καλά, εὐχαριστῶ.
níkos:	páte-s-ton-ginimatóghrafo vlépo.	Πάτε στὸν κινηματόγραφο, βλέπω.
	ma-prín eláte-na-sas-pó-en-astío.	Μὰ πρὶν ἐλᾶτε νὰ σᾶς πῶ ἕν' ἀστεῖο.

Record 10B, beginning.

	o-yánis mya-méra dhúleve-s-to-khtíma-tu.	Ὁ Γιάννης, μιὰ μέρα, δούλευε στὸ χτῆμα του.
	tone-vlépi-ena-korítsi ke-léi:	Τόνε βλέπει ἕνα κορίτσι καὶ λέει:
	kaliméra-sas, tí-kánete?	"Καλημέρα σας, τί κάνετε;"
	ky-o-yánis:	Κι ὁ Γιάννης:
	dhé-vlépete? dhulévo.	"Δὲ βλέπετε; Δουλεύω."
ta-pedhyá:	khá! khá! khá! khá!	Χά! χά! χά! χά!
pétros:	lipúme-polí, ma-dhén-do-katálava to-astío-sas.	Λυποῦμαι πολύ, μὰ δὲν τὸ κατάλαβα τὸ ἀστεῖο σας.

pópi:	to-korítsi-vlépete léi:	Τὸ κορίτσι, βλέπετε, λέει:
	ti-kánete? "How do you do?"	Τί κάνετε; "How do you do?"
	ky-aftós katalavéni:	Κι αὐτὸς καταλαβαίνει:
	ti-kánete? "What are you doing?"	Τί κάνετε; "What are you doing?"

Record 10B, after first spiral.

2. Three Americans, a doctor, an aviator, and a sailor, are riding with a Greek friend along a road in Macedonia.

o-yatrós:	edhó-s-tin-eládha dhén-gáni mite-tóso-zésti mite-tóso-krío sa-s-tin-amerikí.	Ἐδῶ στὴν Ἑλλάδα δὲν κάνει μήτε τόσο ζέστη μήτε τόσο κρύο σὰ στὴν Ἀμερική.
o-aeropóros:	eghó-imuna páno-s-ta-vuná.	Ἐγὼ ἤμουνα πάνω στὰ βουνά.
	ekí íkhame-chyóni-ke-págho.	Ἐκεῖ εἴχαμε χιόνι καὶ πάγο.
o-romyós:	dhén-íkhame-oréo-chimóna-efétos.	Δὲν εἴχαμε ὡραῖο χειμῶνα ἐφέτος.
	ikham-eksínda-mérez-vrochí-ke-paghonyés ke-móno penínda-méres ílyo.	Εἴχαμ' ἑξῆντα μέρες βροχὴ καὶ παγωνιὲς καὶ μόνο πενῆντα μέρες ἥλιο.
o-náftis:	emí-s-tin-galifórnya ekhume-trakósyes eksínda pénde méres ílyo to-khróno.	Ἐμεῖς στὴν Καλιφόρνια ἔχουμε τρακόσιες ἑξῆντα πέντε μέρες ἥλιο τὸ χρόνο.
o-romyós:	káthe-khróno?	Κάθε χρόνο;
o-náftis:	né, káthe.	Ναί, κάθε.
o-yatrós:	thá-thela-na-páo ap-ton-álo-dhrómo.*	Θὰ 'θελα νὰ πάω ἀπ' τὸν ἄλλο δρόμο.
	ine-pyó-steghnós.	Εἶναι πιὸ στεγνός.
o-aeropóros:	m-aftós-o-dhrómos kondá-s-ti-thálasa ine-pyó-oréos.	Μ' αὐτὸς ὁ δρόμος κοντὰ στὴ θάλασσα εἶναι πιὸ ὡραῖος.
o-náftis:	k-i-thálasa ine-pyó-oré-akóma.	Κ' ἡ θάλασσα εἶναι πιὸ ὡραία ἀκόμα.

*On the record *ton-álo-dhrómo*, which may also be heard.

[5–D]

Record 10B, after second spiral.

3. The aviator and the sailor wake up in the morning.

o-aeropóros:	*ti-kakós-kerós!*	Τί κακὸς καιρός!
o-náftis:	*ti-léte! kakós-kerós-aftós?*	Τί λέτε! Κακὸς καιρὸς αὐτός;
o-aeropóros:	*polí-kakós.*	Πολὺ κακός.
	dhe-chyonízi páno-s-ta-vuná?	Δὲ χιονίζει πάνω στὰ βουνά;
	dhe-vréchi káto-ki-s-ti-thálasa?	Δὲ βρέχει κάτω 'κεῖ στὴ θάλασσα;
o-náftis:	*né né, vréchi ke-chyonízi;*	Ναί, ναί, βρέχει καὶ χιονίζει·
	ma-dhén-ine kakós-kerós.	μὰ δὲν εἶναι κακὸς καιρός.
o-aeropóros:	*oréo-keró eghó-tone-léo ota-dhén-echi*	Ὡραῖο καιρὸ ἐγὼ τόνε λέω ὅτα δὲν ἔχει μήτε κρύο
	míte-krío míte-ighrasía.	μήτε ὑγρασία.
o-náftis:	*ist-ap-tin-galifórnya i-apo-álo-zestó-méros*	Εἶστ' ἀπ' τὴν Καλιφόρνια ἢ ἀπὸ ἄλλο ζεστὸ μέρος
	tis-amerikís?	τῆς Ἀμερικῆς;
o-aeropóros:	*óchi pedhí-mu, im-ap-to-Maine.*	Ὄχι, παιδί μου, εἶμ' ἀπ' τὸ Maine.
o-náftis:	*ma-ki-echi-chyóni-ke-págho trakósyes*	Μὰ 'κεῖ ἔχει χιόνι καὶ πάγο τρακόσιες ἑξῆντα μέρες
	eksínda méres to-khróno.	τὸ χρόνο.
o-aeropóros:	*páno-káto.*	Πάνω κάτω.
	ma-ine-spíti-mu.	Μὰ εἶναι σπίτι μου.
	ky-ota-dhén-ime-spíti-mu thélo-zésti k-ílyo.	Κι ὅτα δὲν εἶμαι σπίτι μου, θέλω ζέστη κ' ἥλιο.

SECTION E—CONVERSATION

1. Covering the Greek of Basic Sentences (Individual Study)

Cover the Greek of the *Basic Sentences* and practice saying the Greek equivalents of the English expressions.

2. Vocabulary Check-Up

Give the Greek expressions for the English equivalents in the *Basic Sentences* as the Leader calls for them.

3. Conversation

As you have done in the *Conversation* in the previous Units, begin to converse by following the model outlined below fairly closely; then change the situation somewhat. By now you have a fair amount of material that you can bring into your conversations. Invent new combinations of subject matter.

A conversation with a Greek acquaintance of yours turns on the subject of the weather.

1. You remark that the winters are beautiful here in Greece.
2. He asks whether they are not beautiful in America, too.
3. You reply that America is very big, and that sometimes the winters are nice, but that in your section they have a hard winter.
4. He inquires whether you live down by the sea or up in the mountains.
5. You say that you live up in the mountains, that there it is very cold in winter, and that you have a lot of snow and ice on the roads in winter, but that the weather is fine in summer.
6. You explain that in summer it's pretty hot, but it's always cool in the evening.
7. He comments that your winter is like Macedonia's; he adds that he lived there before, and that it was always snowing and they used to have frosty weather.
8. He says that here, where he and his children live now, the winter is not so hard; they have more rain than snow, more or less as in San Francisco.
9. You ask whether it isn't extremely hot here in the summer.
10. He admits that the sun is very hot, but they have winds that bring rain.
11. You ask him whether he wants to go to the movies this evening.
12. He answers that he is sorry, but his wife's uncle is coming to the house, and he adds that he doesn't want to go to the movies without his children.

Section F—Conversation (*Cont.*)

Continue the conversation started in Section E with a review of parts 1 and 2 of the Section if necessary.

FINDER LIST

A

o aéras	ὁ ἀέρας	wind
aéridhes p.	ἀέριδες	
echi-aéra	ἔχει ἀέρα	it's windy
álos, -i, -o	ἄλλος, –η, –ο	other; another
apo	ἀπό	by
ap-ton-álo-dhrómo	ἀπ' τὸν ἄλλο δρόμο	by the other road
arketós, -í, -ó	ἀρκετός, –ή, –ό	sufficient; *p.* a good many
to astío	τὸ ἀστεῖο	joke
khorís-t-astía	χωρὶς τ' ἀστεῖα	no joking!

C

o chimónas	ὁ χειμῶνας	winter
to-chimóna	τὸ χειμῶνα	in the winter
to chyóni	τὸ χιόνι	snow
chyonízi	χιονίζει	it snows

D

o dhrómos	ὁ δρόμος	road; street
i dhrosyá	ἡ δροσιά	coolness

E

échi	ἔχει	there is
efétos	ἐφέτος	this year
eksínda	ἐξήντα	sixty
érkhome	ἔρχομαι	I come

F

férno	φέρνω	I bring

G

galifórnya see: kalifórnya

I

i ighrasía	ἡ ὑγρασία	humidity
o ílyos	ὁ ἥλιος	sun

K

kakós, -í, -ó	κακός, —ή, —ό	bad
i kalifórnya	ἡ Καλιφόρνια	California
galifórnya		
to kalokéri	τὸ καλοκαίρι	summer
to-kalokéri	τὸ καλοκαίρι	in the summer
kalós, -í, -ó	καλός, —ή, —ό	good
kápote	κάποτε	sometimes
káthe	κάθε	every; each
káto	κάτω	down
see: *páno*		
ke see: *tóso*		
o kerós	ὁ καιρός	time; weather
ine-kerós	εἶναι καιρὸς	it's time
ékho-keró	ἔχω καιρὸ	I have time
khá! khá! khá! khá!	χά! χά! χά! χά!	ha, ha, ha! (*imitation of laughter*)
khorís	χωρίς	without
o khrónos	ὁ χρόνος	year
khrónya n.p.	χρόνια	
to-khróno	τὸ χρόνο	per year
khrónya see: *khrónos*		
to klíma	τὸ κλίμα	climate

to krío	τὸ κρύο	the cold
káni-krío	κάνει κρύο	it's cold
kríos, -a, -o	κρύος, -a, -o	cold

L

ligháki	λιγάκι	a little
líghos, líyi, lígho	λίγος, λίγη, λίγο	little; a little
líyi, líyes, lígha	λίγοι, λίγες, λίγα	few; a few

M

i makedhonía	ἡ Μακεδονία	Macedonia (*district in northern Greece*)
meghálos, -i, -o	μεγάλος, -η, -ο	large; big
i méra	ἡ μέρα	day
to méros	τὸ μέρος	place; part
méri p.	μέρη	region
mikrós, -í, -ó	μικρός, -ή, -ό	small

N

i níkhta	ἡ νύχτα	night
nóstimos, -i, -o	νόστιμος, -η, -ο	pretty; nice

O

óchi see: tóso		
oréos, -a, -o	ὡραῖος, -a, -ο	beautiful; fine

P

i paghonyá	ἡ παγωνιά	frost
o pághos	ὁ πάγος	ice

páno	πάνω	up
páno-se	πάνω σὲ	up in; upon; on
páno-káto	πάνω κάτω	more or less
páo		
na-páme	νὰ πάμε	that we go
piyénete	πηγαίνετε	go!
polí m.s., obj.	πολύ	much
pyós, pyá, pyó	ποιός, ποιά, ποιό	who? what? which?
pyí, pyés, pyá p.	ποιοί, ποιές, ποιά	

S

sán	σὰν	just like
steghnós, -í, -ó	στεγνός, -ή, -ό	dry (dried off)

T

i thálasa	ἡ θάλασσα	sea
tóso	τόσο	so; so much
dhén-ine-ke-tóso	δέν εἶναι καὶ τόσο	is not so very
óchi-ke-tóso	ὄχι καὶ τόσο	not so very
trakósyi, -es, -a	τρακόσιοι, -ες, -α	three hundred

V

varís m.s., subj.	βαρύς	heavy; hard
varí m.s., obj.	βαρύ	
vréchi	βρέχει	it rains
i vrochí	ἡ βροχή	rain
to vunó	τὸ βουνό	mountain

Z

i zésti	ἡ ζέστη	heat
káni-zésti	κάνει ζέστη	it's hot
zestós, -í, -ó	ζεστός, -ή, -ό	warm; hot

[5–F]

UNIT 6

REVIEW

Section A—What Do You Know In Greek?

To the Group Leader: This Unit is intended to furnish the group with a thorough review of all the work done to date: understanding of vocabulary, use of vocabulary, and grammar. Pronunciation should be the object of attention whenever the students are talking. Either the Guide or, if there is no Guide, the Leader and other students should correct faulty pronunciation.

Section A is a true-and-false quiz which is to be read to the group by the Guide or the phonograph records. Each student is to write the numbers from 1 to 80 on a sheet of paper. After hearing each statement in Greek, the students are to mark T opposite the number of that statement if they consider it a true statement, and F if they consider it false. If the students understand the Greek they will have no difficulty in deciding whether or not the statements are true or false.

Use the first item in the quiz as a practice item. When you are ready to start, announce "Statement 1," and give the signal to the Guide to begin, or put on the phonograph record. The Guide or record will then read the Greek statement: "*i-eládha dhén-échi-vuná*" and will repeat the statement once more. Explain to the group that, since the meaning of this statement is: "Greece has no mountains," they should write an F after the figure 1 on their papers. Then announce "Statement 2" and continue with the Guide or phonograph record. Each statement in Greek is to be presented twice. When working with a Guide, continue to call the number of each statement throughout the quiz so that the students will have no trouble keeping the proper place. Take the quiz with the rest of the group.

In the back of the Guide's Manual you will find a list giving the correct answers (T or F) for the Greek items, together with the English translations. After the quiz is over, read to the group the correct answers, T or F for each item. The students are to check their papers. Find the average number of correct answers per student for your group and include your own answers. Any student who gets less than the average number of answers or less than 80% (whichever is higher) correct, needs more thorough study and review of the preceding Units.

Use the rest of the period to repeat the Greek expressions for which students had the wrong answer and give the English equivalents of these statements if they wish to have them. Be sure that the students understand the meaning of all the items which they got wrong; those are the items on which their vocabulary is weak and needs further study.

This Unit provides several tests which will help you to make sure that you have thoroughly covered the work of the first five *Learning Units* of the course. They will show you what you may need to restudy or review.

Section A is a true-false quiz. After you have marked the numbers 1 to 80 on a sheet of paper, your Leader will have the Guide read, or will play the phonograph records containing, a number of statements in Greek. As you hear each sentence, decide whether the statement it makes is true or false. Decide whether the statement is *usually* true or *usually* false. Do not go into particular cases. If you think the statement is true, mark T opposite the number corresponding to the number of the sentence that has just been spoken. If you think it is false, mark F opposite the number. The first item will be a practice item and will show you just how you are to proceed with the rest of the sentences.

After you have done this work, the Leader will go through your answers with you as a group, and will tell you which statements are true and which are false. Score your paper, counting one for each correct answer. The Leader will figure out the average score for your group. If your score falls below the average of the group as a whole, you need more study and review of the previous Units.

Use the rest of the period to go over the sentences again with your Guide or records. For each item on which you are wrong, be sure that you understand why you are wrong, and what the true meaning of the item is.

If you come out well on this quiz, that indicates that you have a pretty good understanding of practically all the work you have covered to date.

SECTION B—HOW WOULD YOU SAY IT?
(Individual Study)

Go through the following English sentences and prepare to say the equivalents for the English at your next group meeting. *Do not write anything down*, but say the Greek equivalents out loud and keep practicing them aloud until you have the Greek down so cold that when the English is fired at you point-blank you can fire the Greek right back without any hesitation.

I

1. Good morning, sir.
2. How are you?
3. Very well, thank you.
4. May I present (to you) Mr. Cook?
5. Delighted.
6. Where is the station, please?

7. The station is to the left.
8. I did not understand.
9. Speak slowly, please.
10. I would like to drink a [cup of] coffee.

II

11. Excuse me, madam, where is the restaurant?
12. The restaurant is to the right.
13. Thank you very much.
14. You're welcome.
15. Give me a beer; and afterwards I want to eat meat and potatoes.
16. I don't want wine; give me milk or water.
17. Have you cigarettes and matches?
18. How much is it?
19. How do you say "toilet" in Greek?
20. What time is it?

III

21. It's eight o'clock.
22. The girl is going to the movies with the soldier.
23. Good-bye. Delighted to have met you.
24. My name is Mary.
25. What can I offer you?
26. His son is called Peter.
27. Is your brother married?
28. No, he is not.
29. In Greece they don't speak English.
30. What kind of work do you do?

IV

31. I am a farmer.
32. He's a good boy.
33. He is an aviator.
34. He works neither in the city nor in the country; he is on a ship.
35. What's the name of the ship you're on ('where you are')?
36. I can't tell you.
37. Are you an American?
38. His father is an office worker.
39. There are three hundred sailors on our ship.
40. We were reading a lot of books.

V

41. Did you have a good job over there?
42. Let's go (together) to the movies.
43. What part of the United States are you from?
44. Who speaks English here?
45. How many miles is it from Athens to Salonica?
46. The hot winds bring rain.
47. What's the weather like?
48. It's fine weather.
49. It's warm.
50. It's snowing up in the mountains.

Section C—How Did You Say It?

To the Group Leader: Simply follow the directions given below.

This Section is a drill on the work you have done in Section B of this Unit. Keep your book closed. The Leader will call on members of the group (but not in any fixed order) to speak the Greek equivalents of the English sentences given in Section B. The work must be kept moving rapidly, and interest should never lag. If the Guide is present, he is to listen and correct your pronunciation and expressions.

This Section is intended to give you a check on your ability to use the vocabulary you have learned.

Section D—How Would You Say It? (*Cont.*)
(Individual Study)

Go through these English sentences and prepare to say the equivalents for the English, just as you did in Section B of this Unit. Do not write anything down, but have everything well fixed in your mind, and ready to speak in the next group meeting.

I

1. Nick's father and mother live in the country.
2. That gentleman over there is Peter's friend.
3. Now the Americans speak Greek like us.
4. John's friends work on a ship.

[6–D] 147

5. My sister's children are small.
6. One of my brothers works in a hotel.
7. Now let's go straight ahead, and then let's go to the left.
8. There is a hotel near the station.
9. Waiter, one coffee and two beers.
10. Give me meat, bread, and wine.

II

11. My sister has children.
12. Her uncle does not have any children.
13. I work in a factory.
14. Their parents are still living.
15. Do you live in the country?
16. She works down there in the town.
17. We work on a farm.
18. They work in an office.
19. When I was a child, I knew English well.
20. What's your name?

III

21. I am very sorry, but I don't know him.
22. Your daughter is a very pretty girl.
23. We work and read a lot.
24. It begins at five.
25. I am a sailor.
26. A friend of mine is a soldier.
27. Is he a student?
28. He is not a good doctor.
29. She, too, is a student.
30. May I tell you a joke?

IV

31. This doctor has five houses and three farms.
32. Do you know my aunt who lives in Athens?
33. He is not a bad boy.
34. Before the war he was a teacher.
35. I know a little Greek.
36. I leave tonight by train.
37. Come with me.
38. It does not rain so much in Athens.
39. Are the roads dry?
40. It is freezing. ('There is frost.')

V

41. You are a Greek, aren't you?
42. This year we had a hard winter.
43. They have a beautiful winter.
44. It's windy on the sea.

45. Around here it is neither [too] hot nor [too] cold.
46. Please tell me, sir, how is the climate in Macedonia?
47. Their winters are very cold.
48. I am coming from Salonica and I am going to Patras.
49. Your roads are beautiful.
50. California is beautiful in the summer; but it is still more beautiful in the winter.

SECTION E—HOW DID YOU SAY IT? (*Cont.*)

To the Group Leader: Simply follow the directions given below.

As in Section C, the Leader will go around the group and ask various members to supply (with books closed) the Greek equivalents for the sentences given in Section D. If the Guide is present, he will listen and correct pronunciation and expressions.

This Section is intended to give you a check on your understanding of the way the language is built and functions.

SECTION F—CONVERSATION

The members of the group will carry on short conversations lasting not more than 1 to 2 minutes, in which the entire contents of the preceding Units should be used. Everyone should have a chance to take part as many times as possible. The situations of the conversations should be varied and combined as much as possible. Each conversation should begin with greetings and inquiries after each other's health, and should end with formal leave-taking. Here are just a few out of many possibilities for conversations:

1. Meeting friends on the street.
   (Include: questions about each other's health, health of parents, health of brother and sister, where they are living now.)

2. Meeting a stranger.
   (Include: statement of names, questions and answers about where you come from, where you work, where you are living now, what you are doing.)

3. Introducing people.
   (Include: introducing a friend or relative to someone, questions back and forth as to where people are from, what languages they speak, the offering of coffee, questions as to where you are going now.)

4. Inviting a friend to have a drink.
   (Include: questions as to where your friend is going, suggestion that you both go get a beer, discussion of where it is best to go, what each likes to drink, ordering of drinks.)

5. Trades.
   (Include: what your trade is, what your father's is —or was, what your brother's or your sister's is, what work you used to do before the war.)

6. Weather.
   (Include: questions about the climate in the region where you are now, whether there is great humidity in the summer, whether the winter is always hard, where there is the most snow or rain, with comparisons to places back home.)

7. In a restaurant.
   (Include: questions and answers about what you want or do not want, about Greek names of food and drink, ordering a meal, asking prices, paying.)

8. Finding your way.
   (Include: how to find a restaurant, hotel, station, boat, or house of a friend.)

9. Talking about Athens, Salonica, and Patras.
   (Include: desire to go to these cities, their size, beauty, distance between them, relatives and friends living there.)

10. Speaking Greek.
    (Include: how you speak Greek, your understanding it or not, asking someone to speak slowly, asking about Greek equivalents of English words, your knowledge of other languages.)

PART TWO

UNIT 7

GETTING A ROOM

SECTION A—BASIC SENTENCES

Go once through the *Basic Sentences* in unison, then the *Hints on Pronunciation*, and then go twice more through the *Basic Sentences* individually.

1. Basic Sentences

Record 13A, beginning.

John Cook has been assigned to shore duty and is looking for a place to live; he goes to a modest hotel and addresses the woman who owns it.

ENGLISH EQUIVALENTS	AIDS TO LISTENING	CONVENTIONAL SPELLING
John	yánis	Γιάννης
rooms	dhomátia	δωμάτια
Do you have any rooms?	échete-dhomátia?	Ἔχετε δωμάτια;
anything	típota	τίποτα
At the other hotel they didn't have a thing.	s-to-álo-ksenodhochío dhen-íkhane-típota.	Στὸ ἄλλο ξενοδοχεῖο δὲν εἴχανε τίποτα.
The innkeeper	i-ksenodhókha	Ἡ ξενοδόχα
individuals	átoma	ἄτομα
For how many persons?	ya-pósa-átoma?	Γιὰ πόσα ἄτομα;
John	yánis	Γιάννης
for myself	ya-ména	γιὰ 'μένα
I only want it for myself.	to-thélo ya-ména-móno.	Τὸ θέλω γιὰ 'μένα μόνο.

[7–A]

The innkeeper	i-ksenodhókha	Ἡ ξενοδόχα
I only have Number 10.	ekho-móno-to-dhéka.	Ἔχω μόνο τὸ δέκα.
the first floor	to-próto-pátoma	τὸ πρῶτο πάτωμα
It's on the second* floor.	ine-s-to-próto-pátoma.	Εἶναι στὸ πρῶτο πάτωμα.
John	yánis	Γιάννης
that I see	na-dhó	νὰ δῶ
Can I see it?	boró-na-to-dhó?	Μπορῶ νὰ τὸ δῶ;
The innkeeper	i-ksenodhókha	Ἡ ξενοδόχα
This is it here.	aftó-edhó-ine.	Αὐτὸ ἐδῶ εἶναι.
windows	paráthira	παράθυρα
It has three windows.	echi-tría-paráthira.	Ἔχει τρία παράθυρα.
It has a high ceiling. ('It is high.')	ine-psiló.	Εἶναι ψηλό.
It's sunny and airy.	echi-ílyo ky-aéra.	Ἔχει ἥλιο κι ἀέρα.
Do you like it? ('Is it pleasing to you?')	sas-arési?	Σᾶς ἀρέσει;
John	yánis	Γιάννης
the bed	to-kreváti	τὸ κρεββάτι
hard	skliró	σκληρό
The bed's a little hard.	to-kreváti-ine-liǵaki-skliró.	Τὸ κρεββάτι εἶναι λιγάκι σκληρό.

*In Greece they do not count the ground floor in reckoning the number of stories to a house.

The innkeeper	i-ksenodhókha	Ἡ ξενοδόχα
what do you mean?	tí-léte	τί λέτε
soft	malakó	μαλακό
What do you mean, sir? It's soft.	tí-léte kírie, ine-malakó.	Τί λέτε, κύριε, εἶναι μαλακό.
better	kalítero	καλύτερο
all the hotel	ólo-to-ksenodhochío	ὅλο τὸ ξενοδοχεῖο
I haven't another better in the whole hotel.	dhén-ekho-álo-kalítero s-ólo-to-ksenodhochío.	Δὲν ἔχω ἄλλο καλύτερο σ' ὅλο τὸ ξενοδοχεῖο.
you sleep	kimáste	κοιμᾶστε
You'll sleep well on this.	s-aftó kimáste-kalá.	σ' αὐτὸ κοιμᾶστε καλά.
the furniture	ta-épipla	τὰ ἔπιπλα
And don't you like the furniture—	ke-ta-épipla dhé-sas-arésune—	καὶ τὰ ἔπιπλα δὲ σᾶς ἀρέσουνε—
the table	to-trapézi	τὸ τραπέζι
a wardrobe	mya-dulápa	μιὰ ντουλάπα
three chairs	trís-karékles	τρεῖς καρέκλες
—the table, a wardrobe, and three chairs?	—to-trapézi mya-dulápa ke-trís-karékles?	—τὸ τραπέζι, μιὰ ντουλάπα καὶ τρεῖς καρέκλες;

Record 13B, beginning.

John	yánis	Γιάννης
noise	thórivos	θόρυβος
in the night	ti-níkhta	τὴ νύχτα
the quiet	i-isichía	ἡ ἡσυχία
Is it noisy at night or quiet?	ine-thórivos-ti-níkhta í-isichía?	Εἶναι θόρυβος τὴ νύχτα ἢ ἡσυχία;

[7–A] 153

The innkeeper
ever
No, it's never noisy at night.

anybody
wakes up
Nobody wakes up at night.

John
Where's the toilet?

The innkeeper
the third door
The third door on the left.

the second
the bath(room)
And the second is the bath.

John
well
Well then, how much [for] the room?

The innkeeper
I take
a hundred
per day
For Number 10 I get a hundred drachmas a day.

i-ksenodhókha
poté
óchi, dhén-ine-thórivos poté-ti-níkhta.

kanénas
ksipnái
kanénaz-dhen-gzipnái ti-níkhta.

yánis
pú-ine-to-méros?

i-ksenodhókha
i-tríti-pórta
i-tríti-pórt-aristerá.

i-dhéfteri
to-bányo
k-i-dhéfteri ine-to-bányo.

yánis
lipón
lipón, póso-to-dhomátio?

i-ksenodhókha
pérno
ekató
tin-iméra
ya-to-dhéka pérno-ekató-dhrakhmés tin-iméra.

Ἡ ξενοδόχα
ποτέ
Ὄχι, δὲν εἶναι θόρυβος ποτὲ τὴ νύχτα.

κανένας
ξυπνάει
Κανένας δὲν ξυπνάει τὴ νύχτα.

Γιάννης
Ποῦ εἶναι τὸ μέρος;

Ἡ ξενοδόχα
ἡ τρίτη πόρτα
Ἡ τρίτη πόρτ' ἀριστερά.

ἡ δεύτερη
τὸ μπάνιο
Κ' ἡ δεύτερη εἶναι τὸ μπάνιο.

Γιάννης
λοιπὸν
Λοιπόν, πόσο τὸ δωμάτιο;

Ἡ ξενοδόχα
παίρνω
ἑκατὸ
τὴν ἡμέρα
Γιὰ τὸ δέκα παίρνω ἑκατὸ δραχμὲς τὴν ἡμέρα.

per cent	tis-ekató	τοῖς ἑκατό
you pay	plirónete	πληρώνετε
for the service	ya-tin-ipiresía	γιὰ τὴν ὑπηρεσία
And you pay ten per cent for the service.	ke-dhéka-tis-ekató plirónete ya-tin-ipiresía.	Καὶ δέκα τοῖς ἑκατὸ πληρώνετε γιὰ τὴν ὑπηρεσία.
cheap	ftinó	φτηνό
It's very reasonable.	ine-polí-ftinó.	Εἶναι πολὺ φτηνό.

John / yánis / Γιάννης

expensive	akrivó	ἀκριβό
All right, it's not expensive.	kalá, dhén-in-akrivó.	Καλά, δὲν εἶν' ἀκριβό.
I do not know yet	dhén-gzéro-akóma	δὲν ξέρω ἀκόμα
when?	póte	πότε
it is necessary	prépi	πρέπει
that I leave	na-fígho	νὰ φύγω
I don't know yet when I have to leave.	dhén-gzéro-akóma póte-prépi-na-fígho.	Δὲν ξέρω ἀκόμα πότε πρέπει νὰ φύγω.
it is possible	borí	μπορεῖ
that I stay	na-míno	νὰ μείνω
for a long time	polín-geró	πολὺν καιρό
I may stay for a long time.	borí-na-míno polín-geró.	Μπορεῖ νὰ μείνω πολὺν καιρό.

Record 14A, beginning.

The innkeeper / i-ksenodhókha / Ἡ ξενοδόχα

you wake up	ksipnáte	ξυπνᾶτε
What time do you wake up?	tí-ora-ksipnáte?	Τί ὥρα ξυπνᾶτε;

[7–A]   155

John	yánis	Γιάννης
that we work	na-dhulévume	νὰ δουλεύουμε
On the ship I'm on ('where I am') we have to work hard.	s-to-vapóri-pu-íme prépi-na-dhulévume-polí.	Στὸ βαπόρι ποὺ εἶμαι πρέπει νὰ δουλεύουμε πολύ.
that I wake up	na-ksipnó	νὰ ξυπνῶ
at four o'clock	s-tis-téseris	στὶς τέσσερεις
I have to wake up at four.	prépi-na-ksipnó s-tis-téseris.	Πρέπει νὰ ξυπνῶ στὶς τέσσερεις.
tomorrow	ávrio	αὔριο
that I work	na-dhulépso	νὰ δουλέψω
But tomorrow I don't have to work.	ma-ávrio dhén-ekho-na-dhulépso.	Μὰ αὔριο δὲν ἔχω νὰ δουλέψω.
that you wake me up	na-me-ksipnísete	νὰ μὲ ξυπνήσετε
Can you wake me up at seven?	boríte-na-me-ksipnísete s-tis-eftá?	Μπορεῖτε νὰ μὲ ξυπνήσετε στὶς ἑφτά;
The innkeeper	i-ksenodhókha	Ἡ ξενοδόχα
Of course!	pós?	Πῶς;
Do you have the key?	échete-to-klidhí?	Ἔχετε τὸ κλειδί;
John	yánis	Γιάννης
I have it	tó-kho	τό 'χω
in the pocket	s-tin-dzépi	στὴν τσέπη
Yes, I have it in my pocket.	né, tó-kho-s-tin-dzépi-mu.	Ναί, τό 'χω στὴν τσέπη μου.

Before you go through the *Basic Sentences* a second time, read the following:

2. Hints on Pronunciation

1. THE SOUNDS *t*, *k*, AND *p* AFTER *n*.

Of all the changes of sounds that take place when words run together in a phrase in Greek, perhaps the most striking is the effect produced when one word ends with an *n* and the next word begins with *t*, *k*, or *p*. This section is a review for you, since this matter was discussed in Unit 2. But in order either to recognize combinations of familiar words when you hear them spoken or to pronounce them convincingly in a phrase yourself, you should repeat some typical combinations of this kind till you can make the changes without thinking about them.

Record 14A, after first spiral.
PRACTICE 1

(a) *n + t* becomes *nd* as pronounced in English *candle*.

to-vlépo.	I see it.	*dhén-do-vlépo.*	I don't see it.
tí-ine?	What is it?	*san-dí-ine?*	What is it, exactly? ('Just what is it?')
i-tríti-pórta	the third door (subj.)	*tin-dríti-pórta*	the third door (obj.)

(b) *n + k* becomes *ng* as pronounced in English *finger*.

enas-kafés	a coffee (subj.)	*enan-gafé*	a coffee (obj.)
o-kírios	the gentleman (subj.)	*ton-gírio*	the gentleman (obj.)
i-kóri-mu	my daughter (subj.)	*tin-góri-mu*	my daughter (obj.)
k-esás	and you (obj.)	*san-g-esás*	like you
káni-krío.	It's cold.	*dhén-gáni-krío.*	It isn't cold.

(c) *n + p* becomes *mb* as pronounced in English *number*.

o-papús-tis	her grandfather (subj.)	*tom-bapú-tis*	her grandfather (obj.)
i-pórta	the door (subj.)	*tim-bórta*	the door (obj.)
prépi-na-fígho.	I must leave.	*dhém-brépi-na-fígho.*	I must not leave.

Record 14A, after second spiral.
PRACTICE 2

2. THE SOUNDS *ts*, *ks*, AND *ps* AFTER *n*.

i-tsépi-sas	your pocket (subj.)	*s-tin-dzépi-sas*	in your pocket
kséro	I know	*dhén-gzéro*	I don't know
i-ksenodhókha	the (woman) innkeeper (subj.)	*tin-gzenodhókha*	the (woman) innkeeper (obj.)
ksipnái-kanénas?	Does anybody wake up?	*kanénaz-dhen-gzipnái.*	Nobody wakes up.
i-psilí-pórta	the high door (subj.)	*tim-bzilí-pórta*	the high door (obj.)

You will notice that the changes that occur in the phrases above are very much like the ones you have just practiced in Section 1. And this is natural. In the clusters *ts*, *ks*, and *ps* the change of *t* to *d*, *k* to *g*, and *p* to *b* brings with it the change of the following *s* to *z*. All this is quite familiar to you from English, where you have *pots* beside *pods*, *locks* beside *logs*, and *cups* beside *cubs*.

Don't be surprised, however, if you hear pronunciations like *s-ti-dzépi*, *dhé-gzéro*, *ti-bzilí-pórta*. The consonant groups *ndz*, *ngz*, *mbz* in combinations of words (and *ndz* within a word) are often reduced to *dz*, *gz*, *bz* in the speech of many Greeks.

SECTION B—WORD STUDY AND REVIEW OF BASIC SENTENCES
1. Word Study (Individual Study)
COMMENT 1

THE VERB *ksipnó*. Up to this point in the course all verbs with the accent on the last syllable in the *I*-form have been like *miló* 'I speak' (with the second person *milíte* 'you speak', and the third person *milí* 'he speaks'). But although these verbs like *miló* are in very common use, they are really not nearly as numerous as the verbs which follow the model of *ksipnó*. Let's look at the forms of this verb:

		Endings:
I wake up	*ksipnÓ*	-ó
you wake up	*ksipnÁTE*	-áte
he wakes up	*ksipnÁI*	-ái
we wake up	*ksipnÚME*	-úme
they wake up	*ksipnÚNE*	-úne

In three of the forms the endings are like those of

miló. But tnere the resemblance stops, for the second person ends in -*áte* (instead of -*íte*), and the third person ends in -*ái* (instead of -*í*). Notice that from the ending -*ó* of the first person singular, under which verbs are entered in the *Finder List*, you cannot tell whether any given verb has forms like *miló* or like *ksipnó*. Since this is so, and since, as has been stated, the *ksipnó* verbs are far more numerous than the ones like *miló*, the two kinds of verbs with accent on the last syllable will be distinguished in the *Finder Lists* on this basis: after the first person singular of a verb like *miló* there will be added in parentheses the third person singular ending -*í*; on the other hand verbs like *ksipnó* will go unmarked so that you can take it for granted that any such verb has a third person singular in -*ái*. Thus typical entries would be: *miló* (-*í*), but simply *ksipnó*. Here is a complete list of the verbs like *miló* which have been introduced by now: *boró* (-*í*), *efkharistó* (-*í*), *parakaló* (-*í*), and *zó* (-*í*).

The verbs like *ksipnó* are so much in the majority that they tend to influence the relatively few verbs which go like *miló*, so don't be surprised if you hear, for example, *milái* instead of *milí*, or *miláte* instead of *milíte*.

COMMENT 2

THE VERB *kimúme*. The following sentences show the forms of *kimúme* 'I sleep', which you have met in the present Unit:

otan-ékho-keró, kimúme.
s-aftó kimáste-kalá.
kanénaz-dhen-gimáte ti-níkhta.
to-kalokéri dhén-gimúmaste-kalá.
s-to-ksenodhochío-mu kimúnde-kalá.

When I have time, I sleep.
You'll sleep ('You sleep') well on this.
Nobody sleeps at night.
We don't sleep well in summer.
In my hotel they sleep well.

Here is a summary of the forms:

		Endings:
I sleep	*kimÚME*	-*úme*
you sleep	*kimÁSTE*	-*áste*
he sleeps	*kimÁTE*	-*áte*
we sleep	*kimÚMASTE*	-*úmaste*
they sleep	*kimÚNDE*	-*únde*

As you see, this verb is of the same general type as certain other verbs which you have learned, such as *ergházome* 'I work' or *érkhome* 'I come', with two exceptions: first, the endings are somewhat different; secondly, the accent is on the ending not only in the *we*-form, as in *erghazómaste* or *erkhómaste*, but in all the forms.

COMMENT 3

-o VERBS AND -me VERBS. Since you have learned the verbs *kséro* 'I know' and *ergházome* 'I work', you must already have seen that Greek verbs may be divided into two totally different sets of forms: the first set comprises verbs like *kséro*, *léo*, *miló*, or *ksipnó*, which aside from many differences in detail have one thing in common, that they all end in the same way, namely, in -o, -te, -i*, -me, -ne; similarly, the verbs of the second set, like *ergházome* or *kimúme*, end in -me, -ste, -te**, -maste, -nde**. This is a fundamental line of division in the Greek verb-system, and it will be convenient to take it into account by referring to a verb as being either of the -o type (like *kséro*, *léo*, *miló*, or *ksipnó*) or of the -me type (like *ergházome* or *kimúme*).

COMMENT 4

HOW TO EXPRESS IN GREEK 'I WANT TO', 'I HAVE TO', 'I MAY', 'I CAN', ETC.

(a) *na-dhulévo* 'that I (always) work'. In this Unit there occurred the following sentences:

s-to-vapóri-pu-íme prépi-na-dhulévume-polí.	On the ship I'm on we have to work ('it is necessary that we [always] work' *or* 'it is necessary for us to work') hard.
prépi-na-ksipnó s-tis-téseris.	I have to wake up at four. ('It is necessary that I [always] wake up at four.')

While *dhulévume* and *ksipnó* used by themselves mean 'we work; we are working' and 'I wake up; I am waking up', the combinations *na-dhulévume* and *na-ksipnó* mean literally 'that we (always) work', 'that I (always) wake up'.

(b) *na-dhulépso* 'that I work (this once)'. In this Unit you have also met these sentences:

ávrio dhén-ekho-na-dhulépso.	Tomorrow I don't have to work. ('Tomorrow I do not have that I work.')
boríte-na-me-ksipnísete s-tis-eftá?	Can you wake me up at seven? ('Are you able that you wake me up at seven?')

---

*In the speech of those who say, for example, *ksipná* instead of *ksipnái*, the *-i* has been reduced to zero.
**The form *íne* 'he (she, it) is; they are' is unique.

The striking thing about these sentences, in contrast to the ones analyzed in the preceding section, is that in the verb-forms that come after *na* the endings are added onto an entirely different stem: that is, we have not *dhulévo* in the first sentence above, but *dhulépso*, and not *ksipnáte* but *ksipnísete*. Now, this difference of stem goes along with a difference of meaning which you should grasp clearly. While *prépi-na-dhulévo* would mean "It is necessary that I (always) work, that I be working," the sentence *prépi-na-dhulépso* means "It is necessary that I work (this once)." And while *boríte-na-me-ksipnáte?* would mean "Can you (always) wake me up?" the sentence *boríte-na-me-ksipnísete?* means "Can you wake me up (this once)?" Thus the stems *dhulev-* and *ksipn-* apply to acts in process or repeated or customary or to some enduring state of things and are called *imperfective* (meaning 'unfinished'); on the contrary the stems *dhuleps-* and *ksipnis-* apply to single acts and are called *perfective* (meaning 'finished').

Almost every Greek verb has two stems with this difference of meaning, the imperfective stem and the perfective stem. This is very characteristic of Greek; in fact, this feature is the very backbone of the Greek verb-system. You will meet this contrast again and again. Thus the form *dhulépso*, which we just discussed, is based on the perfective stem *dhuleps-;* but since it never stands by itself but only after *na* 'that' and a few other little words of this kind, generally in dependent clauses, we shall call it the *perfective dependent*. On the other hand there is the form *dhulévo* based on the imperfective stem *dhulev-;* this form can be used either by itself, meaning 'I work; I am working', or after *na* and the other particles in a dependent clause. This form we shall call the *imperfective present*. The imperfective present is the stem under which you learn all verbs in the *Finder Lists*.

The mastery of each Greek verb really depends on one's knowing both stems and using now one, now the other in the proper situations. If a person knows one stem, he can often form the other; but it must be admitted that this is not always possible. The formation of the perfective stem from the imperfective stem, or vice versa, will be studied in more detail later. The important thing now is for you to make a beginning by noting the form and meaning of the perfective dependents that come in the following sentences which you have had; the imperfective present, as it would occur in the *Finder List*, is given at the left for contrast.

Imperfective present	Perfective dependent	
ksipnó	*boríte-na-me-ksipnísete s-tis-eftá?*	Can you wake me up at seven?
dhulévo	*ávrio dhén-ekho-na-dhulépso.*	Tomorrow I don't have to work.
parusiázo	*boró-na-sas-parusiáso-tin-giría-burbúli?*	May I present (to you) Mrs. Bourboulis?

méno	*borí-na-míno polín-geró.*	I may stay for a long time.
prosférno	*tí-boró-na-sas-prosféro?*	What can I treat you to?
févgho	*póte-prépi-na-fígho?*	When do I have to leave?
vlépo	*boró-na-to-dhó?*	Can I see it?
léo	*dhém-boró-na-sas-to-pó.*	I can't tell you (it).

You will observe that the endings of the perfective dependent are the same as in the imperfective present of verbs like *kséro*, except for monosyllables like *dhó* or *pó*, which have the same endings as *zó* 'I live'.

Examples of the perfective dependent:

na-míno	that I stay;	(for me)	to stay	*na-pó*	that I say;	(for me)	to say
na-mínete	that you stay;	(for you)	to stay	*na-píte*	that you say;	(for you)	to say
na-míni	that he stay;	(for him)	to stay	*na-pí*	that he say;	(for him)	to say
na-mínume	that we stay;	(for us)	to stay	*na-púme*	that we say;	(for us)	to say
na-mínune	that they stay;	(for them)	to stay	*na-púne*	that they say;	(for them)	to say

Watch also the change of *gh* to *y* before *e* and *i* in the perfective dependent *fígho*, a change which you encountered in the imperfective present *févgho* in Unit 2.

na-fígho	that I leave;	(for me)	to leave
na-fíyete	that you leave;	(for you)	to leave
na-fíyi	that he leave;	(for him)	to leave
na-fíghume	that we leave;	(for us)	to leave
na-fíghune	that they leave;	(for them)	to leave

As to *na* you will get accustomed to its use in the common groups *thélo-na* 'I want to', *ékho-na* 'I have to', *prépi-na* 'it is necessary to', *boró-na* 'I am able to; I can', *borí-na* 'it is possible to'. It is often very convenient to use our English infinitives, such as 'to work' or 'to wake up', in translating these combinations, but it should always be remembered that *na* is literally 'that' introducing a personal verb-form, that is, a verb-form preceded by 'I', 'you', 'he', etc.; Greek has no infinitive. Thus *thélo-na-dhulévo* 'I want to work' is really 'I want that I work'; *théli-na-dhulévo* 'he wants me to work' is really 'he wants that I work'; and *thélo-na-dhulépsete ávrio* 'I want you to work tomorrow' is really 'I want that you work tomorrow'.

COMMENT 5

How to say 'no one (nobody)', 'nothing', and 'never' in Greek. Just as, in English, there is a clear relationship between the pairs 'anyone (anybody)' and 'no one (nobody)', 'anything' and 'nothing', and 'ever' and 'never', so in Greek there is a similar relationship that may be studied in the following sentences, which are taken from this Unit or are based on the material of this or earlier Units:

QUESTION:	FULL ANSWER:	SHORT ANSWER:
kimáte-kanenas-edhó?	*óchi, dhen-gimáte-kanénas-edhó.* or *óchi, kanénaz-dhen-gimát-edhó.*	*kanénas.*
Does anybody sleep here?	No, nobody sleeps here. ('No, not anybody sleeps here.')	Nobody.
ksipnái-kanenas ti-níkhta?	*óchi, dhen-gzipnái-kanénas ti-níkhta.* or *óchi, kanénaz-dhen-gzipnái ti-níkhta.*	*kanénas.*
Does anybody wake up at night?	No, nobody wakes up at night. ('No, not anybody wakes up at night.')	Nobody.
íkhane-típota s-to-álo-ksenodhochío?	*óchi, dhen-íkhane-típota s-to-álo-ksenodhochío.* or *típota-dhen-íkhane s-to-álo-ksenodhochío.*	*típota.*
Did they have anything at the other hotel?	No, they had nothing at the other hotel. ('No, they did not have anything at the other hotel.')	Nothing.
katalávate-típota?	*óchi, dhen-gatálava-típota.* or *típota-dhen-gatálava.*	*típota.*

[7–B]

Did you understand anything?	No, I understood nothing.	Nothing.
	('No, I did not understand anything.')	
ine-thórivos poté-ti-níkhta?	*óchi, dhén-ine-thórivos poté-ti-níkhta.*	*poté.*
	or	
	óchi, poté-dhen-ine-thórivos ti-níkhta.	
Is it ever noisy at night?	No, it's never noisy at night.	Never.
	('No, it is not ever noisy at night.')	

From these sentences you see that in Greek the equivalents for the negative expressions 'no one (nobody)', 'nothing', and 'never' are really combinations of *dhén* 'not' plus such words for 'anyone (anybody)', 'anything', and 'ever' as may be used in questions. Notice also that the order of the two parts may vary: for 'nobody sleeps' one may say *dhen-gimáte-kanénas*, literally 'not sleeps anybody', or one may say *kanénaz-dhen-gimáte*, literally 'anybody not sleeps'. And the same variation of word order holds for *típota* (*dhen . . . típota* or *típota-dhen . . .*) and *poté* (*dhen . . . poté* or *poté-dhen . . .*). In the short answers the 'not' is taken for granted and left out. In all these combinations, whether *dhén* is expressed or omitted, there is a particularly heavy stress on the element (*kanénas, típota*, etc.) combining with *dhén*.

COMMENT 6

HOW TO SAY 'ONE O'CLOCK', 'THREE O'CLOCK', AND 'FOUR O'CLOCK' IN GREEK. Consider these expressions of time:

ine-mía.	It's one.	*s-ti-mía*	at one
ine-dhío	It's two.	*s-tiz-dhío*	at two
ine-trís.	It's three.	*s-tis-trís*	at three
ine-téseris.	It's four.	*s-tis-téseris*	at four
ine-pénde.	It's five.	*s-tis-pénde*	at five

You remember that when you are simply counting up you start out, "*éna, dhío, tría, tésera, pénde.*" Now when you do this, you are really using the neuter form of those numerals which happen to have more than one form, namely, those for 'one', 'three', and 'four'. But when you tell time in Greek you do not use *éna, tría,* or *tésera*. There is a good reason for this. "It's one" is often expressed in a fuller form as *ine-mía-i-óra*, literally "It is one, the hour." Since *óra* 'hour' is feminine, the form for 'one' to be used with it must be *mía;* similarly in *ine-trís* and *ine-téseris* or in *s-tis-trís* and *s-tis-téseris* the plural *óres* 'hours' is taken for granted and left out.

The forms *trís* and *téseris* serve not only as feminine but also as masculine. The numeral *dhío* 'two' and the other numerals you have learned from five through ten have only one form for all genders.

Here is a table which illustrates all the forms (in the subject case) of the numerals from one through five, using them with *ándras* 'man', *yinéka* 'woman', and *pedhí* 'child'.

	masc.	fem.	neut.
1:	énas-ándras	myá-yinéka	éna-pedhí
3:	trís-ándres	tríz-yinékes	tría-pedhyá
4:	téseris-ándres	téseriz-yinékes	tésera-pedhyá
but			
2:	dhyó-ándres	dhyó-yinékes	dhyó-pedhyá
5:	pénde-ándres	pénde-yinékes	pénde-pedhyá

As to the double pronunciations *mía* and *myá*, you may take this as a general rule, that *myá* always goes closely with the following word, as in *myá-yinéka* 'one woman', but that *mía* stands alone at the end of a phrase, as in *ine-mía* "It's one (o'clock)," although if one is being particularly emphatic about the accuracy of counting he may say *mía yinéka* 'one woman'. It is the same with *dhyó* and *dhío*, for if someone asks *pósa-pedhyá-échi?* "How many children has he?" the answer might be either *dhyó-pedhyá* 'two children' or *dhío* 'two', unless the speaker wanted to say emphatically *dhío pedhyá* '*two* children'.

2. Covering English and Greek of Word Study (Individual Study)

Check yourself on your knowledge of the *Word Study* by covering first the English, then the Greek, and making sure you know everything thoroughly.

3. Review of Basic Sentences

With the Guide or records, review the first half of the *Basic Sentences* as in previous Units.

Section C—Review of Basic Sentences (*Cont.*)

1. Review of Basic Sentences (*Cont.*)

Review the second half of the *Basic Sentences*.

2. Covering the English of Basic Sentences (Individual Study)

Go through the *Basic Sentences*, covering up the English and reading aloud the Greek. Check up on anything you do not know, until you are sure of everything.

3. What Would You Say? (Individual Study)

I. Fill each blank with one or more of the following words expressing possession: *mu, sas, tu, tis, mas, tus.*

1. *i-ghonís* —— *ménune s-tin-amerikí.* 2. *aftós-in-o-fílos* ——. 3. *kaliméra mikré* ——. 4. *i-yinéka* —— *ergházete se-ghrafío.* 5. *févyi léi o-yatró* ——. 6. *ta-khtimatá* —— *dhén-ine-meghála.* 7. *i-mitéra* —— *ine-polí-kalí.* 8. *o-patéraz* —— *ky-o-patéra* —— *in-ap-ti-makedhonía.* 9. *to-tésera ine-to-dhomatió* ——. 10. *to-klidhí* —— *tó-kho-s-tin-dzépi* ——.

II. How would you say in Greek:

1. How do you say 'when?' in Greek? 2. How do you say 'never' in Greek? 3. I sleep well in my bed. 4. What time does the train leave? 5. When do you wish to leave for Salonica? 6. Every day he comes at four o'clock. 7. Sometimes they do not pay for the service. 8. At this hotel you pay a hundred drachmas and you don't sleep well. 9. Give them (*neuter*). 10. Have you a room for two persons?

III. Match each phrase in the left-hand column with one or more appropriate phrases in the right-hand column.

1. *to-dhomatió-sas*
2. *to-dhéftero-pátoma s-tin-amerikí*
3. *dhém-boró-na-érkhome káthe-méra*
4. *to-vapóri-févyi*
5. *tí-ora*

a. *ya-tría-átoma?*
b. *s-aftó-to-dhomátio?*
c. *thélete-na-sas-ksipníso?*
d. *í-me-to-tréno.*
e. *ya-tin-ipiresía.*

6. *échete-dhomátio*
7. *boríte-na-páte me-to-vapóri*
8. *lipúme-polí, ma*
9. *pó-sas-arésune-ta-épipla*
10. *prépi-na-plirónete-dhéka-dhrakhmés*

f. *ine-to-tría.*
g. *ine-to-próto-pátoma s-tin-eládha.*
h. *dhén-ekho-dhomátio-me-bányo.*
i. *ávrio-to-vrádhi.*
j. *m-aftó-to-krío.*

Section D—Listening In

1. What Did You Say?

Give your answers in Greek for each of the exercises in the preceding sections, when the Leader calls for them. Then, as the Leader calls for them, give the English equivalents of all the expressions in the exercise.

2. Word Study Check-Up

As you have done in the previous Units, go back to the *Word Study* and give the correct Greek for each English expression, without having to read it from the book. The Leader or one of the members of the group should read the English.

3. Listening In

With your book closed, listen to the following conversations as read by the Guide or phonograph record. Repeat the Greek immediately after hearing it. After the first repetition of each conversation, check up on the meaning of anything you do not understand, by asking someone else or by going back to the *Basic Sentences* if no one knows. Repeat each conversation if necessary, then take parts and carry on the conversation.

Record 14A, after third spiral.

1. John and Peter discuss the hotels in which they live.

pétros: *dhe-mu-léte yáni, pú-ménete?*
yánis: *eghó? méno-se-ksenodhochío.*
pétros: *k-eghó méno-se-ksenodhochío, s-to-madzéstik.*

Δὲ μοῦ λέτε, Γιάννη, ποῦ μένετε;
Ἐγώ; Μένω σὲ ξενοδοχεῖο.
Κ' ἐγὼ μένω σὲ ξενοδοχεῖο, στὸ Μαζέστικ.

yánis: *to-madzéstik to-kséro.*
       íne-kaló?
pétros: *dhén-ine-ke-tóso-kakó.*
       m-arési.

Τὸ Μαζέστικ τὸ ξέρω.
Εἶναι καλό;
Δὲν εἶναι καὶ τόσο κακό.
Μ' ἀρέσει.

Record 14B, beginning.

2. John and Peter go into the hotel where Peter lives.

pétros: *to-dhomatió-mu ine-to-peninda-pénde.*
       ine-s-to-dhéftero-pátoma.
       s-tin-eládha vlépete to-dhéftero-pátoma in-aftó-
          pu-ne-s-tin-amerikí to-tríto.
yánis: *to-kséro to-kséro.*
pétros: *eláte-na-to-dhíte.*
       in-i-próti-pórta-dheksyá.

Τὸ δωμάτιό μου εἶναι τὸ πενήντα πέντε.
Εἶναι στὸ δεύτερο πάτωμα.
Στὴν Ἑλλάδα, βλέπετε, τὸ δεύτερο πάτωμα εἶν' αὐτὸ ποὺ 'ναι στὴν Ἀμερικὴ τὸ τρίτο.
Τὸ ξέρω, τὸ ξέρω.
Ἐλᾶτε νὰ τὸ δῆτε.
Εἶν' ἡ πρώτη πόρτα δεξιά.

Record 14B, after first spiral.

3. They go into the room.

pétros: *aftó-ine-to-dhomatió-mu.*
       dhén-ine-polí-meghálo.
       ine-ya-éna-átomo-móno.
       sas-arési?
yánis: *m-arési párapoli.*
       echi-meghálo-paráthiro k-ena-soró-épipla.
       échete vlépo ke-dulápa.
       to-kreváti-ine-malakó.

Αὐτὸ εἶναι τὸ δωμάτιό μου.
Δὲν εἶναι πολὺ μεγάλο.
Εἶναι γιὰ ἕνα ἄτομο μόνο.
Σᾶς ἀρέσει;
Μ' ἀρέσει πάρα πολύ.
Ἔχει μεγάλο παράθυρο κ' ἕνα σωρὸ ἔπιπλα.
Ἔχετε, βλέπω, καὶ ντουλάπα.
Τὸ κρεββάτι εἶναι μαλακό.

pétros:	né, to-kreváti-ine-kaló. ma-dhén-gimúme-kalá. t-aftokínita kánune-meghálo-thórivo ti-níkhta.
yánis:	echete-myá-karékla kondá-s-to-kreváti ke-mya-áli ya-to-trapézi.
pétros:	ky-áli-tríti s-to-bányo.
yánis:	échete-bányo s-to-dhomatió-sas? s-tin-eládha móno-lígha-ksenodhochía ekhune-dhomátia-me-bányo. ine-éna-bányo se-káthe-pátoma i éna-bányo ya-ólo-to-ksenodhochío i echete-ti-thálasa ya-bányo.
pétros:	dhén-do-íkser-aftó.
yánis:	tí-ora-sas-ksipnúne?
pétros:	s-to-ksenodhochío me-ksipnúne s-tis-éksi ma-o-thórivo-s-to-dhrómo me-ksipnái s-tis-pénde.

Ναί, τὸ κρεββάτι εἶναι καλό.
Μὰ δὲν κοιμοῦμαι καλά.
Τ' αὐτοκίνητα κάνουνε μεγάλο θόρυβο τὴ νύχτα.
Ἔχετε μιὰ καρέκλα κοντὰ στὸ κρεββάτι καὶ μιὰ ἄλλη γιὰ τὸ τραπέζι.
Κι ἄλλη τρίτη στὸ μπάνιο.
Ἔχετε μπάνιο στὸ δωμάτιό σας;
Στὴν Ἑλλάδα μόνο λίγα ξενοδοχεῖα ἔχουνε δωμάτια μὲ μπάνιο.
Εἶναι ἕνα μπάνιο σὲ κάθε πάτωμα
ἢ ἕνα μπάνιο γιὰ ὅλο τὸ ξενοδοχεῖο
ἢ ἔχετε τὴ θάλασσα γιὰ μπάνιο.
Δὲν τὸ ἤξερ' αὐτό.
Τί ὥρα σᾶς ξυπνοῦνε;
Στὸ ξενοδοχεῖο μὲ ξυπνοῦνε στὶς ἕξι,
μὰ ὁ θόρυβος στὸ δρόμο μὲ ξυπνάει στὶς πέντε.

Record 14B, after second spiral.

4. They speak about John's hotel.

yánis:	s-to-ksenodhochío-mu in-isichía.
pétros:	in-akrivó?
yánis:	óchi, ine-polí-ftinó. pliróno ekató-dhrakhmés tin-iméra ya-to-dhomátio ke-dhéka-tis-ekató ya-tin-ipiresía.
pétros:	sas-arési-lipón to-ksenodhochío-sas?

Στὸ ξενοδοχεῖο μου εἶν' ἡσυχία.
Εἶν' ἀκριβό;
Ὄχι, εἶναι πολὺ φτηνό.
Πληρώνω ἑκατὸ δραχμὲς τὴν ἡμέρα γιὰ τὸ δωμάτιο καὶ δέκα τοῖς ἑκατὸ γιὰ τὴν ὑπηρεσία.
Σᾶς ἀρέσει λοιπὸν τὸ ξενοδοχεῖο σας;

yánis: to-dhomatió-mu echi-lígha-épipla.
Τὸ δωμάτιό μου ἔχει λίγα ἔπιπλα.
to-kreváti-mu ine-skliró.
Τὸ κρεββάτι μου εἶναι σκληρό.
s-to-bányo dhén-echi-zestó-neró.
Στὸ μπάνιο δὲν ἔχει ζεστὸ νερό.
ke-to-méros dhén-echi-klidhí.
Καὶ τὸ μέρος δὲν ἔχει κλειδί.
ma-i-ksenodhókha ine-polí-kalí-yinéka.
Μὰ ἡ ξενοδόχα εἶναι πολὺ καλὴ γυναῖκα.
tí-thélo-kalíterol
Τί θέλω καλύτερο!

Section E—Conversation

1. Covering the Greek of Basic Sentences (Individual Study)

Cover the Greek of the *Basic Sentences* and practice saying the Greek equivalents of the English expressions.

2. Vocabulary Check-Up

Give the Greek expressions for the English equivalents in the *Basic Sentences* as the Leader calls for them.

3. Conversation

As you have done in the *Conversation* in the previous Units, begin to converse by following the models outlined below fairly closely; then change the situations somewhat. Invent new combinations of subject matter.

I. *At a small inn you ask about a place to live.*

1. You ask whether they have a room.
2. The innkeeper asks you to come with her, saying that she has only one room now, but it's a fine one.
3. She shows it to you and describes the furniture.
4. You object to one of the chairs, saying it is too small for you, and too hard.
5. She says that she has another bigger one.
6. You ask her where the bathroom is.
7. She shows it to you and adds that they don't always have hot water.
8. Well then, you say, how much for the room?

9. She tells you that she gets a hundred drachmas a day and that three other Americans are staying at her hotel.
10. You say that it is reasonable and that you want to stay here the whole summer.

II. *At a somewhat larger hotel which you enter with a friend of yours.*
1. You ask your friend where the office is.
2. He answers that he sees an employee over there near the big window.
3. You tell the clerk that you want a room.
4. He asks whether it is for two persons.
5. You say no, that it is only for you, that your friend here only wanted to see it.
6. You ask whether they have a room with bath.
7. The clerk says they don't have any rooms with bath, but that they have one near the bathroom.
8. You ask where they have rooms with bath.
9. At the Majestic, he says.
10. Your friend interrupts to say that he knows the Majestic, but that it's a very expensive hotel.
11. The clerk asks whether you want to stay long.
12. You say that you may stay for a long time, but you don't know yet.
13. Finally he says that he has a good room but that another man is staying in it; he leaves tomorrow, however. Do you still want the room?
14. You say you do, that you are coming tomorrow, and that such and such is your name.

11. You ask her whether the room has a key.
12. She answers that it has and that she had it in her pocket but now she doesn't know where it is.

Section F—Conversation (*Cont.*)

Continue the conversations started in Section E with a review of parts 1 and 2 of the Section if necessary.

FINDER LIST

A

o aéras	ὁ ἀέρας	air; wind
akóma	ἀκόμα	still; yet
dhen ... akóma	δὲν ... ἀκόμα	⎫
akóma-dhen ...	ἀκόμα δὲν ...	⎬ not yet

akrivós, -í, -ó	ἀκριβός, —ή, —ό	expensive
arési	ἀρέσει	it is pleasing
m-arési	μ' ἀρέσει	it is pleasing to me; I like it
ta-épipla m-arésune	τὰ ἔπιπλα μ' ἀρέσουνε	I like the furniture
to átomo	τὸ ἄτομο	individual; person
ávrio	αὔριο	tomorrow

B

to bányo	τὸ μπάνιο	bath; bathroom
borí	μπορεῖ	it is possible

D

dhéfteros, -i, -o	δεύτερος, —η, —ο	second
dhó see: vlépo		
to dhomátio	τὸ δωμάτιο	room
dhulépso see: dhulévo		
dhulévo	δουλεύω	I work
na-dhulépso	νὰ δουλέψω	that I work
i dulápa	ἡ ντουλάπα	wardrobe
dzépi see: tsépi		

E

ekató	ἑκατό	one hundred
tis-ekató	τοῖς ἑκατό	per cent
ékho		
tó-kho	τό 'χω	I have it
eména		
ya-ména	γιὰ 'μένα	for myself
ta épipla	τὰ ἔπιπλα	furniture

F

févgho   φεύγω   I leave
    na-fígho   νά φύγω   that I leave
fígho see: *févgho*
ftinós, -í, -ó   φτηνός, —ή, —ό   cheap; reasonable

G

geró see: *polín-geró*
gzéro see: *kséro*
gzipnái see: *ksipnó*

I

iméra
    tin-iméra   τὴν ἡμέρα   per day
i ipiresía   ἡ ὑπηρεσία   service
i isichía   ἡ ἡσυχία   the quiet

K

kalíteros, -i, -o   καλύτερος, —η, —ο   better
kanénas   κανένας   anyone; anybody; a person
    dhen ... kanénas   δὲν ... κανένας
    kanénaz-dhen ...   κανένας δὲν ...   } no one; nobody
i karékla   ἡ καρέκλα   chair
kerós see: *polín-geró*
kho see: *ékho*
kimúme   κοιμοῦμαι   I sleep
to klidhí   τὸ κλειδί   key
to kreváti   τὸ κρεββάτι   bed

i ksenodhókha	ἡ ξενοδόχα	(woman) innkeeper
kséro	ξέρω	I know
dhén-gzéro	δὲν ξέρω	I don't know
ksipnó	ξυπνῶ	I wake up
dhén-gzipnái	δὲν ξυπνάει	doesn't wake up
nà-ksipníso	νὰ ξυπνήσω	that I wake up

L

léo	λέω	I say
tí-léte	τί λέτε	what do you mean?
lipón	λοιπόν	well; then

M

malakós, -í, -ó	μαλακός, —ή, —ό	soft
ména see: *eména*.		
méno	μένω	I stay
na-míno	νὰ μείνω	that I stay
míno see: *méno*		

N

i níkhta	ἡ νύχτα	night
ti-níkhta	τὴ νύχτα	in the night; at night

O

ólos, -i, -o	ὅλος, —η, —ο	all; whole
ólo-to-ksenodhochío	ὅλο τὸ ξενοδοχεῖο	the whole hotel

P

to paráthiro	τὸ παράθυρο	window

to pátoma	τὸ πάτωμα	floor
pérno	παίρνω	I take
pliróno	πληρώνω	I pay
polín-geró	πολὺν καιρό	for a long time
i pórta	ἡ πόρτα	door
pós?	πῶς;	of course!
pósos, -i, -o	πόσος, -η, -ο	how much?
pósi, -es, -a	πόσοι, -ες, -α	how many?
póte	πότε	when?
poté	ποτέ	ever
dhen ... poté	δὲν ... ποτέ	} never
poté-dhen ...	ποτὲ δὲν ...	
prépi	πρέπει	it is necessary
prótos, -i, -o	πρῶτος, -η, -ο	first
psilós, -í, -ó	ψηλός, -ή, -ό	high; tall

S

sklirós, -í, -ó	σκληρός, -ή, -ό	hard

T

téseris m. and f	τέσσερεις	four
tésera n.	τέσσερα	
o thórivos	ὁ θόρυβος	noise
típota	τίποτα	anything
dhen ... típota	δὲν ... τίποτα	} nothing
típota-dhen ...	τίποτα δὲν ...	

to (neuter article)		
to-dhéka	τὸ δέκα	Number 10
to trapézi	τὸ τραπέζι	table
trítos, -i, -o	τρίτος, –η, –ο	third
i tsépi	ἡ τσέπη	pocket
s-tin-dzépi	στὴν τσέπη	in the pocket

V

vlépo	βλέπω	I see
na-dhó	νὰ δῶ	that I see

Y

ya	γιὰ	for; about
see: *eména*		

UNIT 8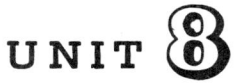

SPRUCING UP

Section A—Basic Sentences

Go once through the *Basic Sentences* in unison, then the *Hints on Pronunciation*, and then go twice more through the *Basic Sentences* individually.

1. Basic Sentences

Record 15A, beginning.

John Cook addresses the innkeeper.

ENGLISH EQUIVALENTS	AIDS TO LISTENING	CONVENTIONAL SPELLING
John	yánis	Γιάννης
that you give me	na-mu-dhósete	νὰ μοῦ δώσετε
some	merikés	μερικές
pieces of information	pliroforíes	πληροφορίες
Can you give me some information?	boríte-na-mu-dhósete-merikés-pliroforíes?	Μπορεῖτε νὰ μοῦ δώσετε μερικὲς πληροφορίες;
The innkeeper	i-ksenodhókha	Ἡ ξενοδόχα
I'd be glad to. ('Gladly.')	efkharístos.	Εὐχαρίστως.
John	yánis	Γιάννης
the shoes	ta-papútsya	τὰ παπούτσια
clean	kathará	καθαρά
My shoes aren't clean.	ta-papútsya-mu dhén-ine-kathará.	Τὰ παπούτσια μου δὲν εἶναι καθαρά.

[8–A] 177

white	áspra	άσπρα
black	mávra	μαύρα
My white ones are black and my black ones [are] white.	ta-áspra-mu-ine-mávra ke-ta-mávra-mu-áspra.	Τὰ ἄσπρα μου εἶναι μαῦρα καὶ τὰ μαῦρα μου ἄσπρα.
that they shine them for me	na-mu-ta-yalísune	νὰ μοῦ τὰ γυαλίσουνε
Where's there a chance of my getting them shined?	pú-borí-na-mu-ta-yalísune?	Ποῦ μπορεῖ νὰ μοῦ τὰ γυαλίσουνε;

The innkeeper — i-ksenodhókha — Ἡ ξενοδόχα

that I show	na-dhíkso	νὰ δείξω
Let me show you.	na-saz-dhíkso.	Νὰ σᾶς δείξω.
they go	piyénune	πηγαίνουνε
the harbor	to-limáni	τὸ λιμάνι
You know how you go down to the harbor?	ksérete pos-piyénune káto-s-to-limáni?	Ξέρετε πῶς πηγαίνουνε κάτω στὸ λιμάνι;

John — yánis — Γιάννης

Yes, I believe [so]. — né, pistévo. — Ναί, πιστεύω.

The innkeeper — i-ksenodhókha — Ἡ ξενοδόχα

nearby	kondá	κοντά
It's not far.	ine-kondá.	Εἶναι κοντά.
that you lose	na-khásete	νὰ χάσετε
You can't miss it ('the road').	dhém-boríte-na-khásete-to-dhrómo.	Δὲν μπορεῖτε νὰ χάσετε τὸ δρόμο.

ask!	rotíste	ρωτήστε
the policeman	ton-astifílaka	τὸν ἀστυφύλακα
on the Street of England	s-tin-odhón*-anglías	στὴν Ὁδὸν Ἀγγλίας
Ask the policeman on England St.	rotíste-ton-astifílaka s-tin-odhón-anglías.	Ρωτήστε τὸν ἀστυφύλακα στὴν Ὁδὸν Ἀγγλίας.
many	polí	πολλοί
bootblacks	lústri	λοῦστροι
Down by the harbor there are a lot of bootblacks.	káto-s-to-limáni ine-polí-lústri.	Κάτω στὸ λιμάνι εἶναι πολλοὶ λοῦστροι.
they give to them	tuz-dhínune	τοὺς δίνουνε
Everybody here gives his shoes to them.	óli-edho tuz-dhínune ta-papútsya-tus.	Ὅλοι ἐδῶ τοὺς δίνουνε τὰ παπούτσια τους.

Record 15B, beginning.

John	yánis	Γιάννης
they wash	plénune	πλένουνε
the clothes	ta-rúkha	τὰ ροῦχα
And will you please tell me where people get their laundry done here?	ke-dhe-mu-léte parakaló, pú-plénun-edhó-ta-rúkha?	Καὶ δὲ μοῦ λέτε, παρακαλῶ, ποῦ πλένουν ἐδῶ τὰ ροῦχα;
The innkeeper	i-ksenodhókha	Ἡ ξενοδόχα
I can do your washing for you.	boró-eghó-na-sas-ta-pléno.	Μπορῶ ἐγὼ νὰ σᾶς τὰ πλένω.

---
*i-odhós, used before names of streets, is a peculiar feminine noun with masculine endings; notice that the object case is *odhón*. The following street-name is in the restrictive case without the definite article.

what else? What else do you want?	tí-alo tí-alo-thélete?	τί ἄλλο Τί ἄλλο θέλετε;
John	*yánis*	Γιάννης
that you clean that you iron the uniform Can you clean and press my uniform for me?	na-katharísete na-sidherósete ti-stolí boríte-na-mu-katharísete ke-na-mu-sidherósete ti-stolí-mu?	νὰ καθαρίσετε νὰ σιδερώσετε τὴ στολή Μπορεῖτε νὰ μοῦ καθαρίσετε καὶ νὰ μοῦ σιδερώσετε τὴ στολή μου;
It's dirty.	ine-vrómiki.	Εἶναι βρώμικη.
that I put Where can I put it?	na-válo pú-boró-na-tine-válo?	νὰ βάλω Ποῦ μπορῶ νὰ τήνε βάλω;
The innkeeper	*i-ksenodhókha*	Ἡ ξενοδόχα
to a tailor to a cleaning establishment To get your uniform done ('For your uniform') you have to go to a tailor or a cleaner's.	se-ráfti se-katharistírio ya-ti-stolí-sas prépi-na-páte se-ráfti í-se-katharistírio.	σὲ ράφτη σὲ καθαριστήριο Γιὰ τὴ στολή σας πρέπει νὰ πάτε σὲ ράφτη ἢ σὲ καθαριστήριο.
John	*yánis*	Γιάννης
any barber cuts the hair Do you know any barber that gives a good haircut?	kanenan-guréa kóvi ta-malyá kséréte-kanenan-guréa pu-kóvi-kalá-ta-malyá?	κανέναν κουρέα κόβει τὰ μαλλιά Ξέρετε κανέναν κουρέα ποὺ κόβει καλὰ τὰ μαλλιά;

The innkeeper	i-ksenodhókha	Ἡ ξενοδόχα
opposite to	andíkri-se	ἀντίκρυ σὲ
the best	o-kalíteros	ὁ καλύτερος
The barber across from the movie theater is the best.	o-kuréas andíkri-s-ton-ginimatóghrafo in-o-kalíteros.	Ὁ κουρέας ἀντίκρυ στὸν κινηματόγραφο εἶν' ὁ καλύτερος.
much	polís	πολύς
world	kózmos	κόσμος
the barber shop	to-kurío	τὸ κουρεῖο
Lots of people go to his place.	piyéni-polís-kózmo-s-to-kurío-tu.	Πηγαίνει πολὺς κόσμος στὸ κουρεῖο του.
[At the barber's.]	[s-tu-kuréa.]	[Στοῦ κουρέα.]
The barber	o-kuréas	Ὁ κουρέας
Sit down, please.	kathíste parakaló.	Καθίστε, παρακαλῶ.
that I shave	na-ksuríso	νὰ ξουρίσω
that I cut	na-kópso	νὰ κόψω
Do you want (me to give you) a shave or a haircut?	thélete-na-sas-ksuríso í-na-sas-kópso-ta-malyá?	Θέλετε νὰ σᾶς ξουρίσω ἢ νὰ σᾶς κόψω τὰ μαλλιά;

Record 16A, beginning.

John	yánis	Γιάννης
cut!	kópste	κόψτε
Give me a haircut, please.	kópste-mu-ta-malyá parakaló.	Κόψτε μου τὰ μαλλιά, παρακαλῶ.

	The barber	o-kuréas	Ὁ κουρέας
short		kondá	κοντά
long		makriá	μακρειά
Shall I take a lot off or just give you a trim? ('Do you want them short or long?')		ta-thélete-kondá i-makriá?	Τὰ θέλετε κοντὰ ἢ μακρειά;

	John	yánis	Γιάννης
Just a trim.		makriá.	Μακρειά.
razor blades		lámes	λάμες
Do you have razor blades?		échete-lámes?	Ἔχετε λάμες;

	The barber	o-kuréas	Ὁ κουρέας
I sell		puló	πουλῶ
No, I don't sell [them].		óchi, dhém-buló.	Ὄχι, δὲν πουλῶ.
the variety-stand		to-kyóski	τὸ κιόσκι
in front of		brostá-se	μπροστὰ σὲ
They sell [them] at the news-stand in front of the barber shop.		s-to-kyóski brostá-s-to-kurío pulúne.	Στὸ κιόσκι μπροστὰ στὸ κουρεῖο πουλοῦνε.
you find		vrískete	βρίσκετε
whatever		óti	ὅ,τι
There you'll find whatever you want.		ekí-vrískete óti-thélete.	Ἐκεῖ βρίσκετε ὅ,τι θέλετε.

	John	yánis	Γιάννης
that I find		na-vró	νὰ βρῶ
a letter		ena-ghráma	ἕνα γράμμα
I'd like to find a letter from Phroso.		thá-thela-na-vró ena-ghrám-ap-ti-fróso.	Θά 'θελα νὰ βρῶ ἕνα γράμμ' ἀπ' τὴ Φρόσω.

Before you go through the *Basic Sentences* a second time, read the following:

2. Hints on Pronunciation

p, t, AND *k*. In English words like *appeal, return, akin,* you pronounce the consonants *p, t, k* with quite a strong puff of breath after them. This almost explosive quality is never a feature of *p, t, k* as pronounced in Greek, and in order to say these sounds as you should in Greek words you will have to practice speaking them less vigorously. Then they will sound like the *p, t, k* that we have in *speed, stern, skill.*

Record 16A, after first spiral.

PRACTICE 1

pághos	ice	*tésera*	four	*karékla*	chair
trapézi	table	*típota*	anything	*kakós*	bad
vapóri	ship	*tóra*	now	*akóma*	still
prótos	first	*tría*	three	*kríos*	cold

k BEFORE *e* OR *i*. When pronounced before *a, o,* or *u* the Greek *k* is made with the tongue touching the roof of the mouth in about the same position as it takes for our English *k*. But before *e* or *i* the Greek *k* is pronounced with the tongue very forward in the mouth. In fact, if you listen closely to your Guide, you will hear almost *kye, kyi* rather than *ke, ki*.

Record 16A, after second spiral.

PRACTICE 2

kápote	sometimes	*kerós*	weather
kózmos	world	*kalokéri*	summer
kuréas	barber	*kírie*	sir

l BEFORE *e* OR *i*. Our *l* in English, as in *fill, sell, all,* is an *l* that sounds "dark," dull, or hollow. Even before *a, o,* or *u* the Greek *l* does not seem to be pronounced as far back in the mouth; and when it comes before *e* or *i* the *l* in Greek is a "bright," clear one made with the tongue in the front of the mouth, with the tip of the tongue against the teeth.

Record 16A, after third spiral.
PRACTICE 3

thélete	you wish		*fíli*	friends
léne	they say		*milí*	speaks
pléno	I wash		*pliróno*	I pay

THE GREEK *r*. The sound *r* in Greek is not at all like any of the *r* sounds we have in English. The Greek *r* is rolled or trilled with the tip of the tongue against the palate, with just the beginning of the vibration which telephone operators use when saying **thrrree,** or which small boys make in imitating an **automobile** or an **aeroplane**.

Record 16A, after fourth spiral.
PRACTICE 4

neró	water		*pórta*	door
rúkha	clothes		*ghráma*	letter
óra	hour		*tréno*	train

SECTION B—WORD STUDY AND REVIEW OF BASIC SENTENCES

1. Word Study (Individual Study)

COMMENT 1

MORE ABOUT THE IMPORTANT WORD *na*. In any language many of the things a person wants most to be able to express are introduced by phrases for 'I want to', 'I'd like to', 'I need to', 'I must', 'I may', 'I can'. Now in Greek, as you learned in Unit 7, these expressions all call for a verb plus *na*. You remember, however, what a difference there is between, for example, *prépi-na-dhulévo* 'I have to work (generally *or* all the time); I have to be working; I have to keep working', and *prépi-na-dhulépso* 'I have to work (this time)'. A Greek speaker doesn't have to stop and think whether he ought to use *na-dhulévo* or *na-dhulépso*; in any given situation he comes out with the right form as quick as a flash and quite unconsciously. But a foreigner has to hear a good many verb-forms after *na* and at first he has to think a good deal about the way they are used, before he can understand them and use them right himself. The following sentences from this Unit or from earlier ones will give you a chance to review the use of *na*.

(a) *na* WITH THE IMPERFECTIVE PRESENT.

***prépi**-na-dhulévume-polí.*	We have to work ('It is necessary that we [always] work' *or* 'It is necessary for us to work') hard.
***prépi**-na-ksipnó s-tis-téseris.*	I have to wake up at four. ('It is necessary that I [always] wake up at four.')
boró-eghó-na-sas-ta-pléno.	I can do your washing for you. ('I am able that I [always] wash them for you.')

In the English of these sentences you notice that you could add the word 'always' or the words 'every day' or some similar phrase meaning 'all along' or 'each time' without spoiling the sense of the sentence. Well, that is a good proof that you have here the *imperfective present* after the word *na*.

(b) *na* WITH THE PERFECTIVE DEPENDENT. In the following examples from this Unit or from earlier ones the imperfective present, as it would occur in the *Finder Lists*, is given at the left for contrast.

Imperfective present	Perfective dependent	
tróo	*pú-boró-na-fáo?*	Where can I eat?
píno	*thélo-na-pyó.*	I want to drink.
piyéno	*né, thá-thela-na-páo.*	Yes, I'd like to go.
	tha-thélate-na-páte s-ti-saloníki?	Would you like to go to Salonica?
	prépi-na-páte se-ráfti.	You have to go to a tailor.
ksipnó	*boríte-na-me-ksipnísete s-tis-eftá?*	Can you wake me up at seven?

[8–B]

dhulévo	ávrio dhén-ekho-na-dhulépso.	Tomorrow I don't have to work.
parusiázo	boró-na-sas-parusiáso-tin-giría-burbúli?	May I present (to you) Mrs. Bourboulis?
méno	borí-na-míno polín-geró.	I may stay for a long time.
prosférno	tí-boró-na-na-na-sas-prosféro?	What can I treat you to?
févgho	póte-prépi-na-fígho?	When do I have to leave?
vlépo	boró-na-to-dhó?	Can I see it?
léo	dhém-boró-na-sas-to-pó.	I can't tell you (it).
dhíno	boríte-na-mu-dhósete merikés-pliroforíes?	Can you give me some information?
váno	pú-boró-na-tine-válo?	Where can I put it?
yalízo	pú-borí-na-mu-ta-yalísune?	Where's there a chance of my getting them shined? ('Where is it possible that they shine them for me?')
kháno	dhém-boríte-na-khásete-to-dhrómo.	You can't miss it ('the road').
katharízo	boríte-na-mu-katharísete-ti-stolí-mu?	Can you clean my uniform for me?
sidheróno	boríte-na-mu-sidherósete-ti-stolí-mu?	Can you press my uniform for me?
kóvo	thélete-na-sas-kópso-ta-malyá?	Do you want (me to give you) a haircut?
ksurízo	thélete-na-sas-ksuríso?	Do you want (me to give you) a shave?

In these sentences you notice that the combination *na* plus the verb-form always applies to some definite, single occasion. Thus *pú-borí-na-mu-ta-yalísune?* means "Where's there a chance of my getting them shined (now that they are dirty)?" Similarly *pú-boró-na-tine-válo?* means "Where can I put it (now that it needs cleaning)?" And *boríte-na-mu-katharísete-ti-stolí-mu?* means "Can you clean my uniform for me (this time)?"

The test of *na* with the *perfective dependent* is that if there is no word of definite time (like *tóra* 'now' or *ávrio* 'tomorrow') in the sentence already, you could add to the English of the sentence the word 'now' or the words 'this once' or 'this time' without spoiling the sense of the sentence. Occasionally there will be an example that doesn't seem clear, but it *can* be explained.

COMMENT 2

How to find the perfective stem of verbs of the -o type. By now you have heard a good number of perfective dependents and it is time to learn how you can form the perfective stem from the imperfective stem. You find the imperfective stem very easily if you drop the ending -o of the *I*-form (the first person singular); for example, if you have *miló* 'I speak', the imperfective stem is *mil-*, and so forth. Most of the perfective forms you have learned were forms used after *na;* but there are also others (of which you have already had *katálava* 'I understood', *katalávate* 'you understood', *ípate* 'you said', and forms of command like *rotíste* 'ask!' or *dhóste* 'give!' or *kópste* 'cut!'), and since the endings are always the same and can easily be attached to the perfective stem, all you have to know is the perfective stem. Thus if you have found out that the perfective stem of *miló* is *milis-*, you have only to put *na* before it and attach the ending -o in order to get the form *na-milíso*.

First let's look at some verbs that go according to a few very common patterns.

1. Imperfective present

		Perfective dependent	Perfective stem
dhyaváZo	'I read'	*na-dhyaváSo*	*dhyavas-*
parusiáZo	'I present'	*na-parusiáSo*	*parusias-*
archíZo	'I start'	*na-archíSo*	*archis-*
chyoníZi	'it snows'	*na-chyoníSi*	*chyonis-*
katharíZo	'I clean'	*na-katharíSo*	*katharis-*

[8–B]

ksurízo	'I shave'	*na-ksuríso*	*ksuris-*
yalízo	'I shine'	*na-yalíso*	*yalis-*

SUMMARY: Where the imperfective stem ends in *-z*, the perfective stem ends in *-s*.

2. Imperfective present   Perfective dependent   Perfective stem

dhulévo	'I work'	*na-dhulépso*	*dhuleps-*
pistévo	'I believe'	*na-pistépso*	*pisteps-*
kóvo	'I cut'	*na-kópso*	*kops-*

SUMMARY: Where the imperfective stem ends in *-v*, the perfective stem ends in *-ps*.

3. Imperfective present   Perfective dependent   Perfective stem

pliróno	'I pay'	*na-pliróso*	*pliros-*
sidheróno	'I iron'	*na-sidheróso*	*sidheros-*

SUMMARY: Where the imperfective stem ends in *-on*, the perfective stem ends in *-os*.

4. Imperfective present   Perfective dependent   Perfective stem

efkharistó	'I thank'	*na-efkharistíso*	*efkharistis-*
ksipnó	'I wake up'	*na-ksipníso*	*ksipnis-*
miló	'I speak'	*na-milíso*	*milis-*
puló	'I sell'	*na-pulíso*	*pulis-*
rotó	'I ask'	*na-rotíso*	*rotis-*
zó	'I live'	*na-zíso*	*zis-*

SUMMARY: Where the imperfective present is accented on the ending rather than on the stem (that is, where the I-form ends in accented *-ó*), *-is* has to be added to the imperfective stem to form the perfective stem.

The kinds of verbs just listed, those whose imperfective stem ends in *-z*, *-v*, or *-on*, or is unaccented, are extremely common in the language. Each of the four varieties is represented by hundreds upon hundreds of verbs. As you go on and meet more verbs with an imperfective stem in *-v* (like *dhulev-*), you can safely assume that the perfective stem will end in *-ps* (like *dhuleps-*), and so with the other kinds of verbs illustrated above. That is not to say that you will not meet any exceptions to these formations, but the exceptions will be relatively few.

But on the other hand there are a good many verbs in Greek that do not have many other verbs like them, so that their parts must simply be learned by heart. The following is a list of the *-o* verbs you have had so far that do not fit into any of the four patterns (1. *-z*: *-s*, 2. *-v*: *-ps*, 3. *-on*: *-os*, 4. unaccented imperfective stem: addition of *-is*) that you have just studied.

Imperfective present		Perfective dependent	Perfective stem
kháno	'I lose'	na-kháso	khas-
boró	'I can'	na-boréso	bores-
parakaló	'I beg'	na-parakaléso	parakales-
sikhoró	'I pardon'	na-sikhoréso	sikhores-
vréchi	'it rains'	na-vréksi	vreks-
dhíkhno	'I show'	na-dhíkso	dhiks-
káno	'I do'	na-kámo	kam-
váno	'I put'	na-válo	val-
katalavéno	'I understand'	na-katalávo	katalav-
pléno	'I wash'	na-plíno	plin-
méno	'I stay'	na-míno	min-
dhíno	'I give'	na-dhóso	dhos-
férno	'I bring'	na-féro	fer-
pérno	'I take'	na-páro	par-
févgho	'I leave'	na-fígho	figh-
tróo	'I eat'	na-fáo*	fa-

*The forms of *fáo* go just like those of *páo*.

piyéno	'I always go; I am going'	*na-páo*	*pa-*
léo	'I say'	*na-pó*	*p-*
píno	'I drink'	*na-pyó*	*py-*
vlépo	'I see'	*na-dhó*	*dh-*

In this *Word Study* you have now met the two stems you need to know for all verbs of the -*o* type that have occurred up to this point in the Units. If any verb has not been discussed, it is because such a verb (like *ékho, kséro, thélo, arési,* or *prépi*) has only an imperfective stem. Starting with this Unit, for any new verb that occurs the *Finder Lists* will give the first person singular of the imperfective present and the *stem* of the perfective, which will be put between obliques, as follows: *pistévo /pisteps/, rotó /rotis/, léo /p/.*

2. Covering English and Greek of Word Study (Individual Study)

Check yourself on your knowledge of the *Word Study* by covering first the English, then the Greek, and making sure you know everything thoroughly.

3. Review of Basic Sentences

With the Guide or records, review the first half of the *Basic Sentences* as in previous Units.

Section C—Review of Basic Sentences (*Cont.*)

1. Review of Basic Sentences (*Cont.*)

Review the second half of the *Basic Sentences*.

2. Covering the English of Basic Sentences (Individual Study)

Go through the *Basic Sentences* covering up the English and reading aloud the Greek. Check up on anything you do not know, until you are **sure of** everything.

3. What Would You Say? (Individual Study)

Say the following sentences without any hesitation, after making sure that you can supply the Greek for the english words in parentheses:

1. *pú* (do they clean) *stolés edho-péra?* (At the tailor's) *andíkri-s-to-kurío.* 2. *eláte-tóra,* (sit down). 3. *ine-thórivos-ti-níkhta s-to* (hotel) *sas?* 4. *dhén-íthele* (to tell me) *pu-íne.* 5. *prépi-na-tone-dhó* (at three o'clock). 6. (Do you sleep) *kalá s-aftó-to-kreváti?* 7. (Ask) *ton-astifílaka káto-s-to-limáni.* 8. *s-tin-eládha* (many) *lústri ine-pedhyá-akóma.* 9. (You told me) *na-to-kámo-ávrio.* 10. *aftós-o-kafés ine* (good), *ma-o-álos itane* (better).

II. Pick out the right line.

1. John tells the barber that he wants a haircut:
   a. *ta-malyá-mu ine-makriá.*
   b. *kópste-mu-ta-malyá parakaló.*
   c. *boríte-na-me-ksurísete?*
   d. *o-kuréas kóvi-ta-malyá.*

2. The barber asks him if he wants a shave:
   a. *ta-malyá-sas ine-mávra.*
   b. *boríte-na-mu-plínete-ta-malyá?*
   c. *thélete-na-sas-ksuríso?*
   d. *kathíste-na-sas-kópso-ta-malyá.*

3. John asks where he can find a variety-stand:
   a. *pú-pái-ólos-aftós-o-kózmos?*
   b. *boríte-na-mu-dhíksete edho-kondá ena-kyóski?*
   c. *dhé-thélo-na-kháso-to-dhrómo.*
   d. *tí-pulúne s-ta-kyóskya?*

4. John is at a variety-stand and asks for razor blades:
   a. *echete-lámes parakaló?*
   b. *póso-kánune óla-mazí?*
   c. *dhóste-mu tría-sigharéta.*
   d. *i-láme-sas in-akrivés.*

III. How do you say in Greek:

1. I know a woman who washes (the) clothes. 2. He used to go to her restaurant. 3. You must go to a cleaner's. 4. He always puts the key into his pocket. 5. At the variety-stands they sell blades. 6. I didn't understand what he wanted. 7. They don't know anything. 8. Do I have to pay you now, or can I pay you tomorrow? 9. I always take it with me. 10. Can I get my shoes shined? They are dirty.

Section D—Listening In

1. What Did You Say?

Give your answers in Greek for each of the exercises in the preceding section, when the Leader calls for them. Then, as the Leader calls for them, give the English equivalents of all the expressions in the exercise.

2. Word Study Check-Up

As you have done in the previous Units, go back to the *Word Study* and give the correct Greek for each English expression, without having to read it from the book. The Leader or one of the members of the group should read the English.

3. Listening In

With your book closed, listen to the following conversations as read by the Guide or phonograph record. Repeat the Greek immediately after hearing it. After the first repetition of each conversation, check up on the meaning of anything you do not understand, by asking someone else or by going back to the *Basic Sentences* if no one knows. Repeat again if necessary, then take parts and carry on the conversation.

Record 16A, after fifth spiral.

1. In John's hotel.

i-ksenodhókha:	kírie-Cook kírie-Cook!	Κύριε Cook, κύριε Cook!
	in-eftá-i-óra.	Εἶν' ἐφτὰ ἡ ὥρα.
	prépi-na-ksipnísete-tóra.	Πρέπει νὰ ξυπνήσετε τώρα.
yánis:	thá-thela-na-mínoligháki-s-to-krevváti.	Θὰ 'θελα νὰ μείνω λιγάκι στὸ κρεββάτι.
i-ksenodhókha:	ma-mu-ípate-na-sas-ksipníso s-tis-eftá.	Μὰ μοῦ εἴπατε νὰ σᾶς ξυπνήσω στὶς ἐφτά.
yánis:	dhé-me-katalávate-kalá.	Δὲ μὲ καταλάβατε καλά.
	eghó-íthela-na-me-ksipnísete s-tis-eftá-to-vrádhi.	Ἐγὼ ἤθελα νὰ μὲ ξυπνήσετε στὶς ἐφτὰ τὸ βράδυ.
i-ksenodhókha:	ke-ton-gafé-sas s-tis-eftá-to-vrádhi tone-thélete?	Καὶ τὸν καφέ σας στὶς ἐφτὰ τὸ βράδυ τόνε θέλετε;
yánis:	óchi, ton-gafé-mu tone-thélo tóra.	Ὄχι, τὸν καφέ μου τόνε θέλω τώρα.

Record 16B, beginning.

2. John finds two bootblacks.

yánis:	dhe-mu-léte pedhyá, pyós-apo-sás katharízi-áspra-papútsya?	Δὲ μοῦ λέτε, παιδιά, ποιὸς ἀπὸ 'σᾶς καθαρίζει ἄσπρα παπούτσια;
o-prótoz-lústros:	eghó.	Ἐγώ.
o-dhéfteros:	k-eghó.	Κ' ἐγώ.
yánis:	thélo o-énas na-mu-katharísi-ta-áspra-mu-papútsya ky-o-álos na-mu-yalísi-ta-mávra.	Θέλω ὁ ἕνας νὰ μοῦ καθαρίσῃ τὰ ἄσπρα μου παπούτσια κι ὁ ἄλλος νὰ μοῦ γυαλίσῃ τὰ μαῦρα.
o-prótos:	eghó pérno-ta-mávra.	Ἐγὼ παίρνω τὰ μαῦρα.
o-dhéfteros:	k-eghó sas-katharízo-ta-áspra.	Κ' ἐγὼ σᾶς καθαρίζω τὰ ἄσπρα.
yánis:	ine-polí-vrómika. eghó prépi-na-páo-tóra-s-to-ksenodhochío-mu. to-vlépete? in-eki-káto s-tin-odhón-anglías. eláte-na-me-vríte-ekí.	Εἶναι πολὺ βρώμικα. Ἐγὼ πρέπει νὰ πάω τώρα στὸ ξενοδοχεῖο μου. Τὸ βλέπετε; Εἶν' ἐκεῖ κάτω στὴν Ὁδὸν Ἀγγλίας. Ἐλᾶτε νὰ μὲ βρῆτε ἐκεῖ.

Record 16B, after first spiral.

3. John asks a gentleman for directions about finding a few places in the city.

yánis:	me-sikhoríte kírie, boríte-na-mu-píte pú-plénun-edhó-ta-rúkha?	Μὲ συχωρεῖτε, κύριε, μπορεῖτε νὰ μοῦ πῆτε ποῦ πλένουν ἐδῶ τὰ ροῦχα;
o-kírios:	kséro-mya-yinéka pu-ta-pléni. dhén-in-akriví. méni s-ena-mikró-spíti kondá-s-to-ksenodhochío.	Ξέρω μιὰ γυναῖκα ποὺ τὰ πλένει. Δὲν εἶν' ἀκριβή. Μένει σ' ἕνα μικρὸ σπίτι κοντὰ στὸ ξενοδοχεῖο.

[8–D]

yánis:	ke-pú-katharízune ke-sidherónune-stolés?	Καὶ ποῦ καθαρίζουνε καὶ σιδερώνουνε στολές;
o-kírios:	prépi-na-vrít-ena-ráfti.	Πρέπει νὰ βρῆτ' ἕνα ράφτη.
	ma-dhén-gzéro-kanéna-ráfti-edho-kondá.	Μὰ δὲν ξέρω κανένα ράφτη ἐδῶ κοντά.
yánis:	ke-pú-boró-na-páo ya-bányo?	Καὶ ποῦ μπορῶ νὰ πάω γιὰ μπάνιο;
	to-thélo-zestó.	Τὸ θέλω ζεστό.
o-kírios:	ekhume-polí-oréo ke-polí-zestó-bányo edhó-to-kalokéri.	Ἔχουμε πολὺ ὡραῖο καὶ πολὺ ζεστὸ μπάνιο ἐδῶ τὸ καλοκαίρι.
	ekhume-ti-thálasa.	Ἔχουμε τὴ θάλασσα.

Record 16B, after second spiral.

4. Mr. Kontos meets Mr. Makres; they talk about a letter.

kondós:	ikha-ghrám-ap-to-yórgho.	Εἶχα γράμμ' ἀπ' τὸ Γιώργο.
	ine-fílo-sas pistévo.	Εἶναι φίλος σας, πιστεύω.
makrís:	o-yórghos? in-o-kaliteróz-mu-fílos!	Ὁ Γιώργος; Εἶν' ὁ καλύτερός μου φίλος!
kondós:	i-zoí mu-léi s-tin-anglía in-akriví.	Ἡ ζωή, μοῦ λέει, στὴν Ἀγγλία εἶν' ἀκριβή.
	ine-polís-kózmos tóra-ekí.	Εἶναι πολὺς κόσμος τώρα ἐκεῖ.
	ma-vrískune óti-thélune.	Μὰ βρίσκουνε ὅ,τι θέλουνε.
	o-yós-tu ine-s-tin-italía.	Ὁ γιός του εἶναι στὴν Ἰταλία.
makrís:	tí-alo-léi-s-to-ghráma-tu?	Τί ἄλλο λέει στὸ γράμμα του;
kondós:	mu-dhíni-merikés-pliroforíes ya-tin-amerikí.	Μοῦ δίνει μερικὲς πληροφορίες γιὰ τὴν Ἀμερική.
makrís:	thá-thela-na-to-dhyaváso to-ghráma-tu.	Θά 'θελα νὰ τὸ διαβάσω τὸ γράμμα του.
	boríte-na-mu-to-dhósete?	Μπορεῖτε νὰ μοῦ τὸ δώσετε;
kondós:	efkharístos, ma-dhén-do-ékho s-tin-dzépi-mu.	Εὐχαρίστως, μὰ δὲν τὸ ἔχω στὴν τσέπη μου.

makrís:	pú-thélete-na-to-válo?	Ποῦ θέλετε νὰ τὸ βάλω;
	brostá-s-tim-bórta-tu-spityú-sas.	Μπροστὰ στὴν πόρτα τοῦ σπιτιοῦ σας.
	k-eghó érkhome ke-to-pérno.	Κ' ἐγὼ ἔρχομαι καὶ τὸ παίρνω.

SECTION E—CONVERSATION

1. Covering the Greek of Basic Sentences (Individual Study)

Cover the Greek of the *Basic Sentences* and practice saying the Greek equivalents of the English expressions.

2. Vocabulary Check-Up

Give the Greek expressions for the English equivalents in the *Basic Sentences* as the Leader calls for them.

3. Conversation

As you have done in the *Conversation* in the previous Units, begin to converse by following the models outlined below fairly closely; then change the situations somewhat. Invent new combinations of subject matter.

I. *At the barber's.*

1. You ask whether you can have a haircut.
2. The barber admires your beautiful hair, and adds that it is white like snow.
3. You reply that you had beautiful hair as a child; it was long and black, but now you have only a little hair.
4. He asks you whether you want him to wash your hair.
5. You say, no thanks, ask how much it is and inquire where you can get your shoes shined.
6. He answers that there are two bootblacks on America St., (the) one in front of Kladas's cleaning place and the other near the station.
7. You say that in Italy, where you were [before], there were bootblacks in the hotels who used to clean (the) shoes.
8. He asks you if you like Italy.
9. You say yes, it has a very good climate, but you like Greece still more.
10. Yes, he says, Greece is beautiful, it has mountains and sea, and very beautiful cities.

II. *At the laundress's.*
1. The girl at the door asks you what you want.
2. You say you have a lot of dirty clothes and inquire if she could wash them.
3. She says yes, her mother washes (the) clothes, but she is not here now, and then she offers you a seat.
4. You ask her if her mother cleans uniforms.
5. She answers that she irons them, but she does **not** clean them; you have to go to a tailor.
6. You ask who the best tailor is, around here.
7. She says that George Aravantinos is the best, and that he is her uncle.
8. To change the conversation you ask her what kind of job *she* does.
9. She says that she works in an office, but in the evening she goes to her brother's variety-stand and sells cigarettes, and matches, and razor blades, and whatever else you want.
10. She adds that before the war her brother was a factory worker and used to work hard. Afterwards he was a soldier and now he can not work so very much.

Section F—Conversation (*Cont.*)

Continue the conversations started in Section E, with a review of Parts 1 and 2 of the Section if necessary.

FINDER LIST

A

akrivós		
in-akriví	εἶν' ἀκριβή	she charges high prices
álo n.	ἄλλο	else
ti-alo	τί ἄλλο	what else?
andíkri-se	ἀντίκρυ σὲ	opposite to; across from
i anglía	ἡ Ἀγγλία	England
áspros, -i, -o	ἄσπρος, —η, —ο	white
o astifílakas	ὁ ἀστυφύλακας	policeman

B

brostá-se	μπροστὰ σὲ	in front of

D

dhíkhno δείχνω I show
  /*dhiks*/ δειξ–

dhíkso see: *dhíkhno*

dhíno δίνω I give
  /*dhos*/ δωσ–

dhóso see: *dhíno*

dhyaváso see: *dhyavázo*

dhyavázo διαβάζω I read
  /*dhyavas*/ διαβασ–

E

edhó
  edho-péra ἐδὼ πέρα around here

efkharístos εὐχαρίστως gladly

G

to ghráma τὸ γράμμα letter

K

kalíteros, -i, -o καλύτερος, –η, –ο better
  o-kalíteros ὁ καλύτερος ⎫
  i-kalíteri ἡ καλύτερη ⎬ the best
  to-kalítero τὸ καλύτερο ⎭

kámo see: *káno*

kanenas m. κανένας any
  kanenan obj. κανέναν

káno κάνω I do
  /*kam*/ καμ–

kathaííso see: *katharízo*		
to *katharistírio*	τὸ καθαριστήριο	cleaning establishment
katharízo	καθαρίζω	I clean
/*katharis*/	καθαρισ–	
katharós, -í, -ó	καθαρός, –ή, –ό	clean
kathíste	καθίστε	sit down!
kháno	χάνω	I lose
/*khas*/	χασ–	
kháso see: *kháno*		
kondá	κοντά	nearby
kondós, -í, -ó	κοντός, –ή, –ό	short
kondós	Κοντός	Kontos (*family name*)
kópso see: *kóvo*		
kópste see: *kóvo*		
kóvo	κόβω	I cut
/*kops*/	κοψ–	
kópste	κόψτε	cut!
o *kózmos*	ὁ κόσμος	world; people
see: *polís*		
ksuríso see: *ksurízo*		
ksurízo	ξουρίζω	I shave
/*ksuris*/	ξουρισ–	
o *kuréas*	ὁ κουρέας	barber
kuréidhes p.	κουρέιδες	
to *kurío*	τὸ κουρεῖο	barber shop
to *kyóski*	τὸ κιόσκι	variety-stand; news-stand

L

i láma	ἡ λάμα	razor blade
to limáni	τὸ λιμάνι	harbor
o lústros	ὁ λούστρος	bootblack

M

makriá see: *makrís*

makrís m.	μακρύς	long
makriá n.p.	μακρειά	
makrís	Μακρής	Makres (*family name*)
ta mallyá	τὰ μαλλιά	hair
mávros, -i, -o	μαῦρος, –η, –ο	black
merikí, -és, -á p.	μερικοί, –ές, –ά	some

O

i odhós (used only before names of streets)	ἡ Ὁδός	Street
i-odhós-anglías	ἡ Ὁδὸς Ἀγγλίας	England St.
s-tin-odhón-anglías	στὴν Ὁδὸν Ἀγγλίας	on England St.
óti	ὅ,τι	whatever

P

to papútsi	τὸ παπούτσι	shoe
péra see: *edhó*		
pistévo	πιστεύω	I believe
/*pisteps*/	πιστεψ–	
piyéno	πηγαίνω	I go
/*pa*/	πα–	

pléno	πλένω	I wash
/*plin*/	πλυν–	
plíno see: *pléno*		
pliroforíes f.p.	πληροφορίες	pieces of information; information
pliróno	πληρώνω	I pay
/*pliros*/	πληρωσ–	
pliróso see: *pliróno*		
polí see: *polís*		
polís m.	πολύς	much
polí m.p.	πολλοί	many
polís-kózmos	πολὺς κόσμος	many people
puló (*-í*)	πουλῶ (–εῖ)	I sell
/*pulis*/	πουλησ–	

R

o *ráftis*	ὁ ράφτης	tailor
ráftes p.	ράφτες	
s-tu-ráfti	στοῦ ράφτη	at the tailor's
rotíste see: *rotó*		
rotó	ρωτῶ	I ask
/*rotis*/	ρωτησ–	
rotíste	ρωτήστε	ask!
ta *rúkha*	τὰ ροῦχα	clothes

S

sidheróno	σιδερώνω	I iron
/*sidheros*/	σιδερωσ–	
sidheróso see: *sidheróno*		
i *stolí*	ἡ στολή	uniform

T

tus	τοὺς	to them

V

válo see: váno		
váno	βάνω	I put
/val/	βαλ–	
vrísko	βρίσκω	I find; I get (*in shopping*)
na-vró (-í)	νὰ βρῶ (-ῇ)	that I find
vró see: vrísko		
vrómikos, -i, -o	βρώμικος, –η, –ο	dirty

Y

yalíso see: yalízo		
yalízo	γυαλίζω	I shine
/yalis/	γυαλισ–	

UNIT 9

LET'S EAT

Section A—Basic Sentences

Go once through the *Basic Sentences* in unison, then the *Hints on Pronunciation*, and then go twice more through the *Basic Sentences* individually.

1. Basic Sentences

Record 17A, beginning.

John Cook has invited his friends, George and Mary Bourboulis and Phroso Adamantiou, to dinner. He is looking for a place to eat.

—— ENGLISH EQUIVALENTS ——	—— AIDS TO LISTENING ——	—— CONVENTIONAL SPELLING ——
John	yánis	Γιάννης
this drugstore	aftó-to-farmakío	αὐτὸ τὸ φαρμακεῖο
Shall we all go to this drugstore [over] here?	páme-mazí s-aftó-edho-to-farmakío?	Πάμε μαζὶ σ' αὐτὸ ἐδὼ τὸ φαρμακεῖο;
Mary	maría	Μαρία
are you by any chance . . . ?	min-íste . . . ?	μὴν εἶστε . . . ;
sick	árostos	ἄρρωστος
Are you sick, by any chance?	min-ist-árostos?	Μὴν εἶστ' ἄρρωστος;
John	yánis	Γιάννης
No, but I'm hungry.	óchi, ma-pinó.	Ὄχι, μὰ πεινῶ.

202 [9–A]

Phroso	fróso	Φρόσω
we eat	tróme	τρώμε
We in Greece don't eat at drugstores.	emi-s-tin-eládha dhén-dróme-se-farmakía.	Ἐμεῖς στὴν Ἑλλάδα δὲν τρώμε σὲ φαρμακεῖα.
John	yánis	Γιάννης
any tavern	kamya-tavérna	καμιὰ ταβέρνα
Do you happen to know any good tavern?	min-gzérete kamya-kalí-tavérna?	Μὴν ξέρετε καμιὰ καλὴ ταβέρνα;
George	yórghos	Γιώργος
I know lots [of them].	kséro-polés.	Ξέρω πολλές.
Mary	maría	Μαρία
to me	eména	ἐμένα
of "Uncle" John	tu-barba-yáni	τοῦ μπάρμπα-Γιάννη
I like "Uncle" John's tavern.	eména-m-arés-i-tavérna-tu-barba-yáni.	Ἐμένα μ' ἀρέσ' ἡ ταβέρνα τοῦ μπάρμπα-Γιάννη.
[At "Uncle" John's.]	[s-tu-barba-yáni.]	[Στοῦ μπάρμπα–Γιάννη.]
John	yánis	Γιάννης
the menu	ti-lísta	τὴ λίστα
Waiter, the menu, please.	pedhí, ti-lísta parakaló.	Παιδί, τὴ λίστα, παρακαλῶ.
say to us!	péste-mas	πέστε μας
that we take	na-párume	νὰ πάρουμε
And now, George, you tell us what to get.	ke-tóra yórgho, péste-mas-esís-ti-na-párume.*	Καὶ τώρα, Γιώργο, πέστε μας ἐσεῖς τί νὰ πάρουμε.

*On the record *tí-na-párume?* "What shall we get?"

George	*yórghos*	Γιώργος
that he bring	na-féri	νὰ φέρῃ
first	próta	πρῶτα
a [serving of] soup	mya-súpa	μιὰ σούπα
Do you want him to bring us a [plate of] soup first?	thélete-na-mas-féri próta mya-súpa?	Θέλετε νὰ μᾶς φέρῃ πρῶτα μιὰ σούπα;
Phroso	*fróso*	Φρόσω
No ('Not') soup, please.	óchi-súpa parakaló.	Ὄχι σούπα, παρακαλῶ.
Mary	*maría*	Μαρία
Why?	yatí?	Γιατί;
Phroso	*fróso*	Φρόσω
fat	pachyá	παχειά
It makes me fat.	me-káni-pachyá.	Μὲ κάνει παχειά.
I['ll] take fish.	eghó pérno-psári.	Ἐγὼ παίρνω ψάρι.
Mary	*maría*	Μαρία
And I['ll take] chicken.	k-eghó kotópulo.	Κ' ἐγὼ κοτόπουλλο.
John	*yánis*	Γιάννης
And I['ll take] (a) steak.	k-eghó mya-brizóla.	Κ' ἐγὼ μιὰ μπριζόλα.
George	*yórghos*	Γιώργος
lamb	arní	ἀρνί
roasted	psitó	ψητό
vegetables	lákhana	λάχανα
Roast lamb, potatoes, and vegetables for me, please.	ya-ména arní-psitó parakaló, patátes ke-lákhana.	Γιὰ 'μένα ἀρνὶ ψητό, παρακαλῶ, πατάτες καὶ λάχανα.

Record 17B, beginning.

And what are you going to have to drink ('are you drinking')?	ke-ti-pínete?	Καὶ τί πίνετε;
dark wine	mávro-krasí	μαῦρο κρασί
Red or white wine?	mávro i-áspro-krasí?	Μαῦρο ἢ ἄσπρο κρασί;
Phroso	*fróso*	*Φρόσω*
The red's [too] strong.	to-mávro-ine-varí.	Τὸ μαῦρο εἶναι βαρύ.
John	*yánis*	*Γιάννης*
I am thirsty	dhipsó	Διψῶ
I'm awfully thirsty.	dhipsó párapoli.	Διψῶ πάρα πολύ.
Mary	*maría*	*Μαρία*
drink!	pyéte	πιέτε
Drink wine [mixed] with water.	pyéte-krasí-me-neró.	Πιέτε κρασὶ μὲ νερό.
Phroso	*fróso*	*Φρόσω*
they are lacking	lípune	λείπουνε
spoons	kutálya	κουτάλια
knife	machéri	μαχαίρι
fork	pirúni	πιρούνι
Waiter, we're short two spoons, one knife, and one fork.	pedhí, lípune dhío-kutálya éna-machéri k-éna-pirúni.	Παιδί, λείπουνε δύο κουτάλια, ἕνα μαχαίρι κ' ἕνα πιρούνι.
George	*yórghos*	*Γιώργος*
the food	to-faí	τὸ φαΐ
that gentleman	ekínos-o-kírios	ἐκεῖνος ὁ κύριος
Do you know what food that man there had?	ksérete ti-faí-ich-ekínos-eki-o-kírios?	Ξέρετε τί φαΐ εἶχ' ἐκεῖνος ἐκεῖ ὁ κύριος;

[9–A]

eggs	avghá	αὐγά
salad	saláta	σαλάτα
He had eggs and salad.	iche-avghá ke-saláta.	Εἶχε αὐγὰ καὶ σαλάτα.
a glass	ena-potíri	ἕνα ποτήρι
And a glass of wine.	k-ena-potíri-krasí.	Κ' ἕνα ποτήρι κρασί.
suit	foresyá	φορεσιά
I see it, from his suit.	to-vlépo, ap-ti-foresyá-tu.	Τὸ βλέπω, ἀπ' τὴ φορεσιά του.
John	*yánis*	Γιάννης
And now what else do you want (us) to eat?	ke-tóra ti-alo-thélete-na-fáme?	Καὶ τώρα, τί ἄλλο θέλετε νὰ φᾶμε;
George	*yórghos*	Γιῶργος
cheese	tirí	τυρί
at this tavern	se-tútin-din-davérna	σὲ τούτην τὴν ταβέρνα
They have fine cheese at this tavern.	ekhun-oréo-tirí se-tútin-din-davérna.	Ἔχουν ὡραῖο τυρὶ σὲ τούτην τὴν ταβέρνα.
Phroso	*fróso*	Φρόσω
I prefer	protimó	προτιμῶ
fruit	frúta	φροῦτα
I prefer fruit.	eghó protimó-frúta.	Ἐγὼ προτιμῶ φροῦτα.
George	*yórghos*	Γιῶργος
then	tóte	τότε
Well then, cheese, fruit, and four coffees.	tóte-lipón, tirí frúta ke-téseris-kafédhes.	Τότε λοιπόν, τυρί, φροῦτα καὶ τέσσερεις καφέδες.

John	yánis	Γιάννης
the bill	to-logharyazmó	τὸ λογαριασμό
And the check, please.	ke-to-logharyazmó parakaló.	Καὶ τὸ λογαριασμό, παρακαλῶ.

Record 18A, beginning.

George	yórghos	Γιῶργος
don't forget!	mín-gzekhnáte	μὴν ξεχνᾶτε
the tip	to-burbuár	τὸ πουρμπουάρ
Don't ever forget the tip here in Greece.	mín-gzekhnáte-poté-to-burbuár edhó-s-tin-eládha.	Μὴν ξεχνᾶτε ποτὲ τὸ πουρμπουάρ ἐδῶ στὴν Ἑλλάδα.
John	yánis	Γιάννης
Our coffees were strong.	i-kafédhez-mas itane-varyí.	Οἱ καφέδες μας ἤτανε βαρειοί.
that we go for a walk	na-páme-perípato	νὰ πάμε περίπατο
Shall we go for a walk?	thélete-na-páme-perípato?	Θέλετε νὰ πάμε περίπατο;
George	yórghos	Γιῶργος
after	íster-apo	ὕστερ' ἀπὸ
such	tétyo	τέτοιο
Not after a meal like that, my friend.	óchi fíle-mu, íster-apo-tétyo-faï.	Ὄχι, φίλε μου, ὕστερ' ἀπὸ τέτοιο φαΐ.
better	kalítera	καλύτερα
an ice cream	ena-paghotó	ἕνα παγωτό
some kind of pastry	kanena-ghlikó	κανένα γλυκό
Instead let's go [somewhere else] so I [can] treat you to (an) ice cream or some kind of pastry.	páme-kalítera na-sas-prosféro ena-paghotó i-kanena-ghlikó.	Πᾶμε καλύτερα νὰ σᾶς προσφέρω ἕνα παγωτὸ ἢ κανένα γλυκό.

[9–A]   207

Before you go through the *Basic Sentences* a second time, read the following:

2. Hints on Pronunciation

THE POSITION OF THE ACCENT IN GREEK. You have learned that the accent in Greek may come only on one of the last three syllables of a word. But you must find out for any given word whether, as a matter of fact, the accent falls on the last syllable, the next to the last, or the second from the last. In certain sets of forms the accent goes as far back from the end of the word as it possibly can; you have found this to be true for the imperfective past of all verbs of the type of *kséro* (thus *dhúleva, évlepa, árchiza, íksera, katalávena,* etc.), and also for all neuter nouns in *-ma* (thus *ónoma, onómata,* and so with *khtíma, ghráma, pátoma,* etc.). For some other groups of forms a different accent rule prevails; it may be of at least some assistance to you to know that the accent can be either on the last syllable or on the syllable next to the last, but never on the second syllable from the last, in the three following sets: (1) neuter nouns ending in *-i*, like *pedhí* or *trapézi*; (2) verb-forms of the first person singular in *-o*, like *miló* or *dhulévo*, and the third person singular in *-i*, like *milí* or *dhulévi*; (3) masculine nouns and adjectives in *-is*, like *fititís, varís,* or *erghátis, tembélis* 'lazy fellow'. Lastly, you will find that verb-forms of the first person singular in *-me* are stressed either on the second syllable from the last, like *érkhome*, or on the next to the last syllable, like *kimúme*, but never on the last syllable. Many words do not come in such sets, however. And in most cases you must simply fix your attention on the place of the accent and learn the accent as an essential part of the word. Very frequently you will meet two words like *píno* 'I drink' and *pinó* 'I'm hungry' which are quite similar except for the accent. But this exception must be taken seriously; in Greek the position of the accent is enough in itself to distinguish words that are otherwise identical. After all, you have met such pairs of words in English, like *pro*test and pro*test*, *com*pound and com*pound*, shiv*ery* and shiva*ree* (spelled *charivari*). Note well the following examples that have occurred by now in the Units you have studied.

Record 18A, after first spiral.
PRACTICE

pinó	I'm hungry	:	*píno*	I drink
eména	me	:	*émena*	I used to stay
polí m.	many	:	*póli*	town

polís m.	much	:	*pólis*	towns
milí	speaks	:	*míli*	mile
poté	never	:	*póte*	when?
zestí f.	hot	:	*zésti*	heat

Section B—Word Study and Review of Basic Sentences

1. Word Study (Individual Study)

COMMENT 1

ADJECTIVES OF THE TYPE *varís*. In Unit 5 you had a survey of the forms of the adjective *kalós, -í, -ó* (with the slightly different *oréos, -a, -o*). Such adjectives in *-os* are certainly the commonest in Greek. But there is a second type, and an important one for you to know. Look carefully at the following examples:

(a) masculine

sing. subj. *o-chimónas-tus-ekí-ine-varís.* — They have *real* winters there. ('Their winter there is hard.')
     obj. *dhén-ékhume-varí-chimóna.* — We don't have a hard winter.
plur. subj. *i-kafédhez-mas itane-varyí.* — Our coffees were strong.
     ekíni-i-astifílakes ine-polí-pachí. — Those policemen are very fat.
     obj. *esíz-dhén-duz-vrískete-pachyús?* — Don't *you* think they're fat? ('Don't *you* find them fat?')

(b) feminine

sing. subj. *i-súpa ine-pachyá.* — The soup is fat.
     obj. *íthele-na-váli-aftín-di-varyá-karékla kondá-s-to-kreváti-mu.* — She wanted to put that heavy chair next to my bed.
plur. subj. *in-akrivés-tóra-i-varyés-foresyés.* — Heavy suits are expensive now.
     obj. *aftó-to-pedhí tis-protimái-makriés tis-foresyés-tu.* — This boy likes ('prefers') his suits long.

(c) neuter

sing.	subj.	*aftó-to-kréaz-dhén-ine-pachí.*
	obj.	*aftó-to-arní echi-polí-pachí-kréas.*
plur.	subj.	*ta-malyá-tis-tóte itane-makriá ke-mávra.*
	obj.	*ta-thélete aftá-ta-varyá-papútsya?*

This meat isn't fat.
This lamb has very fat meat.

Her hair was long and dark then.
Do you want these heavy shoes?

It will perhaps help you to learn the forms of adjectives like *varís* if you compare them with the forms of nouns that you are familiar with already. The neuter *varí* (pl. *varyá*) is really just like the neuter noun *pedhí* 'boy' (pl. *pedhyá*); and the feminine *varyá* (pl. *varyés*) is just like the feminine noun *paghonyá* 'frost' (pl. *paghonyés*). As for the masculine *varís*, in the singular it is like the masculine noun *fititís* 'student', while in the plural it is like *romyí* 'Greeks'. In so far as it resembles one type of noun in the singular and a different type in the plural, the set of masculine forms is a little difficult.

Here is a table of the adjectives in *-ís:*

varís 'heavy'

		masc.	fem.	neut.
sing.	subj.	*varís*	⎫ *varyá*	⎫ *varí*
	obj.	⎫ *varí*		
	rest.		*varyás*	*varyú*
plur.	subj.	*varyí*	⎫ *varyés*	⎫ *varyá*
	obj.	*varyús*		

pachís 'fat'

		masc.	fem.	neut.
sing.	subj.	*pachís*	⎫ *pachyá*	⎫ *pachí*
	obj.	⎫ *pachí*		
	rest.		*pachyás*	*pachyú*
plur.	subj.	*pachí*	⎫ *pachés*	⎫ *pachyá*
	obj.	*pachyús*		

makrís 'long'

	masc.	fem.	neut.
sing. subj.	*makrís*	}*makriá*	}*makrí*
obj.	}*makrí*		
rest.		*makriás*	*makriú*
plur. subj.	*makrií*	}*makriés*	}*makriá*
obj.	*makriús*		

There are a few things that you should notice about these adjectives. (1) Among the forms of *pachís* there are two that should be noted especially: in the subject case of the masculine plural you find *pachí*, and in the feminine plural *pachés;* there is no *y* (as you have it in *varyí, varyés*) between *ch* and *i* or *e*. (2) After the consonant group *kr* Greeks do not pronounce a *y*, but use *i;* thus beside the two-syllable word *varyá* you have the three-syllable word *makriá*, and beside the two-syllable word *varyés* you have the three-syllable word *makriés*, etc. (3) The restrictive forms are not used much in spoken Greek.

COMMENT 2

HOW TO SAY 'MUCH' AND 'MANY' IN GREEK. You know that in English we use the word 'much' before a singular noun, and the word 'many' before a plural. In Greek, however, there is only one word, of which you have already had numerous examples.

First consider these sentences:

sing. fem. obj.	*káni-polí-zésti-edhó to-kalokéri.*	It's very hot ('It makes much heat') here in summer.
plur. masc. subj.	*káto-s-to-limáni ine-polí-lústri.*	Down by the harbor there are a lot of bootblacks.
plur. masc. obj.	*ekhume-polús-oréuz-dhrómu-s-tin-amerikí.*	We have many fine roads in America.
plur. fem. obj.	*echi-polés-tavérnes edho-péra?*	Are there many taverns around here?
plur. neut. obj.	*imast-ekí polá-khrónya.*	We were there for many years.

In these examples, which comprise the singular of the feminine and the whole plural, the adjective meaning 'much' and 'many' behaves, as you see, like an adjective in -*os*, e.g. *kalós*. This is very easy.

Now look at these sentences:

sing. masc. subj.	*piyéni-polís-kózmo-s-to-kurío-tu.*	Lots of people go to his barber shop.
sing. masc. obj.	*efétos dhén-iche-polí-ílyo.*	This year there wasn't much sunshine.
	prin-ap-tom-bólemo ikhame-polín-gafé.	Before the war we had lots of coffee.
	bori-na-míno polín-geró.	I may stay for a long time.
sing. neut. obj.	*iche-polí-krasí s-tin-davérna-tu.*	He had a lot of wine at his tavern.

You see that these sentences contain examples only of the masculine and the neuter singular in the subject and object cases. These forms, then, behave like the corresponding forms of *varís*.

SUMMARY: the adjective *polís*

	masc.	fem.	neut.
sing. subj.	*polís*	} *polí*	} *polí*
obj.	*polí(n)*		
rest.	*polú*	*polís*	*polú*
plur. subj.	*polí*	} *polés*	} *polá*
obj.	*polús*		

Before a word beginning with *p*, *t*, or *k* you find *polín* in the object case of the masculine singular, as in *polín-dópo* 'a lot of space', or *polím-biretó* 'a high fever'.

This is most common in the set phrase *polín-geró* '(for) a long time'. The restrictive case is not much used.

COMMENT 3

THE WORDS FOR 'THIS' AND 'THAT' BEFORE NOUNS. In this present Unit and in some of the previous ones you have met quite a few sentences containing the words for 'this' or 'that' in Greek. Here are some of those examples together with others made from the material of the lessons.

tútos:
túto-to-paghotó ine-sa-neró.
túti-dho-i-láma dhén-góvi-kalá.

This ice cream is like water.
This razor blade here doesn't cut well.

aftós:
ky-aftós-o-mikrós pyós-íne?
ta-thélete aftá-ta-varyá-papútsya?
aftós-o-kírios ky-aftí-i-kiría, sas-ksérune?
páme-mazí s-aftó-edho-to-farmakío?
dhe-méni-kanénas s-aftó-to-spíti-eki-péra.

ekínos:
ekínos-o-kírios íche-avghá ke-saláta.
páme-s-ekíno-ki-to-trapézi.
ekíni-i-astifílakes íne-polí-pachí.

And who is this little fellow?
Do you want these heavy shoes?
Do they know you—that man and woman?
Shall we all go to this drugstore [over] here?
Nobody lives in that house over there.

That man had eggs and salad.
Let's go to that table there.
Those policemen are very fat.

In regard to the words for 'this' and 'that' which come in the sentences given above there are several things to notice at once: (1) the forms, (2) the way the forms for 'this' or 'that' are linked with the nouns they go with, and (3) the range of meaning that they have.

If you fix your attention for the moment on the forms alone, you will note that none of the endings of the *demonstratives* cited here is any different from the corresponding ending of the familiar adjective *kalós*. But now observe the forms that occur in the following sentences.

tútos:
ekhun-oréo-tirí se-tútin-din-davérna.

aftós:
protimó-aftín-di-saláta.

ekínos:
vlépet-ekínon-don-gírio pu-trói tóso-sighá?

They have fine cheese at this tavern.

I prefer this salad.

Do you see that man who is eating so slowly?

Here you see that in the object case of the singular the ending for the masculine is *-on* and the ending for the feminine is *-in*.* In this respect, then, these words differ from *kalós* and are like the definite article with its forms *ton* and *tin*.

*But you will also hear the endings *-o* and *-i*, in which case *tútos*, *aftós*, and *ekínos* are handled just like *kalós*.

[9–B] 213

This is a summary of the forms of *aftós* before nouns, with the same endings for *tútos* and *ekínos:*

	masc.	fem.	neut.
sing. subj.	*aftós*	*aftí*	*aftó*
obj.	*aftón*	*aftín*	*aftó*
rest.	*aftú*	*aftís*	*aftú*
plur. subj.	*aftí*	*aftés*	*aftá*
obj.	*aftús*	*aftés*	*aftá*

The next thing to remark is that, as you can see from all the sentences above, whenever the Greek words for 'this' or 'that' are combined with a noun, the word for 'the' must stand right before the noun. Thus in the subject case the phrase for 'that man' is *ekínos-o-kírios*, for 'that woman' *ekíni-i-kiría*, for 'that child' *ekíno-to-pedhí*, and the Greek speaker would never employ such phrases without the appropriate forms of the definite article.

Now you have already seen from the grouping of the examples cited above that Greek has not two words, one for 'this' and the other for 'that', but *three* such words. Since this is clearly a different system from ours in English, it will be necessary to look closely at the examples, so as to learn just when you are going to use *tútos*, when *aftós*, and when *ekínos*.

First let's take the examples of *tútos:* in them you find that the English word corresponding to *tútos* is always 'this'; furthermore you see that *tútos* may be used with *edhó* 'here', as in the phrase *túti-dho-i-láma* 'this razor blade here', and you will find that *tútos* is never used with *ekí* 'there'; *tútos*, therefore, refers to what is physically close to the speaker.

Secondly, let's turn to the examples of *ekínos:* in them you find that the English word corresponding to *ekínos* is always 'that'; furthermore you see that *ekínos* may be used with *ekí*, as in the phrase *ekíno-ki-to-trapézi* 'that table there', and you will find that *ekínos* is never used with *edhó; ekínos*, therefore, refers to what is remote from the speaker.

Now let's examine the examples in which *aftós* figures: to a speaker of English the surprising thing is that one and the same word *aftós* may stand sometimes for 'this', sometimes for 'that'; this is underlined by the fact that *aftós* may be used either with *edhó*, as in the phrase *aftó-edho-to-farmakío* 'this drugstore [over] here', or with *ekí*, as in the phrase *aftó-to-spíti-eki-péra* 'that house over there'. In the examples given the persons or things pointed out by *aftós* are evidently fairly near—a few steps away, or across a room, or across a street; in addition, *aftós* is the word used to refer to what is near in thought because it has been mentioned before. It is fair to conclude that *aftós* covers a middle ground between what is right in one's hand or right next to one and what is far off or at quite a distance. Since it is convenient to be able to refer to persons or things with a word for 'this' or 'that' which is not too specific, the speakers of Greek make more use of the general word *aftós* than of either of the other two demonstratives.

COMMENT 4

tróo 'I EAT'. In Unit 2, as you remember, you learned two important verbs the stem of which ended in a vowel. They were *páo* 'I go' and *léo* 'I say'. Now here in this Unit a new verb of this kind has appeared which behaves exactly like the others. It is *tróo* 'I eat'.

These are the forms:

tróo	I eat
tróte	you eat
trói	he eats
tróme	we eat
tróne	they eat

The perfective stem, incidentally, is /fa/, and the form *fáo*, to be used after *na*, behaves exactly like *páo*; e.g. *tí-thélete-na-fáte?* "What do you wish to eat?" or *páme-na-fáme* "Let's go eat," or *óra-na-fáme* "It's time (for us) to eat."

2. Covering English and Greek of Word Study (Individual Study)

Check yourself on your knowledge of the *Word Study* by covering first the English, then the Greek, and making sure you know everything thoroughly.

3. Review of Basic Sentences

With the Guide or records, review the first half of the *Basic Sentences* as in previous Units.

SECTION C—REVIEW OF BASIC SENTENCES (*Cont.*)

1. Review of Basic Sentences (*Cont.*)

Review the second half of the *Basic Sentences*.

2. Covering the English of Basic Sentences (Individual Study)

Go through the *Basic Sentences* covering up the English and reading aloud the Greek. Check up on anything you do not know, until you are sure of everything.

3. What Would You Say?

I. Pick out the right sentence:

1. Bourboulis and Roilos are ordering a meal in a restaurant. Bourboulis calls the waiter:
   a. *s-tin-amerikí dhén-ekhume-tétya-lákhana.*
   b. *min-gzérete kanena-kaló-estiatório?*
   c. *pedhí!*
   d. *tróte-avghá ke-tirí?*
2. Roilos asks for the menu:
   a. *to-kréas ine-pachí.*
   b. *to-mávro-krasí ine-varí.*
   c. *ti-lísta parakaló.*
   d. *lípune-tría-pirúnya.*
3. The waiter asks if they would like a beer:
   a. *thélete-na-sas-féro próta mya-bíra?*
   b. *mi-thélete-ghlikó?*
   c. *mín-dróte-tóso-polí to-vrádhi.*
   d. *ton-gafé-mu tone-thélo-varí.*
4. Bourboulis orders fish:
   a. *tí-thélete-na-pyíte?*
   b. *dhóste-mu-ena-potíri-ghála parakaló.*
   c. *se-tútin-din-davérna trói-kanenas-kalá.*
   d. *ya-ména psári parakaló.*
5. Roilos orders lamb and potatoes:
   a. *eghó pérno-arní-me-patátes.*
   b. *mya-brizóla ya-ton-gírio.*
   c. *dhóste-mas áspro-krasí.*
   d. *echete-frúta ke-tirí?*
6. The two guests ask for the check:
   a. *póso-ekho-na-plirόso ya-tin-ipiresía?*
   b. *s-tin-eládha dhínune-pánda-burbuár.*
   c. *ta-meghála-kutálya ta-léme-kutálya-ti-súpas.*
   d. *pedhí, to-logharyazmó parakaló.*
7. They remark that the dinner was heavy but good:
   a. *túto-to-paghotó ine-sa-neró.*
   b. *to-faí itane-varí ma-kaló.*
   c. *ta-kotópula m-arésune-psitá.*
   d. *i-romyí ekhun-estiatória s-ólo-ton-gózmo.*

[9–C]

II. Say each of the following sentences using the *you-*, *he-*, *we-*, *they*-forms instead of the *I*-form:
1. *protimó-aftín-di-saláta.* 2. *tróo-polí.* 3. *prépi-na-fígho to-vrádhi.* 4. *dhém-boró-na-ksekháso-tin-eládha.*
5. *ergházome se-ghrafío.* 6. *kimúm-eftá-óres.*

Section D—Listening In

1. What Did you Say?

Give your answers in Greek for each of the exercises in the preceding section, when the Leader calls for them. Then, as the Leader calls for them, give the English equivalents of all the expressions in the exercise.

2. Word Study Check-Up

As you have done in the previous Units, go back to the *Word Study* and give the correct Greek for each English expression, without having to read it from the book. The Leader or one of the members of the group should read the English.

3. Listening In

With your book closed, listen to the following conversations as read by your Guide or phonograph record. Repeat the Greek immediately after hearing it. After the first repetition of each conversation, check up on the meaning of anything you do not understand, by asking someone else or by going back to the *Basic Sentences* if no one knows. Repeat again if necessary, then take parts and carry on the conversation.

Record 18A, after second spiral.

1. John and Peter are feeling hungry.

yánis: *dhipsó ke-pinó.*
pétros: *k-eghó thá-thela-na-fáo ke-na-pyó.*
yánis: *tóte-lipón, páme-na-fáme.*
pétros: *páme-s-ekíno-ki-to-farmakío.*
yánis: *imaste-s-tin-eládha fíle-mu,*
 mín-do-ksekhnát-aftó.
 edhó móno-otan-in-árostos-kanenas
  pái-s-to-farmakío.

Διψῶ καὶ πεινῶ.
Κ' ἐγὼ θά 'θελα νὰ φάω καὶ νὰ πιῶ.
Τότε λοιπόν, πάμε νὰ φάμε.
Πάμε σ' ἐκεῖνο 'κεῖ τὸ φαρμακεῖο.
Εἴμαστε στὴν Ἑλλάδα, φίλε μου,
μὴν τὸ ξεχνᾶτ' αὐτό.
Ἐδῶ μόνο ὅταν εἶν' ἄρρωστος κανένας πάει στὸ
 φαρμακεῖο.

pétros: *dhén-do-íkser-aftó.*   Δὲν τὸ ἤξερ' αὐτό.
yánis: *kséro-ena-estiatório pu-dhén-ine-makriá-apo-dhó.*   Ξέρω ἕνα ἐστιατόριο ποὺ δὲν εἶναι μακρειὰ ἀπὸ 'δώ.
       ine-s-to-dhéftero-dhrómo aristerá.   Εἶναι στὸ δεύτερο δρόμο ἀριστερά.
       ine-katharó.   Εἶναι καθαρό.

Record 18B, beginning.

2. John and Peter speak about the guests in the restaurant.

pétros: *echi-ena-soro-fayá-edho-péra.*   Ἔχει ἕνα σωρὸ φαγιὰ ἐδῶ πέρα.
yánis: *né, ma-ólos-o-kózmos trói-súpa.*   Ναί, μὰ ὅλος ὁ κόσμος τρώει σούπα.
pétros: *pós-to-kséret-esís-aftó?*   Πῶς τὸ ξέρετ' ἐσεῖς αὐτό;
yánis: *ap-to-thórivo pu-kánune.*   Ἀπ' τὸ θόρυβο ποὺ κάνουνε.
pétros: *khá! khá! khá! khá!*   Χά! χά! χά! χά!
yánis: *vlépet-ekínon-don-gírio pu-trói-to-tirí me-to-machéri?*   Βλέπετ' ἐκεῖνον τὸν κύριο ποὺ τρώει τὸ τυρὶ μὲ τὸ μαχαίρι;
pétros: *né, tone-vlépo.*   Ναί, τόνε βλέπω.
yánis: *dhém-bíni-poté-neró.*   Δὲν πίνει ποτὲ νερό.
pétros: *yatí?*   Γιατί;
yánis: *trói káthe-méra s-aftó-to-estiatório*   Τρώει κάθε μέρα σ' αὐτὸ τὸ ἐστιατόριο
       k-étsi píni-arketó-neró me-to-ghála-tu.   κ' ἔτσι πίνει ἀρκετὸ νερὸ μὲ τὸ γάλα του.
pétros: *eláte-tóra.*   Ἐλᾶτε τώρα.
       arketá-astía-ípate.   Ἀρκετὰ ἀστεῖα εἴπατε.
       pyéte-mya-bíra.   Πιέτε μιὰ μπίρα.

Record 18B, after first spiral.

3. John and Peter speak about Greek food.

yánis: *ksérete ti-m-arési-eména-edhó-s-tin-eládha?*   Ξέρετε τί μ' ἀρέσει ἐμένα ἐδῶ στὴν Ἑλλάδα;

pétros:	i-thálasa.
yánis:	né, ke-tí-álo?
pétros:	ta-korítsya-tus.
yánis:	né, ine-polí-nóstima-kápote.
	ke-tí-álo?
pétros:	dhén-gzéro ti-álo-sas-arési edho-béra.
yánis:	to-faí-tus fíle-mu m-arési,
	to-mávro-tus-krasí ky-o-kafés-tus otan-ine-varís.
pétros:	eména-m-arésune-ta-frúta-tus.
yánis:	se-mya-tavérna pu-ímuna-me-tus-fíluz-mu
	ikhan-avghá kréas-psitó-me-patátes ke-kotópula.
pétros:	isaste-poté s-tin-davérna-tu-barba-spíru?
yánis:	óchi, poté.
pétros:	prépi-na-páme-mazí.
	ekhune-tis-kalíterez-brizóles-eki-péra.
yánis:	páme-ávrio-to-vrádhi.
	ávrio ékho-keró.
pétros:	ke-tí-thélete-na-fáme-tóra?
yánis:	eghó pérno-psári-me-saláta.
	k-ístera ena-paghotó.
pétros:	eghó protimó-arní-me-lákhana.
	k-ístera ena-ghlikó.

Ἡ θάλασσα.
Ναί, καὶ τί ἄλλο;
Τὰ κορίτσια τους.
Ναί, εἶναι πολὺ νόστιμα κάποτε.
Καὶ τί ἄλλο;
Δὲν ξέρω τί ἄλλο σᾶς ἀρέσει ἐδῶ πέρα.
Τὸ φαΐ τους, φίλε μου, μ' ἀρέσει,
τὸ μαῦρο τους κρασὶ κι ὁ καφές τους ὅταν εἶναι βαρύς.
Ἐμένα μ' ἀρέσουνε τὰ φροῦτα τους.
Σὲ μιὰ ταβέρνα ποὺ ἤμουνα μὲ τοὺς φίλους μου
εἶχαν αὐγά, κρέας ψητὸ μὲ πατάτες καὶ κοτόπουλλα.
Ἤσαστε ποτὲ στὴν ταβέρνα τοῦ μπάρμπα-Σπύρου;
Ὄχι, ποτέ.
Πρέπει νὰ πάμε μαζί.
Ἔχουνε τὶς καλύτερες μπριζόλες ἐκεῖ πέρα.
Πάμε αὔριο τὸ βράδυ.
Αὔριο ἔχω καιρό.
Καὶ τί θέλετε νὰ φάμε τώρα;
Ἐγὼ παίρνω ψάρι μὲ σαλάτα.
Κ' ὕστερα ἕνα παγωτό.
Ἐγὼ προτιμῶ ἀρνὶ μὲ λάχανα.
Κ' ὕστερα ἕνα γλυκό.

Record 18B, after second spiral.

4. Peter wants to smoke.

pétros: ksérete pu-boró-na-vró-sigharéta?

Ξέρετε ποῦ μπορῶ νὰ βρῶ σιγαρέτα;

yánis:	*s-ta-kyóskya-pulúne.*	Στὰ κιόσκια πουλοῦνε.
pétros:	*ekhune-polí-kala-sigharéta-edho-péra.*	Ἔχουνε πολὺ καλὰ σιγαρέτα ἐδὼ πέρα.
yánis:	*né, ma-ine-ligháki-varyá.*	Ναί, μὰ εἶναι λιγάκι βαρειά.
	ta-kalítera-sigharéta ine-tiz-makedhonías.	Τὰ καλύτερα σιγαρέτα εἶναι τῆς Μακεδονίας.
pétros:	*ma-ekhun-erghostásia ke-s-ála-méri-tis-eládhas.*	Μὰ ἔχουν ἐργοστάσια καὶ σ' ἄλλα μέρη τῆς Ἑλλάδας.
	kséro-éna kondá-s-tim-bátra.	Ξέρω ἕνα κοντὰ στὴν Πάτρα.
yánis:	*póso-makriá-ine?*	Πόσο μακρειὰ εἶναι;
pétros:	*ine-móno-okhtó-mílya-me-to-vapóri,*	Εἶναι μόνο ὀχτὼ μίλια μὲ τὸ βαπόρι
	k-ístera eksínda-chilyómetra-me-to-tréno.	κ' ὕστερα ἑξῆντα χιλιόμετρα μὲ τὸ τρένο.

SECTION E—CONVERSATION

1. Covering the Greek of Basic Sentences (Individual Study)

Cover the Greek of the *Basic Sentences* and practice saying the Greek equivalents of the English expressions.

2. Vocabulary Check-Up

Give the Greek expressions for the English equivalents in the *Basic Sentences* as the Leader calls for them.

3. Conversation

As you have done in the *Conversation* in the previous Units, begin to converse by following the models outlined below fairly closely; then change the situations somewhat. Invent new combinations of subject matter.

I. *You speak with a friend about Greek taverns.*

1. You ask your friend whether he eats only in restaurants or whether he goes to drugstores, too.
2. He is astonished and replies that in Greece they never eat in drugstores but sometimes they go to taverns.
3. You ask him what a tavern is in Greece.
4. He says that a tavern is a small restaurant in the town or in the country, and that you always find bread and cheese and eggs and salad there. They don't always have a menu.

5. You inquire if they have other dishes, too.
6. Sure, he says, they have meat and vegetables and potatoes and fish and whatever else you want.
7. You would like to know if they have also milk in these taverns.
8. No, he says, they don't. But they sell good red or white wine, and he adds: "Let's go to 'Uncle' John's tavern which has the best wine in our town."
9. To this you answer that you are very sorry but you don't drink either wine or beer.

II. *You sit with a friend in a restaurant and discuss American and Greek eating habits.*

1. Your friend asks you what you drink when you wake up.
2. You say that at eight o'clock you drink a glass of milk, or coffee with milk, and eat bread and eggs.
3. Your friend is surprised and says that in Greece they don't eat so much, they only drink coffee with milk and eat a little bread.
4. Later on, he continues, at ten o'clock, they drink a cup of coffee and a glass of water. After two or three hours, at one o'clock, they eat a lot, soup and meat or fish, cheese, fruit and sometimes pastry.
5. Now it is your turn to be surprised, and you say that the Americans don't eat at one o'clock but one hour before and that they do not eat much. They haven't time to eat.
6. We have time, says the Greek, and in the summer when it's hot we sleep one or two hours, after the meal.
7. At six o'clock in the evening, you tell your friend, the American goes to his home. In the evening he does not work. He eats his steak or chicken or roast meat and drinks a cup of coffee. First he cuts a little meat with his knife, then takes his fork and eats very slowly. Then with his spoon he eats his ice cream or his pastry very slowly, too.
8. In Greece, replies the friend, they don't eat slowly. And in the evening they don't eat so much. They eat vegetables, eggs, cheese, and fruit.
9. Finishing your conversation you call the waiter and ask for the bill. You ask your friend whether they give tips in Greece.
10. Yes, he says, ten per cent.

Section F—Conversation (*Cont.*)

Continue the conversations started in Section E, with a review of Parts 1 and 2 of the Section if necessary.

FINDER LIST

A

aftós, -í, -ó	αὐτός, —ή, —ό	this; that
to arní	τὸ ἀρνί	lamb
árostos, -i, -o	ἄρρωστος, —η, —ο	sick
to avghó	τὸ αὐγό	egg

B

barba- (familiarly used before first names of older men)	μπάρμπα—	"Uncle"
i brizóla	ἡ μπριζόλα	steak
to burbuár (unchangeable)	τὸ πουρμπουάρ	tip

D

dhipsó /dhipsas/	διψῶ διψασ—	I am thirsty

E

ekínos, -i, -o	ἐκεῖνος, —η, —ο	that
eména	ἐμένα	to me

F

to faí	τὸ φαΐ	food; dish; meal
to farmakío	τὸ φαρμακεῖο	drugstore
férno /fer/	φέρνω φερ—	I bring
féro see: férno		
i foresyá	ἡ φορεσιά	suit
ta frúta	τὰ φροῦτα	fruit

G

to ghlikó	τὸ γλυκό	pastry
gzekhnáte see: *ksekhnó*		

I

ístera		
íster-apo	ὕστερ' ἀπὸ	after

K

kalítera	καλύτερα	better; rather
kamyá see: *kanenas*		
kanenas, kamyá, kanena	κανένας, καμιά, κανένα	any; some; some kind of
to kotópulo	τὸ κοτόπουλλο	chicken
krasí see: *mávros, varís*		
ksekhnó	ξεχνῶ	I forget
/*ksekhas*/	ξεχασ–	
to kutáli	τὸ κουτάλι	spoon

L

ta lákhana	τὰ λάχανα	vegetables
léo	λέω	I say
/*p*/	π–	
péste	πέστε	say!
lípi	λείπει	is lacking
/*lips*/	λειψ–	
lipón see: *tóte*		
i lísta	ἡ λίστα	menu
o logharyazmós	ὁ λογαριασμὸς	bill; check

M

to machéri	τὸ μαχαίρι	knife
mas	μᾶς	to us
mávros		
mávro-krasí	μαῦρο κρασί	red wine
mín	μὴν	(do) not
mín-gzekhnáte	μὴν ξεχνᾶτε	don't forget!
min	μὴν	by any chance

O

óchi	ὄχι	not (*before anything but a verb*)

P

pachís, pachyá, pachí	παχύs, παχειά, παχύ	fat
to paghotó	τὸ παγωτό	ice cream
páro see: pérno		
o perípatos	ὁ περίπατος	walk
páo-perípato	πάω περίπατο	I go for a walk
pérno	παίρνω	I take
/par/	παρ–	
péste see: léo		
pino	πίνω	I drink
/py/	πι–	
pyéte	πιέτε	drink!
pinó	πεινῶ	I am hungry
/pinas/	πεινασ–	
to pirúni	τὸ πιρούνι	fork

224   [9–F]

to potíri	τὺ ποτήρι	glass
ena-potíri-ghála	ἕνα ποτήρι γάλα	a glass of milk
próta	πρῶτα	first
protimó	προτιμῶ	I prefer
/protimis/	προτιμησ–	
to psári	τὸ ψάρι	fish
psitós, -í, -ó	ψητός, –ή, –ό	roasted
pyéte see: píno		

S

i saláta	ἡ σαλάτα	salad
i súpa	ἡ σούπα	soup

T

i tavérna	ἡ ταβέρνα	restaurant (*country style, with wine*)
tétyos, -a, -o	τέτοιος, –α, –ο	such
to tirí	τὸ τυρί	cheese
tóte	τότε	then
tóte-lipón	τότε λοιπόν	well then
tróo	τρώω	I eat
/fa/	φα–	
tútos, -i, -o	τοῦτος, –η, –ο	this

V

varís, varyá, varí	βαρύς, βαρειά, βαρύ	heavy
varí-krasí	βαρὺ κρασί	strong wine

UNIT 10

SEEING THE SIGHTS

Section A—Basic Sentences

Go once through the *Basic Sentences* in unison, then go twice through the *Basic Sentences* individually.

1. Basic Sentences

Record 19A, beginning.

John Cook is taken around by his friends.

———— ENGLISH EQUIVALENTS ————	———— AIDS TO LISTENING ————	———— CONVENTIONAL SPELLING ————
Phroso	fróso	Φρόσω
today	símera	σήμερα
closed	klistó	κλειστό
Today the museum's closed.	símera to-musío ine-klistó.	Σήμερα τὸ μουσεῖο εἶναι κλειστό.
Mary	maría	Μαρία
we shall show to him	tha-tu-dhíksume	θὰ τοῦ δείξουμε
the fortress	to-kástro	τὸ κάστρο
We'll show him the town and the fortress.	tha-tu-dhíksume tim-bóli ke-to-kástro.	Θὰ τοῦ δείξουμε τὴν πόλι καὶ τὸ κάστρο.
George	yórghos	Γιώργος
as far as the square	ísa-me-tim-blatía	ἴσα μὲ τὴν πλατεῖα
five minutes	pénde-leftá	πέντε λεφτά
From here up to the square it's only five minutes.	apo-dhó ísa-me-tim-blatía ine-móno-pénde-leftá.	Ἀπὸ 'δῶ ἴσα μὲ τὴν πλατεῖα εἶναι μόνο πέντε λεφτά.

with the feet Let's walk.	me-ta-pódhya páme-me-ta-pódhya-mas.	μὲ τὰ πόδια Πάμε μὲ τὰ πόδια μας.

John
the broad road
the trees
I like this wide street and the trees.

yánis
o-platíz-dhrómos
ta-dhéndra
aftós-o-platíz-dhrómoz-me-ta-dhéndra
m-arési.

Γιάννης
ὁ πλατὺς δρόμος
τὰ δέντρα
Αὐτὸς ὁ πλατὺς δρόμος μὲ τὰ δέντρα μ' ἀρέσει.

Mary
coffee-houses
the most beautiful houses
Here are our best coffee-shops* and our finest houses.

maría
kafenía
ta-pyó-oréa-spítya
edhó ine-ta-kaliterá-mas-kafenía
ke-ta-pyó-oréa-ma-spítya.

Μαρία
καφενεῖα
τὰ πιὸ ὡραῖα σπίτια
Ἐδὼ εἶναι τὰ καλύτερά μας καφενεῖα καὶ τὰ πιὸ ὡραῖα μας σπίτια.

George
hears
the music
Everyone goes for a walk here in the evening and listens to the band-concert.

yórghos
akúi
ti-musikí
ólos-o-kózmos pái-perípato-edhó-to vrádhi ky-akúi-ti-musikí.

Γιώργος
ἀκούει
τὴ μουσική
Ὅλος ὁ κόσμος πάει περίπατο ἐδὼ τὸ βράδυ κι ἀκούει τὴ μουσική.

Phroso
tired
I'm a bit tired.

fróso
kurazméni
ime-liǵaki-kurazméni.

Φρόσω
κουρασμένη
Εἶμαι λιγάκι κουρασμένη.

---
*On the record 'coffee-houses'.

[10–A]

George
we shall sit	tha-kátsume	θὰ κάτσουμε
we shall take	tha-párume	θὰ πάρουμε
a taxi	ena-taksí	ἕνα ταξί

First we'll sit, down by the harbor, and later we'll take a taxi.
tha-kátsume próta káto-s-to-limáni k-ístera tha-párum-ena-taksí.
Θὰ κάτσουμε πρῶτα κάτω στὸ λιμάνι κ' ὕστερα θὰ πάρουμ' ἕνα ταξί.

they sit — *káthonde* — κάθονται
[They sit in a coffee-house.] [*káthonde s-ena-kafenío.*] [Κάθονται σ' ἕνα καφενεῖο.]

John / yánis / Γιάννης
vessels — *karávya* — καράβια
There aren't many ships in the harbor.
dhén-ine-polá-karávya s-to-limáni.
Δὲν εἶναι πολλὰ καράβια στὸ λιμάνι.

old — *palyá* — παλιά
And some are very, very old.
ke-meriká ine-polí-polí-palyá.
Καὶ μερικὰ εἶναι πολὺ πολὺ παλιά.

Record 19B, beginning.

George / yórghos / Γιώργος
any more	álo	ἄλλο
they will make a trip	tha-taksidhépsune	θὰ ταξιδέψουνε

They won't sail any more.
dhé-tha-taksidhépsune-álo.
Δὲ θὰ ταξιδέψουνε ἄλλο.

Mary / maría / Μαρία
a little while	lígho	λίγο
we shall have again	thá-khume-páli	θά 'χουμε πάλι

But we'll soon have a lot of them again.
ma-se-lígho thá-khume-páli-polá.
Μὰ σὲ λίγο θά 'χουμε πάλι πολλά.

they will be sailing And our ships will once more be sailing all over the world.	tha-taksidhévune ke-páli ta-karávya-mas tha-taksidhévune s-ólo-ton-gózmo.	θὰ ταξιδεύουνε Καὶ πάλι τὰ καράβια μας θὰ ταξιδεύουνε σ' ὅλο τὸν κόσμο.

John — yánis — Γιάννης

new
That one there is newer.

How old is it?

kenúryo
aftó-ekí-ine-pyó-kenúryo.

póso-khronóne-íne?

καινούργιο
Αὐτὸ ἐκεῖ εἶναι πιὸ καινούργιο.

Πόσω χρονῶνε εἶναι;

George — yórghos — Γιώργος

It's thirteen years old.

It goes back to (the) nineteen thirty-two.

ine-dheka-trió-khronóne.

in-ap-to-chílya-enyakósya-trianda-dhío.

Εἶναι δεκατριῶ χρονῶνε.

Εἶν' ἀπ' τὸ χίλια ἐννιακόσια τριάντα δύο.

Phroso — fróso — Φρόσω

that we go up
Come on, let's go up to the fortress.

n-anevúme
eláte-n-anevúme páno-s-to-kástro.

ν' ἀνεβοῦμε
Ἐλᾶτε ν' ἀνεβοῦμε πάνω στὸ κάστρο.

Mary — maría — Μαρία

they stop
the store
The taxis stop in front of Kladas's store.

at the peak
[At the top of the hill.]

stamatúne
to-maghazí
ta-taksí stamatúne brostá-s-to-maghazí tu-kladhá.

s-tin-gorfí
[s-tin-gorfí-tu-vunú.]

σταματοῦνε
τὸ μαγαζί
Τὰ ταξὶ σταματοῦνε μπροστὰ στὸ μαγαζὶ τοῦ Κλαδᾶ.

στὴν κορφή
[Στὴν κορφὴ τοῦ βουνοῦ.]

[10–A]

George	yórghos	Γιώργος
meters	métra	μέτρα
high up	psilá	ψηλά
We're four hundred meters up.	ímaste tetrakósya métra psilá.	Εἴμαστε τετρακόσια μέτρα ψηλά.
John	yánis	Γιάννης
church	eklisyá	ἐκκλησιά
What church is that one there?	tí-eklisyá-in-ekíni-kí?	Τί ἐκκλησιὰ εἶν' ἐκείνη 'κεῖ;
Phroso	fróso	Φρόσω
the ruins	ta-erípia	τὰ ἐρείπια
of an ancient temple	enos-archéu-naú	ἑνὸς ἀρχαίου ναοῦ
It's the ruins of an ancient temple.	ine-ta-erípia enos-archéu-naú.	Εἶναι τὰ ἐρείπια ἑνὸς ἀρχαίου ναοῦ.

Record 20A, beginning.

John	yánis	Γιάννης
at the wharf	s-tim-brokiméa	στὴν προκυμαία
they are lighting	anávune	ἀνάβουνε
the lights	ta-fóta	τὰ φῶτα
Down by the wharf they're lighting the lights.	káto-s-tim-brokiméa anávune-ta-fóta.	Κάτω στὴν προκυμαία ἀνάβουνε τὰ φῶτα.
George	yórghos	Γιώργος
they return	yirízune	γυρίζουνε
the fishermen	i-psarádhes	οἱ ψαράδες
boats	várkes	βάρκες
The fishermen are coming back with their boats.	yirízun-i-psarádhes me-tiz-várkes-tus.	Γυρίζουν οἱ ψαράδες μὲ τὶς βάρκες τους.

	Mary	maría	Μαρία
It's cold; let's go home.		káni-krío, páme-spíti.	Κάνει κρύο, πάμε σπίτι.

Record 20A, after spiral.

Some More Numbers

In Unit 1 you learned the numbers from 1 to 10. Here is a list of all the remaining numbers you will need. Go through them in the same way as the *Basic Sentences*, repeating each number after your **Guide** or the phonograph record.

eleven	éndeka	ἔντεκα
twelve	dhódheka	δώδεκα
thirteen	dheka-tría	δεκατρία
fourteen	dheka-tésera	δεκατέσσερα
fifteen	dheka-pénde	δεκαπέντε
sixteen	dheká-ksi	δεκάξι
seventeen	dheka-eftá	δεκαεφτά
eighteen	dheka-okhtó	δεκαοχτώ
nineteen	dheka-enyá	δεκαεννιά
twenty	íkosi	εἴκοσι
twenty-one	ikosi-éna	εἴκοσι ἕνα
twenty-two	ikosi-dhío	εἴκοσι δύο
thirty	triánda	τριάντα
forty	saránda	σαράντα
fifty	penínda	πενήντα
sixty	eksínda	ἑξήντα
seventy	evdhomínda	ἑβδομήντα
eighty	oghdhónda	ὀγδόντα

[10–A]

ninety	*enenínda*	ἐνενήντα
a hundred	*ekató*	ἑκατό
a hundred and one	*ekaton-éna*	ἑκατὸν ἕνα
a hundred and two	*ekaton-dhío*	ἑκατὸν δύο
a hundred and three	*ekaton-dría*	ἑκατὸν τρία
two hundred	*dhyakósya*	διακόσια
three hundred	*trakósya*	τρακόσια
four hundred	*tetrakósya*	τετρακόσια
five hundred	*pendakósya*	πεντακόσια
six hundred	*eksakósya*	ἑξακόσια
seven hundred	*eftakósya*	ἐφτακόσια
eight hundred	*okhtakósya*	ὀχτακόσια
nine hundred	*enyakósya*	ἐννιακόσια
a thousand	*chílya*	χίλια
two thousand	*dhyó-chilyádhes*	δυὸ χιλιάδες
a million	*ena-ekatomírio*	ἕνα ἑκατομμύριο
zero	*midhén*	μηδέν
a zero	*ena-midhenikó*	ἕνα μηδενικό

SECTION B—WORD STUDY AND REVIEW OF BASIC SENTENCES

1. Word Study (Individual Study)

COMMENT 1

THE INDIRECT OBJECT. Almost all the following sentences have come in the Units you have studied. As you read them over, observe closely the form and use of the short words that stand at the margin.

mu

dhóste-mu-kafé parakaló.
dhe-mu-léte?
m-arési.
pú-borí-na-mu-ta-yalísune?

boríte-na-mu-katharísete-ti-stolí-mu?
kópste-mu-ta-malyá parakaló.

Give me coffee, please.
Tell me, won't you? ('Won't you say to me?')
I like it. ('It is pleasing to me.')
Where is there a chance of my getting them shined?
  ('Where is it possible that they shine them for me?')
Can you clean my uniform for me?
Give me a haircut, please. ('Cut the hair for me, please.')

sas

sas-arési?
boró-na-sas-parusiáso-ton-gírio-burbúli?
na-saz-dhíkso.
tí-boró-na-sas-prosféro?
dhém-boró-na-sas-to-pó.

Do you like it? ('Is it pleasing to you?')
May I present (to you) Mr. Bourboulis?
Let me show you.
What can I treat you to?
I can't tell you (it). ('I can't tell it to you.')

tu m.

tha-tu-dhíksume-tim-bóli.
tha-t-arési.

We'll show him the town.
He'll like it. ('It will be pleasing to him.')

tis f.

thélo-na-tiz-dhíkso to-vapóri-mu.

I want to show her my ship.

tu n.

ávrio érchete-to-pedhí, tóte tu-dhínete
  t-avghá ke-ta-lákhana.

The boy's coming tomorrow; you ['ll] give him the eggs and the vegetables then.

[10–B] 233

mas

    péste-mas-esís-ti-na-párume.   You tell us what to get.
    thélete-na-mas-féri próta mya-súpa?   Do you want him to bring us a [plate of] soup first?
    dhóste-mas áspro-krasí.   Give us white wine.

tus

    óli-edho tuz-dhínune ta-papútsya-tus.   Everybody here gives his shoes to them. ('All [the people] here give their shoes to them.')

You see that the forms *mu, sas, tu, tis, tu, mas, tus* that occur in the Greek sentences above are the very same ones that are used in phrases like *o-patéraz-mu, i-mitéra-sas, o-adherfós-tu, to-pedhí-tis,* etc., but they are used in a way that is entirely different. In *o-patéraz-mu, i-mitéra-sas,* and other such phrases the words *mu, sas,* etc., go closely with the noun, and they answer the question 'whose?' 'of whom?' 'of what?' But in *dhóste-mu-kafé parakaló* "Give me coffee, please," or *kópste-mu-ta-malyá parakaló* "Give me a haircut, please," or *tí-boró-na-sas-prosféro?* "What can I treat you to?" and other such expressions the words *mu, sas,* etc. go with the verb, and they answer the question 'to whom?' 'for whom?' Of course, we do not always need to use the words 'to' or 'for' in the English of these expressions; we can say "They give *them* their shoes" as well as "They give their shoes *to them*," and we can say "We want you to bring *us* wine" as well as "We want you to bring wine *for us*." Note that the word serving as the actual goal or object of the action of the verb, like *kafé* in the sentence *dhóste-mu-kafé parakaló,* or *to* in the sentence *dhém-boró-na-sas-to-pó,* stands in the object form and is called the direct object. But a pronoun of the set *mu, sas,* etc. may indicate a person on whom the action of the verb takes effect indirectly, and is then called the *indirect object*.

As to the actual forms, you observe, first, that *mas* and *sas*, meaning '(to) us, for us' and '(to) you, for you', respectively, are no different from the direct object forms *mas, sas* (as in *mas-kséri* 'he knows us', or *sas-kséri* 'he knows you'). Secondly, the form *tus,* meaning '(to) them, for them', is identical with the masculine object form for 'them' (as in *tus-kséri* 'he knows them'). But the form *tus* need not refer only to masculine nouns like *ándres* 'men'; it is also the word for '(to) them, for them' when the reference is to feminine nouns like *yinékes* 'women' or neuter nouns like *pedhyá* 'children'. With all the other pronouns the forms of the indirect object are unlike those of the direct.

Here is a table of forms of the personal pronouns, showing the indirect object forms, with the direct object forms drawn up alongside for comparison.

	Indirect object			Direct object
mu	(to) me, for me		*me*	me
sas	(to) you, for you		*sas*	you
tu	(to) him, for him		*tone*	him
tis	(to) her, for her		*tine*	her
tu	(to) it, for it		*to*	it
mas	(to) us, for us		*mas*	us
			tus	them *masc.*
tus	(to) them, for them		*tis*	them *fem.*
			ta	them *neut.*

There is still one further point to notice about the little unaccented personal pronoun objects, and that is the order in which they stand when a verb takes two of them as objects, one direct and one indirect. Look again at these examples:

pú-borí-na-mu-ta-yalísune?   Where's there a chance of my getting them shined? ('Where is it **possible** that they shine them for me?')

dhém-boró-na-sas-to-pó.   I can't tell you (it).

pú-in-o-kaféz-mu? boríte-na-mu-tone-férete?   Where is my coffee? Can you bring it to me?

You see that in every case the indirect object stands before the direct in the Greek.

COMMENT 2

HOW TO SAY 'I'LL COME', 'I'LL SEE', ETC. IN GREEK. Look at the following sentences:

ksérete ti-tha-kámume-símera?   Do you know what we're going to do today?

próta tha-páme-s-tim-blatía.	First we'll go to the square.
tha-tu-dhíksume tim-bóli ke-to-kástro.	We'll show him the town and the fortress.
tha-kátsume próta káto-s-to-limáni k-ístera tha-párum-ena-taksí.	First we'll sit, down by the harbor, and later we'll take a taxi.
ma-se-lígho thá-khume-páli-polá.	But we'll soon have a lot of them again.

All these sentences refer to the future. If you look carefully at the Greek text you will see that every sentence contains the little word *tha*. It is just this word which, placed before the verb, brings about the idea of futurity.

Now look at these two sentences:

dhé-tha-taksidhépsune-álo.	They won't sail any more.
ke-páli ta-karávya-mas tha-taksidhévune s-ólo-ton-gózmo.	And our ships will once more be sailing all over the world.

You see that in the one example we have the form *taksidhépsune*, that is, the perfective dependent, and in the other example the form *taksidhévune*, that is, the imperfective present. This difference of forms after *tha* reminds you, of course, of the same difference of verbal forms after the other little word *na*. And indeed, there is nothing new to you in the fact that Greek can express the future in two ways: if you wish to represent things as *single acts*, you use *tha* + the perfective dependent, as in the sentence *ávrio tha-fáo-psári* "Tomorrow I'll eat fish," but if you wish to say that something will happen *repeatedly*, you use *tha* + the imperfective present, as in the sentence *tha-tróo káthe-méra psári* "I'll eat fish every day."

Here is an example of the two futures of Greek. Let's take the verb *dhulévo* 'I work.'

Perfective future stem: /dhuleps/		Imperfective future stem: /dhulev/	
tha-dhulépso	I'll work (once)	*tha-dhulévo*	I'll work (always)
tha-dhulépsete		*tha-dhulévete*	
tha-dhulépsi		*tha-dhulévi*	
tha-dhulépsume		*tha-dhulévume*	
tha-dhulépsune		*tha-dhulévune*	

Look again at these sentences and observe carefully the order of words:

tha-párum-ena-taksí.	We'll take a taxi.
tha-tu-dhíksume-tim-bóli.	We'll show him the town.

The element *tha* is always placed before the verb. It is a kind of prefix and is separated from the verb only by unstressed personal pronouns.

Now, finally, look at these examples you have already heard:

eghó pérno-psári.	I['ll] take fish.
k-eghó kotópulo.	And I['ll take] chicken.
eghó pérno-ta-mávra.	I['ll] take the black [shoes].
k-eghó sas-katharízo-ta-áspra.	And I['ll] clean the white ones for you.
pú-thélete-na-to-válo?—brostá-s-tim-bórta-tu-spityú-sas,	Where do you want me to put it?—In front of the door of your house; and I['ll] come and get it.
k-eghó érkhome ke-to-pérno.	
févgho to-vrádhi.	I leave tonight.
o-pétros févyi-s-tis-okhtó.	Peter is leaving at eight.

You see from these examples that Greeks often use the imperfective present (without *tha*) instead of the perfective dependent with *tha*.

COMMENT 3

THE FORMS OF THE GREEK NUMERALS. In Unit 7 you learned that *dhío* 'two' and the Greek numbers from five through ten have only one form. Such numbers, of course, are very easy to use. From the higher numbers that are given right after the *Basic Sentences* in this Unit you can increase this list by many more, for there is only one form for eleven and twelve and for each of the teens from fifteen through nineteen and for the tens running from twenty through ninety.

Further, you learned in Unit 7 that when you are simply counting up, starting with *éna, dhío, tría, tésera, pénde*, you are really using the neuter form of those numerals which happen to have more than one form. Now this use of the neuter form for counting up and, for that matter, for almost all the processes of arithmetic, holds for all the Greek numerals, however high you want to count. But when you go to use numerals before nouns in sentences, it is not enough to know only neuter forms—you must know feminines and masculines, too, and for most masculines, in numerals as in ordinary adjectives, the object case is different from the subject case (e.g. *trakósyus-amerikanús* obj. and *trakósyi-amerikaní* subj.).

The forms of *énas*, *trís*, and *téseris*, which you learned some time ago but which will be summarized again for you in the table that accompanies this comment, are exactly the same when they come in compounds: e.g. *ikosi-énas-ándres*, *ikosi-mía-yinékes*, *ikosi-éna-pedhyá*.

Other forms of *énas*, *trís*, and *téseris* occur in the special phrases that are spoken in answer to the question *póso-khronóne-íne* (*íste*, etc.)? "How old is he (are you, etc.)?"—*enós-khronú* 'one year old', *trió-khronóne* 'three years old', *tesáro-khronóne* 'four years old'.

Although the Greek word for 'a hundred' shows no change for gender or case, it does show a variation between *ekató* and *ekatón* on an entirely different basis. When the word stands by itself or with a following noun, its form is *ekató*, as in *to-ekató* 'Number 100', *ekató-ándres* 'a hundred men'; but when the word is followed by a number that is not a noun, its form is *ekatón*, as in *ekatón-éna* 'a hundred and one', *ekaton-dhío* 'a hundred and two', *ekaton-drís* 'a hundred and three',

or *ekatom-benínda* 'a hundred and fifty'. **Notice the phrase *ekató-chilyádhes* 'a hundred thousand', in which *chilyádhes* is really a noun.**

Beyond *ekató* the hundreds are adjectives with **forms** just like the plural of *kalós*, as you have found from the sentences *s-tin-galifórnya ékhume trakósyes eksínda pénde méres ílyo to-khróno* "In California we have three hundred [and] sixty-five days of sunshine a year," and *imaste tetrakósya métra psilá* "We're four hundred meters up." The word for 'a thousand' is the same **sort** of adjective: you say *chílyi-stratyótes* 'a thousand soldiers', *chílyez-yinékes* 'a thousand women', *chílya-pedhyá* 'a thousand children'.

When *chilyádhes* is followed by a noun, the noun stands in the same case as *chilyádhes*. For example, *itane-trís-chilyádhes-amerikaní s-tin-italía* "There were three thousand Americans in Italy," or *kanénaz-mazdhen-gzéri trís-chilyádhes-amerikanús* "None of us knows three thousand Americans."

Finally, *ekatomírio* 'a million', with its compounds, is likewise a noun. It may be used before another noun in exactly the same way as *chilyádhes*, for example, *pyós-apo-sás théli-na-dhí ena-ekatomírio-amerikanús?* "Which of you wants to see a million Americans?" And it may have a plural, as in the phrase *dhyó-ekatomíraromyí* 'two million Greeks'.

Here is a table of those numerals (outside of *ekató*) which have more than one form:

		masc.	fem.	neut.
1	subj.	*énas*	} *myá (mía)*	} *éna*
	obj.	*énan*		
3			*trís*	*tría*
4			*téseris*	*tésera*
200, etc.	subj.	*dhyakósyi*	} *dhyakósyes*	} *dhyakósya*
	obj.	*dhyakósyus*		
1000	subj.	*chílyi*	} *chílyes*	} *chílya*
	obj.	*chílyus*		
1,000,000				*ekatomírio* sing.
				ekatomíria plur.

COMMENT 4

akúo 'I HEAR'. By now you have met three verbs the stem of which ends in a vowel. These are *páo* 'I go', *léo* 'I say', and *tróo* 'I eat'. In this Unit there occurs another of this kind, which behaves in exactly the same fashion as the three earlier verbs. These are the forms:

akúo	I hear
akúte	you hear
akúi	he hears
akúme	we hear
akúne	they hear

2. Covering English and Greek of Word Study (Individual Study)

Check yourself on your knowledge of the *Word Study* by covering first the English, then the Greek, and making sure you know everything thoroughly.

[10–B]

3. Review of Basic Sentences

With the Guide or records, review the first half of the *Basic Sentences* as in previous Units.

Section C—Review of Basic Sentences (*Cont.*)

1. Review of Basic Sentences (*Cont.*)

Review the second half of the *Basic Sentences*.

2. Covering the English of Basic Sentences (Individual Study)

Go through the *Basic Sentences* covering up the English and reading aloud the Greek. Check up on anything you do not know, until you are sure of everything.

3. What Would You Say? (Individual Study)

I. Give the proper answer to each of the following questions. Make complete sentences.

1. *pyóz-yalízi-ta-papútsya s-tin-eládha?*
2. *pú-pulúne-sigharéta?*
3. *tróne-se-farmakía s-tin-eládha?*
4. *tí-ora-thélete-na-sas-ksipníso?*
5. *pós-tone-léne to-yatró-sas?*
6. *póte-tha-fíyete, símera í-ávrio?*
7. *tí-keros-ítane to-chimóna?*
8. *póso-plirónete ya-to-dhomatió-sas?*
9. *yatí-thélete-na-párum-ena-taksí?*
10. *tí-boró-na-sas-prosféro?*

II. How would you say in Greek?

1. It's one o'clock. 2. My daughter is thirteen years old. 3. My room is on the second floor. 4. We are seven hundred sixty-four meters up. 5. It's five thousand four hundred eleven miles from New York to Athens. 6. That castle over there goes back to (is from the) twelve hundred and fifty-seven. 7. In Greece they give ten per cent for the service. 8. My room is number forty-nine. 9. One hundred and twenty persons live in that hotel: eighty-eight Greeks and thirty-two Americans. 10. Four soups, sixteen drachmas; three salads, twelve drachmas; eight eggs, twenty-four drachmas; two coffees, four drachmas; and one beer, five drachmas; all (*n. p.*) together, sixty-one drachmas.

III. Checking your vocabulary.

1. Give the Greek equivalents for the following English words:

   a. *Family:* relatives; parents; father; mother; husband; wife; grandfather; son; daughter; brother; sister; uncle; aunt.

   b. *Professions:* soldier; sailor; aviator; policeman; physician; teacher; (college) student (male); (college) student (female); worker; employee; fisherman; (woman) innkeeper; barber; bootblack.

2. Give the English equivalents for the following Greek words:

   a. Time: *símera; ávrio; efétos; tóra; tóte; pánda; poté; póte; kápote; próta; prin; prin-apo; ístera; íster-apo; se-lígho; páli; akóma.*

   b. Space: *pú; edhó; edho-péra; apo-dhó; ekí; ekí-péra; dheksyá; aristerá; ísya-brostá; brostá-se; andíkri-se; páno; páno-se; káto; káto-se; psilá; kondá; kondá-se; ísa-me.*

Section D—Listening In

1. What Did You Say?

Give your answers for each of the exercises in the preceding section, when the Leader calls for them. Then, as the Leader calls for them, give the English equivalents of all the expressions in the first exercise.

2. Word Study Check-Up

As you have done in the previous Units, go back to the *Word Study* and give the correct Greek for each English expression, without having to read it from the book. The Leader or one of the members of the group should read the English.

3. Listening In

With your book closed, listen to the following conversations as read by the Guide or phonograph record. Repeat the Greek immediately after hearing it. After the first repetition of each conversation, check up on the meaning of anything you do not understand, by asking someone else or by going back to the *Basic Sentences* if no one knows. Repeat again, if necessary, then take parts and carry on the conversation.

Record 20B, beginning.

1. Members of an American family tell a Greek friend about their stay in the Greek countryside.

o-fílos:	sas-arési-lipón-i-eládha?	Σᾶς ἀρέσει λοιπὸν ἡ Ἑλλάδα;
o-patéras:	echi-orées-pólis.	Ἔχει ὡραῖες πόλεις.
i-mitéra:	eghó-protimó-tin-eksochí-me-ta-dhéndra-tis.	Ἐγὼ προτιμῶ τὴν ἐξοχὴ μὲ τὰ δέντρα της.
to-pedhí:	efétos imaste-se-mya-mikrí-póli kondá-s-ti-thálasa.	Ἐφέτος ἤμαστε σὲ μιὰ μικρὴ πόλι κοντὰ στὴ θάλασσα.
i-mitéra:	poté-dhe-tha-ksekháso-aftó-to-kalokéri.	Ποτὲ δὲ θὰ ξεχάσω αὐτὸ τὸ καλοκαίρι.
o-patéras:	ine-pánda-dhrosyá-to-vrádhi.	Εἶναι πάντα δροσιὰ τὸ βράδυ.
i-mitéra:	*i-yinékes ke-ta-pedhyá páne-perípato s-tim-blatía*	Οἱ γυναῖκες καὶ τὰ παιδιὰ πάνε περίπατο στὴν πλατεῖα
	i-káto-s-tim-brokiméa.	ἢ κάτω στὴν προκυμαία.
o-patéras:	i-ándres káthonde-s-ta-kafenía.	Οἱ ἄντρες κάθονται στὰ καφενεῖα.
	móno-lígha-maghazyá-ine-klistá-to-vrádhi.	Μόνο λίγα μαγαζιὰ εἶναι κλειστὰ τὸ βράδυ.
to-pedhí:	s-to-limáni pulúne-psárya.	Στὸ λιμάνι πουλοῦνε ψάρια.
	i-psarádhes févghune me-tiz-várkes-tus.	Οἱ ψαράδες φεύγουνε μὲ τὶς βάρκες τους.
i-mitéra:	polí-érkhonde-ap-tin-eksochí-s-tim-bóli ke-yirízune-spíti-tus ti-níkhta.	Πολλοὶ ἔρχονται ἀπ' τὴν ἐξοχὴ στὴν πόλι καὶ γυρίζουνε σπίτι τους τὴ νύχτα.
	tus-arés-i-musikí ke-páne ke-tin-akúne.	Τοὺς ἀρέσ' ἡ μουσικὴ καὶ πάνε καὶ τὴν ἀκούνε.
o-patéras:	kondá-s-tim-bóli in-ena-vunó m-ena-mikró-naó.	Κοντὰ στὴν πόλι εἶν' ἕνα βουνὸ μ' ἕνα μικρὸ ναό.
i-mitéra:	borí-na-pári-kanenas ena-taksí-isa-m-ekí.	Μπορεῖ νὰ πάρῃ κανένας ἕνα ταξὶ ἴσα μ' ἐκεῖ.
to-pedhí:	o-dhrómoz-dhén-ine-platís ke-t-aftokínita ine-palyá.	Ὁ δρόμος δὲν εἶναι πλατὺς καὶ τ' αὐτοκίνητα εἶναι παλιά.

	stamatúne brostá-se-mya-mikrí-eklisyá ke-prépi-n-anevíte saránda-métra ísa-me-ta-erípia me-ta-pódhya-sas.	Σταματοῦνε μπροστὰ σὲ μιὰ μικρὴ ἐκκλησιὰ καὶ πρέπει ν' ἀνεβῆτε σαράντα μέτρα ἴσα μὲ τὰ ἐρείπια μὲ τὰ πόδια σας.
o-patéras:	ligha-leftá-móno k-ímaste s-tin-archéa-eládha.	Λίγα λεφτὰ μόνο κ' ἤμαστε στὴν ἀρχαία Ἑλλάδα.

Record 20B, after spiral.

2. Two businessmen, an American and a Greek, talk about Athens.

o-amerikanós:	ísaste-s-tin-athína?	Ἤσαστε στὴν Ἀθήνα;
o-romyós:	né, imuna-tésera-khrónya s-aftín-dim-bóli.	Ναί, ἤμουνα τέσσερα χρόνια σ' αὐτὴν τὴν πόλι.
o-amerikanós:	tí-milún-ekí?	Τί μιλοῦν ἐκεῖ;
o-romyós:	s-tis-tavérnes ke-s-ta-mikrá-kafenía milúne-móno-eliniká.	Στὶς ταβέρνες καὶ στὰ μικρὰ καφενεῖα μιλοῦνε μόνο ἑλληνικά.
	s-ta-meghála-ksenodhochía ke-s-ta-meghála-estiatória katalavénune-ky-angliká.	Στὰ μεγάλα ξενοδοχεῖα καὶ στὰ μεγάλα ἐστιατόρια καταλαβαίνουνε κι ἀγγλικά.
o-amerikanós:	pós-ine-ta-spítya-tis?	Πῶς εἶναι τὰ σπίτια της;
o-romyós:	dhén-ine-polí-psilá.	Δὲν εἶναι πολὺ ψηλά.
	ekhune-dhío-patómata ke-kápote-ísa-me-pénde.	Ἔχουνε δύο πατώματα καὶ κάποτε ἴσα μὲ πέντε.
o-amerikanós:	tí-borí-na-dhí-kanena-s-tin-athína?	Τί μπορεῖ νὰ δῇ κανένας στὴν Ἀθήνα;
o-romyós:	echi-archéuz-naús eklisyés musía platíez-me-dhéndra kenúryuz-dhrómus ke-poléz-nóstimez-yinékes.	Ἔχει ἀρχαίους ναούς, ἐκκλησιές, μουσεῖα, πλατεῖες μὲ δέντρα, καινούργιους δρόμους καὶ πολλὲς νόστιμες γυναῖκες.
o-amerikanós:	zúne-polí-amerikaní-ekí?	Ζοῦνε πολλοὶ Ἀμερικανοὶ ἐκεῖ;

o-romyós:	né, ena-soró.	Ναί, ἕνα σωρό.
o-amerikanós:	tí-dhulyá-kánune?	Τί δουλειά κάνουνε;
o-romyós:	merikí dhén-ekhune-dhulyá.	Μερικοὶ δὲν ἔχουνε δουλειά.
	áli ine-dháskali i-fitités.	Ἄλλοι εἶναι δάσκαλοι ἢ φοιτητές.
	ke-polí-páne-s-tin-athína ke-s-ála-méri-tis-eládhas ya-ta-eripiá-tis* móno.	Καὶ πολλοὶ πάνε στὴν Ἀθήνα καὶ σ' ἄλλα μέρη τῆς Ἑλλάδας γιὰ τὰ ἐρείπιά της μόνο.
o-amerikanós:	tí-dhulyá-in-aftí?	Τί δουλειά εἶν' αὐτή;
o-romyós:	ine-ky-aftí-dhulyá.	Εἶναι κι αὐτὴ δουλειά.
o-amerikanós:	k-esís tí-dhulyá-kánate?	Κ' ἐσεῖς, τί δουλειά κάνατε;
o-romyós:	ékana-paghotá.	Ἔκανα παγωτά.
o-amerikanós:	aftí-ine-dhulyá.	Αὐτὴ εἶναι δουλειά.

*On the record *erípya-tis*, which can also be used.

Section E—Conversation

1. Covering the Greek of Basic Sentences (Individual Study)

Cover the Greek of the *Basic Sentences* and practice saying the Greek equivalents of the English expressions.

2. Vocabulary Check-Up

Give the Greek expressions for the English equivalents in the *Basic Sentences* as the Leader calls for them.

3. Conversation

As you have done in the *Conversation* in the previous Units, begin to converse by following the model outlined below fairly closely; then change the situation somewhat. Invent new combinations of subject matter

You describe to a friend an evening in a small Greek town.

1. He inquires whether the women work in the evening.
2. You answer that in the evening the women don't work any more, and don't light the lights in their houses.
3. He is surprised and says, "Well then, what do they do?"
4. You reply that they sit in front of their houses or go to church, and that the children make a lot of noise in the streets.
5. He inquires whether the men go to church, too.
6. No, you say, they go to the barber shop, or sit in the coffee-shops, or drink wine in the taverns.
7. He asks if the young girls go home after their work.
8. You answer that they go and listen to the band-concert, or go shopping (go to the stores), or take a walk at the wharf and talk with the fishermen.
9. He wants to know where the intelligentsia of the town, the teacher and the doctor, go in the evening.
10. You say that the doctor and the teacher sit in the drugstore, and that sometimes a farmer comes there from his farm, too.
11. Does he want to see the doctor, your friend inquires.
12. No, you answer, he wants to speak with the teacher. He has gotten a letter from his brother in America, but he cannot read it, and so he asks (begs) the teacher to read it.
13. Your friend remarks that he wouldn't like to be a doctor's wife in Greece. Her husband has to work a lot and when he doesn't work he goes to the drugstore.
14. But she has her children, you answer, and sometimes a farmer's wife goes to see her. One of her children has been sick but now it is well again. She brings vegetables, eggs, and chicken for the doctor, and pastry for the children. They sit together and talk.
15. To a question on the part of your friend whether these women stay for a long time at the doctor's house or only a few minutes, you reply that they return home only after many hours.
16. You end by saying that at twelve everybody is asleep.

Section F—Conversation (*Cont.*)

Continue the conversation started in Section E, with a review of previous lessons if necessary.

FINDER LIST

A

akúo	ἀκούω	I hear; I listen to
/akus/	ἀκουσ–	
álo	ἄλλο	any more
dhén ... álo	δὲν ... ἄλλο	not ... any more; no longer
anávo	ἀνάβω	I light
/anaps/	ἀναψ–	
anevéno	ἀν<u>ε</u>βαίνω	I go up
n-anevó (-í)	ν' ἀνεβῶ (–ῇ)	that I go up
anevó see: anevéno		
archéos, -a, -o	ἀρχαῖος, –α, –ο	ancient

B

blatía see: platía
brokiméa see: prokiméa

D

to dhéndro	τὸ δέντρο	tree

E

ékho		
thá-khume	θά 'χουμε	we shall have
i eklisyá	ἡ ἐκκλησιά	church
ta erípia	τὰ ἐρείπια	ruins

F

to fós	τὸ φῶς	light
fóta p.	φῶτα	
fóta see: fós		

G

gorfí see: *korfí*

I

ísa-me ἴσα μὲ as far as; up to
    ísa-me-tim-blatía ἴσα μὲ τὴν πλατεῖα   as far as the square

K

to kafenío τὸ καφενεῖο coffee-house
to karávi τὸ καράβι vessel (ship)
to kástro τὸ κάστρο fortress
káthome κάθομαι I sit
    tha-kátso θὰ κάτσω   I shall sit
kátso see: *káthome*
kenúryos, -a, -o καινούργιος, -α, -ο new
khronóne
    íne ... khronóne εἶναι ... χρονῶνε   is ... years old
    póso-khronóne ... πόσω χρονῶνε ...   how old ...?
khume see: *ékho*
klistós, -í, -ó κλειστός, -ή, -ό closed
i korfí ἡ κορφή peak; top
kurazménos, -i, -o κουρασμένος, -η, -ο tired

L

to leftó τὸ λεφτό minute
lígho λίγο a little while
    se-lígho σὲ λίγο   in a little while; soon

[10–F]

M

to maghazí	τὸ μαγαζί	store
to métro	τὸ μέτρο	meter (*about* 1⅒ yd.)
i musikí	ἡ μουσική	music; band-concert
to musío	τὸ μουσεῖο	museum

N

o naós	ὁ ναός	temple

P

páli	πάλι	again
palyós, -á, -ó	παλιός, -ά, -ό	old (*of things*)
i platía	ἡ πλατεῖα	square
platís, platyá, platí	πλατύς, πλατειά, πλατύ	broad; wide
to pódhi	τὸ πόδι	foot
me-ta-pódhya	μὲ τὰ πόδια	on foot
póso see: khronóne		
i prokiméa	ἡ προκυμαία	wharf
o psarás	ὁ ψαρᾶς	fisherman
psilá	ψηλά	high up
pyó	πιό	more
o-pyó ...	ὁ πιὸ ...	⎫
i-pyó ...	ἡ πιὸ ...	⎬ the most ...
to-pyó ...	τὸ πιὸ ...	⎭

S

símera	σήμερα	today
stamató	σταματῶ	I stop
/stamatís/	σταματησ–	

T

to taksí (unchangeable)	τὸ ταξί	taxi
taksidhévo	ταξιδεύω	I make a trip; I travel
/taksidheps/	ταξιδεψ–	
tha	θὰ	*verbal prefix expressing the future*
to		
to-chílya-enyakósya-trianda-dhío	τὸ χίλια ἐννιακόσια τριάντα δύο	the year 1932
ap-to-chílya-enyakósya-trianda-dhío	ἀπ' τὸ χίλια ἐννιακόσια τριάντα δύο	from the year 1932
tu	τοῦ	to him; to it

V

i várka	ἡ βάρκα	boat

Y

yirízo	γυρίζω	I come back; I return
/yiris/	γυρισ–	

[10–F]

UNIT 11

SHOPPING

Section A—Basic Sentences

Go once through the *Basic Sentences* in unison. Then go through the *Hints on Pronunciation*, and twice more through the *Basic Sentences* individually.

1. Basic Sentences

Record 21A, beginning.

Peter Smith goes shopping with Nick Roilos.

——ENGLISH EQUIVALENTS——	——AIDS TO LISTENING——	——CONVENTIONAL SPELLING——
Peter	pétros	Πέτρος
I need	khriázome	χρειάζομαι
things	prámata	πράματα
I need a lot of things.	khriázome ena-soro-prámata.	Χρειάζομαι ἕνα σωρὸ πράματα.
Nick	níkos	Νίκος
that I buy	n-aghoráso	ν' ἀγοράσω
a hat	ena-kapélo	ἕνα καπέλο
that I take measure	na-páro-métro	νὰ πάρω μέτρο
I (too) have to buy a hat and get measured for a coat.	k-eghó prépi-n-aghoráso ena-kapélo ke-na-páro-métro ya-ena-panofóri.	Κ' ἐγὼ πρέπει ν' ἀγοράσω ἕνα καπέλο καὶ νὰ πάρω μέτρο γιὰ ἕνα πανωφόρι.
[At the clothing store.]	[s-to-emborikó.]	[Στὸ ἐμπορικό.]

The clerk	o-ipálilos	Ὁ ὑπάλληλος
pass!	peráste	περάστε
inside	mésa	μέσα
Step [right] in!	peráste-mésa.	Περάστε μέσα.
the cloth	to-ífazma	τὸ ὕφασμα
Here's the cloth for your coat.	edhó-ine-to-ífazma ya-to-panofóri-sas.	Ἐδὼ εἶναι τὸ ὕφασμα γιὰ τὸ πανωφόρι σας.
Nick	níkos	Νίκος
It's English.	in-anglikó.	Εἶν' ἀγγλικό.
The clerk	o-ipálilos	Ὁ ὑπάλληλος
immediately	amésos	ἀμέσως
Our tailor can take your measurements right away.	o-ráftiz-mas borí-na-sas-pári-métro amésos.	Ὁ ράφτης μας μπορεῖ νὰ σᾶς πάρῃ μέτρο ἀμέσως.
Anything else?	álo-típota?	Ἄλλο τίποτα;
Peter	pétros	Πέτρος
of what kind?	tí-loyís	τί λογῆς
shirts	pukámisa	πουκάμισα
What kind of shirts do you have?	tí-loyís-pukámisa-échete?	Τί λογῆς πουκάμισα ἔχετε;
The clerk	o-ipálilos	Ὁ ὑπάλληλος
colored	khromatistá	χρωματιστά
We have white ones and colored ones.	ekhum-áspra ke-khromatistá.	Ἔχουμ' ἄσπρα καὶ χρωματιστά.

[11–A]

Nick	níkos	Νίκος
don't take!	mím-bárete	μὴν πάρετε
take the blue ones!	párte-ta-blé	πάρτε τὰ μπλέ
Don't take the white ones; take the blue ones (instead).	mím-bárete-t-áspra, párte-kalítera-ta-blé.	Μὴν πάρετε τ' ἄσπρα, πάρτε καλύτερα τὰ μπλέ.
Peter	pétros	Πέτρος
brown	kafetí	καφετύ
ugly	áskimo	ἄσκημο
And this brown one isn't bad.	ky-aftó-to-kafetí dhén-in-áskimo.	Κι αὐτὸ τὸ καφετὺ δὲν εἶν' ἄσκημο.
Nick	níkos	Νίκος
How much do they cost?	póso-kostízune?	Πόσο κοστίζουνε;
The clerk	o-ipálilos	Ὁ ὑπάλληλος
Two hundred drachmas each ('the shirt').	dhyakósyez-dhrakhmés-to-pukámiso.	Διακόσιες δραχμὲς τὸ πουκάμισο.
Nick	níkos	Νίκος
how expensive	tí-akrivá	τί ἀκριβά
That's pretty expensive! ('How expensive that they are!')	tí-akrivá-pu-íne!	Τί ἀκριβὰ ποὺ εἶναι!
The clerk	o-ipálilos	Ὁ ὑπάλληλος
you have right	echete-dhíkyo	ἔχετε δίκιο
price	timí	τιμή
You're right, but I haven't [a thing] at any other price.	echete-dhíkyo, ma-dhén-ekho-s-áli-timí.	Ἔχετε δίκιο, μὰ δὲν ἔχω σ' ἄλλη τιμή.

Record 21B, beginning.

Nick
Give them to us for a hundred and eighty drachmas apiece.

The clerk
in order that I may satisfy you
All right, then, three hundred eighty drachmas for the two of them, if that 'll make you any happier.

Peter
stockings
Do you have any socks?

The clerk
colors
We have [them] in all colors.

Peter
a pair
Give me one pair of white ones and five pairs of black.

I need shoes, too.

Nick
what number?
you wear
What size do you wear?

níkos
dhoste-más-ta ya-ekaton-oghdhónda-dhrakhmés-to-éna.

o-ipálilos
ya-na-sas-efkharistíso
kalá-lipón, trakósyes-oghdhónda-dhrakhméz-ya-ta-dhío ya-na-sas-efkharistíso.

pétros
káltses
échete-káltses?

o-ipálilos
khrómata
ékhum-ap-óla-ta-khrómata.

pétros
ena-zevghári
dhóste-mu éna-zevghári-áspres ke-pénde-zevghárya-mávres.

khriázome-ke-apútsya.

níkos
ti-arithmó
foríte
ti-arithmó foríte?

Νίκος
Δώστε μάς τα γιὰ ἑκατὸν ὀγδόντα δραχμὲς τὸ ἕνα.

Ὁ ὑπάλληλος
γιὰ νὰ σᾶς εὐχαριστήσω
Καλὰ λοιπόν, τρακόσιες ὀγδόντα δραχμὲς γιὰ τὰ δύο, γιὰ νὰ σᾶς εὐχαριστήσω.

Πέτρος
κάλτσες
Ἔχετε κάλτσες;

Ὁ ὑπάλληλος
χρώματα
Ἔχουμ' ἀπ' ὅλα τὰ χρώματα.

Πέτρος
ἕνα ζευγάρι
Δώστε μου ἕνα ζευγάρι ἄσπρες καὶ πέντε ζευγάρια μαῦρες.

Χρειάζομαι καὶ παπούτσια.

Νίκος
τί ἀριθμό
φορεῖτε
Τί ἀριθμὸ φορεῖτε;

[11–A]

Peter	pétros	Πέτρος
Nine in America.	enyá s-tin-amerikí.	Ἐννιὰ στὴν Ἀμερική.
I hope	elpízo	ἐλπίζω
the same thing	to-ídhyo	τὸ ἴδιο
I hope (that) it's the same in Greece, too.	elpízo ná-ne-to-ídhyo-ke-s-tin-eládha.	Ἐλπίζω νά 'ναι τὸ ἴδιο καὶ στὴν Ἑλλάδα.
Nick	níkos	Νίκος
all of us	óli-mas	ὅλοι μας
we order	parangélnume	παραγγέλνουμε
from the shoemaker	s-ton-dzangári	στὸν τσαγγάρι
Here all of us order our shoes from the shoemaker.	edhó óli-mas-parangélnume-ta-papútsya-mas s-ton-dzangári.	Ἐδῶ ὅλοι μας παραγγέλνουμε τὰ παπούτσια μας στὸν τσαγγάρι.
poor	ftochí	φτωχοί
And the poor don't wear any shoes.	k-i-ftochí dhé-forúne-papútsya.	Κ' οἱ φτωχοὶ δὲ φοροῦνε παπούτσια.
Peter	pétros	Πέτρος
I thought that ...	élegha-pos	ἔλεγα πὼς
ready	étima	ἔτοιμα
I [always] thought that the ready-made ones were all right ('are all right, they too').	k-eghó-élegha pos-ta-étima ine-kal í-ky-aftá.*	Κ' ἐγὼ ἔλεγα πὼς τὰ ἔτοιμα εἶναι καλὰ κι αὐτά.

Record 22A, beginning.

one [and a] half	myá-misi	μιά 'μισυ
[An hour and a half later.]	[íster-apo-myá-misi-óra.]	["Υστερ' ἀπὸ μιά 'μισυ ὥρα.]

*On the record *kalítera* 'better'.

Nick	níkos	Νίκος
by your watch	me-to-rolói-sas	μὲ τὸ ρολόι σας
Say, what time is it by your watch?	dhe-mu-léte, tí-ora-ine-me-to-rolói-sas?	Δὲ μοῦ λέτε, τί ὥρα εἶναι μὲ τὸ ρολόι σας;
Peter	pétros	Πέτρος
three minus twenty	trís para-íkosi	τρεῖς παρὰ εἴκοσι
It's twenty minutes of three.	ine-trís para-íkosi.	Εἶναι τρεῖς παρὰ εἴκοσι.
Nick	níkos	Νίκος
Already?	kyólas!	Κιόλας!
It's late.	in-arghá.	Εἶν' ἀργά.
three [and a] half	tris-ímisi	τρεῖς ἥμισυ
I have to be home by half past three.	prépi-ná-me-spíti-mu s-tis-tris-ímisi.	Πρέπει νά 'μαι σπίτι μου στὶς τρεῖς ἥμισυ.
Peter	pétros	Πέτρος
at eight and a quarter	s-tis-okhtó-ke-tétarto	στὶς ὀχτὼ καὶ τέταρτο
Well, [I'll see you] tonight at a quarter after eight.	lipón, símera-to-vrádhi s-tis-okhtó-ke-tétarto.	Λοιπόν, σήμερα τὸ βράδυ στὶς ὀχτὼ καὶ τέταρτο.
Nick	níkos	Νίκος
Pope will be home, too.	thá-ne-spíti-k-i-pópi.	Θά 'ναι σπίτι κ' ἡ Πόπη.
Peter	pétros	Πέτρος
at eight minus a quarter	s-tis-okhtó para-tétarto	στὶς ὀχτὼ παρὰ τέταρτο
Well then, [I'll see you] at a quarter to eight.	tóte-lipón, s-tis-okhtó para-tétarto.	Τότε λοιπόν, στὶς ὀχτὼ παρὰ τέταρτο.

Before you go through the *Basic Sentences* a second time, study the following:

2. Hints on Pronunciation

SOMETHING MORE ABOUT WORDS THAT ARE RUN TOGETHER. Look at these sentences almost all of which you have already heard:

otan-ímuna-pedhí tá-ksera-kalá.	When I was a boy, I knew it ('them') well.
thá-thela-na-páo.	I'd like to go.
tó-kho-s-tin-dzépi-mu.	I have it in my pocket.
se-lígho thá-khume-páli-polá.	We'll soon have a lot of them again.
elpízo ná-ne-to-ídhyo-ke-s-tin-eládha.	I hope it's the same in Greece, too.
íster-apo-myá-misi-óra	an hour and a half later
prépi-ná-me-spíti-mu s-tis-tris-ímisi.	I have to be home at half past three.
thá-ne-spíti-k-i-pópi.	Pope will be home, too.
móno-éna-práma dhe-théli-ná-chi-i-yinéka-tu.	There's only one thing he doesn't want his wife to have.

You see that in all these sentences there occur combinations of words: *tá-ksera* consists of *ta* and *íksera*; *thá-thela*, of *tha* and *íthela*; *tó-kho*, of *to* and *ékho*; *thá-khume*, of *tha* and *ékhume*; *ná-ne*, of *na* and *íne*; *myá-misi*, of *mya* and *ímisi*; *ná-me*, of *na* and *íme*; *thá-ne*, of *tha* and *íne*; *ná-chi*, of *na* and *échi*. Here we might mention also the numeral *dheká-ksi*, from *dhéka* and *éksi*.

You remember from Unit 2 that when Greek vowels of different words are run together, generally *a* is stronger than *o, u, e, i; o* stronger than *u, e, i; u* stronger than *e* and *i;* and *e* stronger than *i*. In our sentences, however, we have not only a combination of vowels, but also a very characteristic shift of accent. This, then, is the conclusion we may draw from our examples: If two words are closely run together, the first of which ends in an unstressed vowel and the second of which begins with a stressed vowel, the initial vowel of the second word disappears and the final vowel of the first word takes over its accent, provided that the final vowel of the first word is stronger than the initial vowel of the second word. But, as we said in Unit 2, the pronunciation or omission of vowels in such combinations of words is not a rule but is up to the native speaker.

Record 22A, after first spiral.
PRACTICE

íne	elpízo-ná-ne	ékhume	thá-khume
íne	thá-ne	íksera	tá-ksera
íme	prépi-ná-me	íthela	thá-thela
ékho	tó-kho	ímisi	myá-misi
échi	théli-ná-chi	éksi	dheká-ksi

Section B—Word Study and Review of Basic Sentences

1. Word Study (Individual Study)

COMMENT 1

How to command and how to forbid in Greek. The same difference that you have already learned for verb-forms after *na* and *tha*, the difference between perfective and imperfective, holds also for verb-forms used in commands and prohibitions.

(a) Look first at these examples of commands:

eláte mazí-mu.	Come with me.
dhóste-mu-sigharéta.	Give me cigarettes.
rotíste-ton-astifílaka s-tin-odhón-anglías.	Ask the policeman on England St.
kathíste parakaló.	Sit down, please.
kópste-mu-ta-malyá parakaló.	Give me a haircut, please. ('Cut the hair for me, please.')
péste-mas-esís-ti-na-párume.	You tell us ('say to us') what to get.
pyéte-krasí-me-neró.	Drink wine [mixed] with water.
peráste-mésa.	Step [right] in!
párte-kalítera-ta-blé.	Take the blue ones (instead).

[11–B]

All these commands have occurred in the Units you have studied so far. As you think over the occasions on which each of these orders was given to a person in the course of the conversations, you will see that these particular orders applied only to some definite situation. As you would expect, the verb-forms of command (or *imperatives*, as they are usually called) in the above sentences contain the perfective stem as you have learned to recognize it (/dhos/, /rotis/, /kops/, /peras/, /par/). You see that it is very easy to form the perfective imperative: you have only to add the ending -*te* to the perfective stem and put the accent on the next to the last syllable. There are, of course, some peculiar forms like the following, that must be learned especially.

/dh/	dhéste	see
/figh/	fíyete	go away; leave
/kam/	kámete	do; make
/min/	mínete	stay
/p/	péste	say; tell
/py/	pyéte	drink

and finally,

eláte	come; come on
kathíste	sit down
vréste	find

In contrast to the *perfective imperfectives* which you have just looked at, Greek also has *imperfective imperatives*. In the examples given below, the two different kinds are put down side by side so that you can compare the forms and meanings of them more easily.

Imperfective imperative
ksipnáte-me káthe-méra s-tis-eftá.
Wake me up every day at seven.

Perfective imperative
ksipníste-me ávrio s-tis-eftá.
Wake me up tomorrow at seven.

milíte-sighá parakaló.
Talk slowly, please.
piyénete káthe-vrádhi s-to-spíti-tu.
Go to his house every evening.

First, as to their forms, you see that *ksipnáte, milíte,* and *piyénete* show the imperfective stem and are identical with the forms that mean 'you are waking up', 'you are talking', and 'you are going', respectively, but the rest of the sentence and the situation in which they are used make clear the fact that in the sentences cited here *ksipnáte, milíte,* and *piyénete* are commands. The imperfective imperative is used most frequently when the speaker tells someone to do something always, or repeatedly, as in the example *ksipnáte-me káthe-méra s-tis-eftá.* But such forms are also used when the command applies to a situation of some duration. This is how we must understand the example *milíte-sighá parakaló* "Talk slowly, please (for all the time that we are conversing)," while the form *milíste*, the perfective imperative, can mean only 'have a talk (on a definite occasion or on a definite subject)'. The imperative *piyénete* 'go' demands especial notice.

milíste-tu-esís parakaló.
You have a talk with him ('to him'), please.
págho-thélete? piyénete-s-ti-makedhonía.
You want ice? Go to Macedonia.

Since it is formed from the imperfective stem *piyen-* you will naturally find it used in commands like *piyénete káthe-vrádhi s-to-spíti-tu.* But as is proved by the example *págho-thélete? piyénete-s-ti-makedhonía* "You want ice? Go to Macedonia," the form *piyénete* may also apply to some single occasion; in fact, it can function as a perfective imperative.

Whether the imperative is perfective or imperfective, any pronoun object will come *after* the imperative, as you see from the phrases *d'ióste-mu* 'give me', *péste-mas* 'tell us' ('say to us'). In this regard imperatives are different from all other verb-forms, for you remember how the pronoun objects come before the verb in sentences like *mas-kséri* "He knows us," *sas-arési?* "Do you like it?" ('Is it pleasing to you?') or *dhémboró-na-sas-to-pó* "I can't tell you (it)." Consider the followin imperatives:

kópste-mu-ta-malyá parakaló.	Give me a haircut, please. ('Cut the hair for me, please.')
kópste-ta.	Cut it.
kopste-mú-ta.	Cut it for me.
péste-mas.	Tell us. ('Say to us.')
péste-to.	Tell it. ('Say it.')
peste-más-to.	Tell it to us. ('Say it to us.')

You observe that with imperatives, as with all other verb-forms, the indirect object pronoun stands before the direct. If you listen closely to your Guide, you will notice that in a command like *kopste-mú-ta* or *peste-másto* the main stress is on the indirect object pronoun *mu* or *mas*, though there is a certain amount of stress on *kópste* or *péste*.*

dhe-mu-léte kírie-Smith, esís apo-pyó-méros-tis-amerikís íste?

me-sikhoríte.

Besides the imperative there is a more polite way of giving an order or making a request, as illustrated by the following examples:

Tell me, won't you, Mr. Smith, what part of the United States are *you* from?

Excuse me.

The place of the pronoun objects before the verb-forms here is sufficient proof that these are not true imperatives. The forms *léte* and *sikhoríte* are imperfective presents that ask a question or make a statement with the force of a perfective imperative. This use of the imperfective present is very frequent in Greek.

(b) Now look at these examples of sentences in which you tell someone not to do something.

Imperfective

mín-gzekhnáte-poté-to-burbuár edhó-s-tin-eládha.   Don't ever forget the tip here in Greece.
mín-aghorázete étima-papútsya s-tin-eládha.   Don't buy ready-made shoes in Greece.
mín-da-lét-aftá.   Don't say such things ('those things').
mím-bínete-krasí to-kalokéri.   Don't drink wine in the summer-time.

Perfective

mím-bárete-t-áspra, párte-kalítera-ta-blé.   Don't take the white ones; take the blue ones (instead).
mín-du-to-píte.   Don't tell it to him.
aftó-to-krasí ine-varí, mín-do-pyíte.   This wine is strong; don't drink it.

From these sentences you see that when you forbid someone to do a thing or urge him not to, you use the word *mín* either with the imperfective present or with a certain perfective form, according to the situation.

---

*A good example is *dhoste-más-ta* 'give them to us', at the very beginning of Record 21B.

As you see from the examples, the perfective form that you use after *mín* in a prohibition is the perfective dependent, and not the perfective imperative: *mímbárete* 'don't take', but *párte* 'take'. As for the word *mín*, it appears as *mín*, *mím*, or *mí* just as *dhén* appears as *dhén*, *dhém*, or *dhé*, depending on the following word, according to the rules you learned for final *-n* in Unit 3. Finally, note that this use of stressed *mín* 'not' in prohibitions is completely different from the use of unstressed *min* 'by any chance' in questions like *min-ist-árostos?* "Are you sick, by any chance?" or *min-gzérete kamyá-kalí-tavérna?* "Do you happen to know any good tavern?"

COMMENT 2

How to say 'one and a half', 'two and a half', etc. in Greek. The numbers you have learned in Greek so far have been whole numbers. But it is useful to be able to employ the Greek word for the fraction 'a half' which is added to the full numbers. Here are some examples to study:

1½ *enas-ímisi* (masc., subj.)
    enan-ímisi (masc., obj.)
    myá-misi (fem.)
    ená-misi (neut.)

2½ *dhyó-misi*

3½ *tris-ímisi* (masc.-fem.)
    triá-misi (neut.)

4½ *teseris-ímisi* (masc.-fem.)
    teserá-misi (neut.)

5½ *pendé-misi*

6½ *eksí-misi*

7½ *eftá-misi*

8½ *okhtó-misi*

9½ *enyá-misi*

10½ *dheká-misi*

From this table you see that the word for 'a half' which is added to the whole numbers is *ímisi* whenever the preceding numeral ends in a consonant; whenever it ends in a vowel, that vowel combines with the initial *i-* of *ímisi* according to a process which you have found treated in the *Hints on Pronunciation* in this Unit. You notice that in these phrases you put *ímisi* after the whole numbers without the need of *ke* 'and',

[11–B]   **261**

just as you add *pénde* to *íkosi* to make *íkosi-pénde* 'twenty-five'. Observe also that as the phrase *íkosi-pénde* is pronounced with no stress on the larger number *íkosi*, but with stress on the smaller number *pénde*, which follows, so, for example, *tris-ímisi* is pronounced with no stress on *tris*, but with stress on the smaller number *ímisi*.

COMMENT 3

How to express time in Greek. It will be convenient to divide this portion of the *Word Study* into two parts, leaving for the second part the phrases containing the hours, and treating first the general expressions for time, seasons, and parts of the day.

(a) Look first at the following sentences, which illustrate the more general expressions of time:

ti-ora-ksipnáte?	What time do you wake up?
borí-na-míno polín-geró.	I may stay for a long time.
ímast-ekí polá-khrónya.	We were there for many years.
káni-krío-edhó-to-chimóna?	Is it cold here in the winter?
káni-zésti-edhó-to-kalokéri?	Is it hot here in the summer?
kanénaz-dhen-gzipnái ti-níkhta.	Nobody wakes up at night.
ekí-ine-pánda-dhrosyá-to-vrádhi.	There it's always cool in the evening.

In all these examples the expressions underlined answer the questions 'when?' 'at what time or season?' or 'how long?'. And to judge by the masculine nouns, as in the phrases *polín-geró*, *to-chimóna*, and by the feminine nouns if they are accompanied by the article, as in the phrase *ti-níkhta*, the noun in such expressions always stands in the object case. It is to be noted also that in Greek these phrases are complete in themselves without any word corresponding to our 'at', 'in', or 'for'.

(b) Now consider these examples of the way you tell the hours of the day in Greek:

boríte-na-me-ksipnísete s-tis-eftá?	Can you wake me up at seven?
févgho s-tis-okhtó-to-vrádhi me-to-tréno.	I leave at eight tonight by train.
prépi-ná-me-spíti-mu s-tis-tris-ímisi.	I have to be home by half past three.

lipón, símera-to-vrádhi s-tis-okhtó-ke-tétarto.
tóte-lipón, s-tis-okhtó para-tétarto.
ine-trís para-íkosi.

Well, [I'll see you] tonight at a quarter after eight.
Well then, [I'll see you] at a quarter to eight.
It's twenty minutes of three.

You remember that in Unit 7 you learned that in the phrases *ine-mía* "It's one," *ine-dhío* "It's two," *ine-trís* "It's three," etc., the number 'one' is in the feminine form and the numbers 'three' and 'four' are in the masculine-feminine form, because the feminine noun *óra* is understood. You will also recall that the same word *óra* is implied in the phrases *s-ti-mía* 'at one', *s-tiz-dhío* 'at two', *s-tis-trís* 'at three', etc.

When you say that it is "half past" the hour, you see that you have only to add to the phrase for the full hour the word *ímisi*, whose use you have just studied. It will be well, however, to look closely at the phrases for 'half past one', etc., up through 'half past four'.

ine-myá-misi.	It's half past one.
ine-dhyó-misi.	It's half past two.
ine-tris-ímisi.	It's half past three.
ine-teseris-ímisi.	It's half past four.

Although you say *ine-mía* "It's one," you must use *myá* in the phrase *ine-myá-misi*, and similarly, although you say *ine-dhío* "It's two," you must use *dhyó* in the phrase *ine-dhyó-misi*.

Now, when you speak of quarter-hours and minutes, there is one fundamental thing to observe: up to the half-hour you *add* by using *ke* 'and', while after that point you *subtract* from the next hour by using *para* 'minus'. Thus you find *s-tis-okhtó-ke-tétarto* 'at a quarter after eight', or *ine-dhódheka-ke-íkosi* "It's twenty minutes after twelve," but *s-tis-okhtó para-tétarto* 'at a quarter to eight', and *ine-dhódheka para-íkosi* "It's twenty minutes of twelve."

2. Covering English and Greek of Word Study (Individual Study)

Check yourself on your knowledge of the *Word Study* by covering first the English, then the Greek, and making sure you know everything thoroughly.

3. Review of Basic Sentences

With the Guide or records, review the first half of the *Basic Sentences* as in previous Units.

Section C—Review of Basic Sentences (*Cont.*)

1. Review of Basic Sentences (*Cont.*)

Review the second half of the *Basic Sentences*.

2. Covering the English of Basic Sentences (Individual Study)

Go through the *Basic Sentences* covering up the English and reading aloud the Greek. Check up on anything you do not know, until you are sure of everything.

3. What Would You Say? (Individual Study)

I. Say the following sentences without any hesitation, after making sure that you can supply the Greek for the English words in parentheses.

1. *thélo* (to buy) *mya-foresyá*.
2. *borúme* (to leave) *amésos*.
3. (Don't forget) *poté tus-ftokhús*.
4. *m-arési* (to eat) *kalá*.
5. *borí* (for me to show it to you) *tóra*.
6. *íster-ap-tom-bólemo ta-vapórya-mas* (will travel) *s-óla-ta-méri-tu-kózmu*.
7. (I'll see you) *ávrio*.
8. *efétos* (they'll take) *óla-tus-ta-pedhyá mazí-tus*.
9. (He'll work) *káthe-méra s-to-khtíma-mu*.
10. *ton-dzangári* (you'll find him) *s-to-maghazí-tu símera-to-vrádhi*.

II. Match each phrase in the left-hand column with the appropriate one in the right-hand column. The resulting sentences form a small connected account.

1. *símera*
2. *páo-lipón s-tu-kladhá*
3. *to-emborikó-tu*
4. *ine-kondá-s-tin*
5. *vrísko*

a. *trakósyez-dhrakhmés."*
b. *ya-to-kalokéri í-ya-to-chimóna?"*
c. *eklisyá.*
d. *m-arési-polí."*
e. *"ena-kapélo ya-to-chimóna."*

6. *páo ke-tu-léo:*
7. *aftós-tóte mu-léi*
8. "*to-thélete*
9. "*khriázome,*" *tu-léo,*
10. "*párte-to-mávro,*"
11. "*né, to-mávro*
12. "*kostízi*
13. "*ine-polí-akrivó,*

f. *enan-ipálilo.*
g. *ikha-keró.*
h. *ya-n-aghoráso-ena-kapélo.*
i. *pos-ékhune-polá.*
j. "*khriázom-ena-kapélo.*"
k. *ma-tha-to-páro.*"
l. *mu-léi-tót-aftós.*
m. *ine-to-kalítero s-tim-bóli-mas.*

Section D—Listening In

1. What Did You Say?

Give your answers in Greek for each of the exercises in the preceding section, when the Leader calls for them. Then, as the Leader calls for them, give the English equivalents of all the expressions in the exercise.

2. Word Study Check-Up

As you have done in the previous Units, go back to the *Word Study* and give the correct Greek for each English expression, without having to read it from the book. The Leader or one of the members of the group should read the English.

3. Listening In

With your book closed, listen to the following conversations as read by the Guide or phonograph record. Repeat the Greek immediately after hearing it. After the first repetition of each conversation, check up on the meaning of anything you do not understand, by asking someone else or by going back to the *Basic Sentences* if no one knows. Repeat again if necessary, then take parts and carry on the conversation.

Record 22A, after second spiral.

1. A man passes by a store; the clerk addresses him.

o-ipálilos: *peráste-mésa.*
o-kírios: *échete-pukámisa?*

Περάστε μέσα.
Ἔχετε πουκάμισα;

o-ipálilos:	tí-loyís-thélete?	Τί λογῆς θέλετε;
o-kírios:	khromatistá.	Χρωματιστά.
o-ipálilos:	sas-arési-aftó-to-kafetí?	Σᾶς ἀρέσει αὐτὸ τὸ καφετύ;
o-kírios:	dhén-ine-áskimo.	Δὲν εἶναι ἄσκημο.
	póso-kostízi?	Πόσο κοστίζει;
o-ipálilos:	dhyakósyez-dhrakhmés.	Διακόσιες δραχμές.
	ine-kalí-timí.	Εἶναι καλὴ τιμή.
o-kírios:	óchi, ine-polí-akrivó.	Ὄχι, εἶναι πολὺ ἀκριβό.

Record 22B, beginning.

	min-échete-típota-pyó-ftinó?	Μὴν ἔχετε τίποτα πιὸ φτηνό;
o-ipálilos:	ekho-aftá-ta-blé.	Ἔχω αὐτὰ τὰ μπλέ.
	ma-mín-da-párete.	Μὰ μὴν τὰ πάρετε.
	dhén-da-forúne-álo s-aftó-to-khróma.	Δὲν τὰ φοροῦνε ἄλλο σ' αὐτὸ τὸ χρῶμα.
	álo-típota?	Ἄλλο τίποτα;
o-kírios:	ine-mésa-o-ráfti-sas?	Εἶναι μέσα ὁ ράφτης σας;
	thélo-na-páro-métro ya-mya-foresyá.	Θέλω νὰ πάρω μέτρο γιὰ μιὰ φορεσιά.
o-ipálilos:	lipúme-polí, ma-dhé-dhulévi-to-vrádhi.	Λυποῦμαι πολύ, μὰ δὲ δουλεύει τὸ βράδυ.
o-kírios:	élegha poz-dhulévi-arghá.	Ἔλεγα πὼς δουλεύει ἀργά.
o-ipálilos:	eláte-páli-ávrio.	Ἐλᾶτε πάλι αὔριο.
	ávrio parangélnete óti-thélete.	Αὔριο παραγγέλνετε ὅ,τι θέλετε.
	ke-thá-ne-étimo se-liyez-méres.	Καὶ θά 'ναι ἔτοιμο σὲ λίγες μέρες.

Record 22B, after first spiral.

2. An American and a Greek are talking about time.

o-amerikanós:	i-amerikí ine-polí-megháli.	Ἡ Ἀμερικὴ εἶναι πολὺ μεγάλη.

	otan-ine-dhódheka-s-ti-néa-yórki, ine-éndeka-s-to-sikágho ke-enyá-s-to-sanfrandzísko.	Ὅταν εἶναι δώδεκα στὴ Νέα Ὑόρκη, εἶναι ἕντεκα στὸ Σικάγο καὶ ἐννιὰ στὸ Σὰν Φραντζίσκο.
o-romyós:	aftó-dhen-ine-típota. otan-ine-trí-s-to-rolói-tu-ghrafíu-mu, ine-trís-ke-pénde s-to-meghálo-rolói-tis-platías, trís-ke-tétarto me-to-rolói-mu, tris-ímisi me-to-rolói tu-fílu-mu tu-roilú, ke-téseris para-tétarto me-to-rolói tiz-yinékaz-mu.	Αὐτὸ δὲν εἶναι τίποτα. Ὅταν εἶναι τρεῖς στὸ ρολόι τοῦ γραφείου μου, εἶναι τρεῖς καὶ πέντε στὸ μεγάλο ρολόι τῆς πλατείας, τρεῖς καὶ τέταρτο μὲ τὸ ρολόι μου, τρεῖς ἥμισυ μὲ τὸ ρολόι τοῦ φίλου μου τοῦ Ροϊλοῦ, καὶ τέσσερεις παρὰ τέταρτο μὲ τὸ ρολόι τῆς γυναῖκας μου.
o-amerikanós:	ke-pyós-echi-dhíkyo?	Καὶ ποιὸς ἔχει δίκιο;
o-romyós:	óli-mas. étsi-ímaste-emís-i-romyí. ekhume-pánda-dhíkyo. ke-kánume-óli-mas óti-thélume.	Ὅλοι μας. Ἔτσι εἴμαστε ἐμεῖς οἱ Ρωμιοί. Ἔχουμε πάντα δίκιο. Καὶ κάνουμε ὅλοι μας ὅ,τι θέλουμε.

Record 22B, after second spiral.

3. Two Greek women are gossiping.

1-mía:	ksérete-to-níko-to-makrí?	Ξέρετε τὸ Νίκο τὸ Μακρή;
i-áli:	pós? itane-triánda-khrónya s-tin-amerikí.	Πῶς; Ἤτανε τριάντα χρόνια στὴν Ἀμερική.
i-próti:	i-ghonís-tu ine-yeoryí.	Οἱ γονεῖς του εἶναι γεωργοί.
i-dhéfteri:	otan-ítane-pedhí-o-níkos, dhen-iche-rúkha-na-forési.	Ὅταν ἤτανε παιδὶ ὁ Νίκος, δὲν εἶχε ροῦχα νὰ φορέσῃ.
i-próti:	ma-tóra echi-pénde-zeveghárya-papútsya k-ena-soro-káltses.	Μὰ τώρα ἔχει πέντε ζευγάρια παπούτσια κ' ἕνα σωρὸ κάλτσες.

i-dhéfteri:	echi-áspra-pukámisa ke-khromatistá.	Ἔχει ἄσπρα πουκάμισα καὶ χρωματιστά.
i-próti:	ke-trís kenúryes foresyés.	Καὶ τρεῖς καινούργιες φορεσιές.
i-dhéfteri:	álo-kapélo-forí-to-chimóna ky-álo-to-kalokéri.	Ἄλλο καπέλο φορεῖ τὸ χειμῶνα κι ἄλλο τὸ καλοκαίρι.
i-próti:	to-panofóri-tu prépi-ná-ne ap-anglikó-ífazma.	Τὸ πανωφόρι του πρέπει νά 'ναι ἀπ' ἀγγλικὸ ὕφασμα.
i-dhéfteri:	o-kuréas tone-ksurízi káthe-méra.	Ὁ κουρέας τόνε ξουρίζει κάθε μέρα.
i-próti:	ke-tóra théli-na-pári-ke-yinéka.	Καὶ τώρα θέλει νὰ πάρῃ καὶ γυναῖκα.
i-dhéfteri:	théli-ná-ne-ftochí ma-oréa.	Θέλει νά 'ναι φτωχή, μὰ ὡραία.
	ky-aftós tha-tis-aghorási óla.	Κι αὐτὸς θὰ τῆς ἀγοράσῃ ὅλα.
	échi vlépete éna-ekatomírio-dhrakhmés.	Ἔχει, βλέπετε, ἕνα ἑκατομμύριο δραχμές.
i-próti:	móno-éna-práma dhe-théli-ná-chi-i-yinéka-tu.	Μόνο ἕνα πρᾶμα δὲ θέλει νά 'χῃ ἡ γυναῖκά του.
i-dhéfteri:	tí?	Τί;
i-próti:	mávra-malyá.	Μαῦρα μαλλιά.

Record 22B, after third spiral.

4. Subtracting in Greek.

tésera apo-pénde, éna.	τέσσερα ἀπὸ πέντε, ἕνα.
eftá apo-dheka-okhtó, éndeka.	ἑφτὰ ἀπὸ δεκαοχτώ, ἕντεκα.
dhódheka apo-íkosi, okhtó.	δώδεκα ἀπὸ εἴκοσι, ὀχτώ.
peninda apo-oghdhónda, triánda.	πενήντα ἀπὸ ὀγδόντα, τριάντα.
eksínda apo-ekató, saránda.	ἑξήντα ἀπὸ ἑκατό, σαράντα.
éna apo-éna, midhén.	ἕνα ἀπὸ ἕνα, μηδέν.

Section E—Conversation

1. Covering the Greek of Basic Sentences (Individual Study)

Cover the Greek of the *Basic Sentences* and practice saying the Greek equivalents of the English expressions.

2. Vocabulary Check-Up

Give the Greek expressions for the English equivalents in the *Basic Sentences* as the Leader calls for them.

3. Conversation

As you have done in the *Conversation* in the previous Units, begin to converse by following the models outlined below fairly closely; then change the situations somewhat. Invent new combinations of subject matter.

1. You discuss with a friend whether or not you have time to go to a clothing store. What time is it? I have to be home by a quarter of four; it's late; I need a lot of things.
2. You buy shirts: In Greece shirts are too long; aren't there shorter shirts in the store?
3. You ask the clerk whether he has socks. He tells you that he has socks in all colors, white ones, black ones, and colored ones. You tell him that you need five pairs.
4. You tell your friend that in Greece one does not buy ready-made suits; but one buys the cloth; and there is a tailor in the store who takes your measurements.
5. You tell your friend that you have to buy a new coat, since your old one has always been a little too short. You would like to order a brown one.
6. You have a pair of black shoes which are too hot and ugly in summer. You want to go to a shoemaker and buy a pair of white ones. You don't know what size you wear in Greece.
7. You buy cigarettes and matches at a variety-stand; you express your surprise that you have to pay for matches, and that you have to pay so much.
8. A Greek doesn't know what a "five and ten" is. Explain it to him.

Section F—Conversation (*Cont.*)

Continue the conversations started in Section E, with a review of previous lessons if necessary.

FINDER LIST

A

aghorázo	ἀγοράζω	I buy
/aghoras/	ἀγορασ–	
álos, -i, -o	ἄλλος, –η, –ο	other; different; else
álo-típota?	ἄλλο τίποτα;	anything else?
álos ... álos	ἄλλος ... ἄλλος	one ... another
amésos	ἀμέσως	immediately
anglikós, -í, -ó	ἀγγλικός, –ή, –ό	English
arghá	ἀργά	late
o arithmós	ὁ ἀριθμός	number; size
áskimos, -i, -o	ἄσκημος, –η, –ο	ugly; bad

B

blé (unchangeable)	μπλέ	blue

C

chi see: ékho

D

to dhíkyo	τὸ δίκιο	right
ekho-dhíkyo	ἔχω δίκιο	I am right
dzangári see: tsangáris		

E

efkharistó (-í)	εὐχαριστῶ (–εῖ)	I thank
/efkharistis/	εὐχαριστησ–	
ya-na-sas-efkharistíso	γιὰ νὰ σᾶς εὐχαριστήσω	in order to satisfy you
ékho		
ná-chi	νά 'χῃ	that he (she, it) may have

élegha see: *léo*		
elpízo	ἐλπίζω	I hope
/elpis/	ἐλπισ–	
to emborikó	τὸ ἐμπορικό	clothing store
étimos, -i, -o	ἔτοιμος, –η, –ο	ready; ready-made

F

foró (-í)	φορῶ (–εῖ)	I wear; I put on
/fores/	φορεσ–	
ftokhós, ftochí, ftokhó	φτωχός, –ή, –ό	poor
o-ftokhós	ὁ φτωχός	the *poor* man

I

ídhyos, -a, -o	ἴδιος, –α, –ο	same
to-ídhyo	τὸ ἴδιο	the same thing
to ífazma	τὸ ὕφασμα	cloth
íme		
ná-me	νά 'μαι	that I am *or* be —
na-ne	νά 'ναι	that he (she, it) is *or* be
thá-ne	θά 'ναι	he (she, it) will be
imisi, misi (only after numbers)	ἥμισυ, 'μισυ	half
myá-misi-óra	μιά 'μισυ ὥρα	an hour and a half
tris-ímisi	τρεῖς ἥμισυ	half past three

K

kafetís, kafetyá, kafetí	καφετύς, καφετειά, καφετύ	brown
i káltsa	ἡ κάλτσα	stocking; sock

to kapélo	τὸ καπέλο	hat
khriázome	χρειάζομαι	I need
to khróma	τὸ χρῶμα	color
khromatistós, -í, -ó	χρωματιστός, -ή, -ό	colored
kostízi	κοστίζει	it costs
/kostis/	κοστισ–	
kyólas	κιόλας	already

L

léo	λέω	I say; I think
élegha (imperfective past)	ἔλεγα	
loyís see: *tí*		

M

me see: *íme*

mésa	μέσα	inside
to métro	τὸ μέτρο	measure; measurements
pérno-métro	παίρνω μέτρο	I take (someone's) measurements; I get measured

misi see: *ímisi*

N

ne see: *íme*

O

ólos

óli-mas	ὅλοι μας	all of us

[11–F]

P

to panofóri	τὸ πανωφόρι	coat
para	παρὰ	minus (*in telling time*)
trís para-íkosi	τρεῖς παρὰ εἴκοσι	twenty minutes of three
parangélno	παραγγέλνω	I order
/parangil/	παραγγειλ–	
parangélno s-ton-dzangári	παραγγέλνω στὸν τσαγγάρι	I order from the shoemaker
párte see: pérno		
peráste see: pernó		
pérno	παίρνω	I take
/par/	παρ–	
párte	πάρτε	take!
pernó	περνῶ	I pass
/peras/	περασ–	
peráste	περάστε	pass!
peráste-mésa	περάστε μέσα	step right in!
pos	πὼς	that
élegha pos	ἔλεγα πὼς	I thought that ...
to práma	τὸ πρᾶμα	thing
pu	ποὺ	that
tí-akrivá-pu-íne!	τί ἀκριβὰ ποὺ εἶναι!	how expensive (that) they are!
to pukámiso	τὸ πουκάμισο	shirt

R

to rolói	τὸ ρολόι	watch; clock

[11–F]

T

to tétarto	τὸ τέταρτο	quarter
okhtó-ke-tétarto	ὀχτὼ καὶ τέταρτο	a quarter after eight
okhtó para-tétarto	ὀχτὼ παρὰ τέταρτο	a quarter to eight
tí		
tí-akrivós see: *pu*		
tí-loyís	τί λογῆς	of what kind?
tí-loyís-pukámisa?	τί λογῆς πουκάμισα;	what kind of shirts?
i timí	ἡ τιμή	price
típota see: *álos*		
tis	τῆς	(to) her; for her
o tsangáris	ὁ τσαγγάρις	shoemaker
tsangáridhes p.	τσαγγάριδες	

Y

ya		
ya-na	γιὰ νὰ	in order that

Z

to zevghári	τὸ ζευγάρι	pair
ena-zevghári-káltses	ἕνα ζευγάρι κάλτσες	a pair of socks

[11–F]

UNIT 12

REVIEW

Section A—What Do You Know in Greek?

This Section is a true-false quiz exactly like the one in Unit 6, except that the first item is not a practice item. Prepare paper with numbers from 1 to 80 and mark the statements that you will hear from your Guide or the phonograph record either T or F. After you finish the quiz, the Leader will read out the correct answers for each statement. Check your paper and give your score to your Leader. He will figure out the average for your group. If your score is less than the average number of correct answers or less than 80% correct, you need more review of the previous Units.

Spend the rest of the time going over the items on which you had difficulty.

Section B—How Would You Say It?
(Individual Study)

Prepare to give orally the Greek for each of the following sentences. Do not write anything down.

I

1. Do you have a room for two persons?
2. I like number sixteen, on the second floor.
3. I'll show you the bathroom.
4. I don't like the furniture.
5. Your room is sunny and airy.
6. I don't want to wake up at night.
7. This hotel is cold in the winter and hot in the summer.
8. You pay ten percent for the service.
9. It's reasonable.
10. Don't forget your key.

[12–B]

II

11. It was late, but I didn't want to wake you up.
12. My shoes are dirty.
13. Can you shine them?
14. There is a policeman on the square.
15. Where do people get their laundry done here?
16. Is there a variety-stand around here?
17. Give me a haircut, please.
18. I need razor blades and matches.
19. The barber shop is closed.
20. Sometimes we clean uniforms, too.

III

21. Do you, by any chance, know a drugstore around here?
22. Give me soup, meat, fruit, and cheese.
23. Bring us some white wine.
24. The bread is hard and this chicken is a hundred years old.
25. I can't eat vegetables and salad.
26. Waiter, we are short three knives and three forks.
27. Don't eat much in the summer.
28. In Greece you have to wash (the) fruit.
29. Don't forget the cheese with the beer.
30. Waiter, check, please.

IV

31. What are we going to do today?
32. From here to the harbor it's only ten minutes.
33. The fortress is three hundred meters up.
34. Let's go see the ruins of the ancient temple.
35. Are you tired, by any chance?
36. Sit down at that table over there.
37. The cars stop near the wharf.
38. How old are you?
39. I'm twenty-three.
40. My ship goes back to (the) nineteen (hundred) thirty-nine.

V

41. I need a lot of things—a hat, shirts, and cloth for a suit.
42. Let's go buy them in that clothing store.
43. With pleasure.
44. Do you want me to speak with the clerk?
45. What size do you wear?

46. What kind of socks do you have?
47. How much does that brown coat cost?
48. What time is it?
49. It's half past six.
50. Already? I have to be at my hotel by a quarter of seven.

Section C—How Did You Say It?

Quiz by the Leader on the sentences in Section B, asking various members of the group: "*póz-lét-elinikά . . . ?*"

Section D—How Would You Say It? (*Cont.*)
(Individual Study)

Prepare to give orally the Greek for each of the following sentences:

I

1. My bed is soft.
2. I can't find the key of my wardrobe.
3. He sleeps near the window.
4. This chair is very hard.
5. The toilet is across from the bathroom.
6. I leave at nine o'clock tonight.
7. I'll be in the hotèl at a quarter past eleven.
8. They didn't have anything at the other hotel.
9. I want this room for myself and (for) my wife.
10. Is it noisy at night?

II

11. "I don't sell anything," says the barber.
12. You'll find whatever you want at the variety-stand.
13. Who can give me some information in this town?
14. I'm doing it in order to satisfy you.
15. Don't always put your dirty clothes on your bed.
16. Let's go down to the harbor together.
17. There is still time.
18. Can you bring me my coffee now?
19. You can't get off the road.
20. You'll find him in a coffee-shop on America Street.

III

21. Do you know where there is a good restaurant?
22. At "Uncle" John's you'll find the best wines.
23. In Greece they don't bring the coffee (together) with the meal.
24. Waiter, the menu, please.
25. Today we have fish, roast lamb, and steak(s).

26. I don't want ice cream; I prefer pastry.
27. After such a meal, we must drink a glass of wine.
28. Give him a good tip.
29. It's raining and we can't go for a walk.
30. Let's go to the movies instead.

IV

31. Come on, let's go up to the top of the hill.
32. The fishermen are coming back with their boats.
33. Nobody was in the church.
34. Where are the lights?—I can't see them.
35. Is it far from here to the museum?

36. They have many trees on their farm.
37. A hundred and seventy-five.
38. There are ten thousand soldiers here.
39. Eighteen hundred and twenty-one.
40. That doctor has many millions.

V

41. Can you bring me that letter immediately?
42. I hope (that) they are now in Athens.
43. You'll find me at my office at half past four.
44. I speak, but I can't read Greek.
45. May I offer you a coffee?
46. Why don't you come with us?

47. I am not hungry any more, but I am a little thirsty.
48. They tell me that in Macedonia the winter is very hard.
49. Do you know, by any chance, where the Red Cross has its office(s)?
50. He wants to see his relatives who live in Greece.

SECTION E—HOW DID YOU SAY IT?

Quiz by the Leader on the work you did in Section D. Keep your book closed. The Leader will ask you to take turns in speaking sentences by saying: "*póz-lét-eliniká* . . . ?" If you have a Guide, he will check on your pronunciation and the correctness of your Greek.

Section F—Conversation Review

Hold a series of conversations, from one to two minutes each, on as many of the topics which have been developed in Units 1-11 as you can, combining and varying them as you wish. All members of the group should have a chance to take part. A few suggested topics:

1. You go into a hotel to get a room. After finding out the price, you ask to see the room and the bathroom. You also ask whether the hotel has a restaurant.
2. At the barber shop—you get a haircut, but don't need a shave. The barber talks about the weather, where you come from, where you live, etc.
3. You ask a stranger directions to get to various places. You want to see a few of the sights in and around the town, go to a restaurant and to the movies. You also want to know how to get back to the station.
4. You ask the innkeeper where you can get your shoes shined, your laundry done, and a suit cleaned and pressed. She tells you how to get to the various places.
5. You go to a store and buy some articles of clothing. You ask how much you have to pay and the clerk makes a detailed bill.
6. You go to a restaurant and order a full meal for yourself and a lady.
7. You and a Greek compare the weather in New York and Athens (or any other two cities).
8. A friend is helping you move into your new room in a hotel. He asks you where various things belong, and you tell him. After everything is in the room, you suggest a beer in a cafe. He gladly accepts.
9. You ask your Greek friend is he has gotten a letter from his father in Salonica. He says yes, and tells you what his father says about other relatives and their whereabouts in Greece.
10. You tell a friend you are going out in the evening. Tell him when you have to be where, whom you're going to meet and where, and what you have to do to get ready.

KEY TO EXERCISES AND TESTS

The following pages give in condensed form a Key to the exercises contained in the *What Would You Say?* sections of each regular Unit, and to the tests and exercises contained in the Review Units. You will also find here the tests themselves so that you can read them even if you have no guide.

Each part of the Key is identified by a heading giving the Unit and the page on which the exercise occurs.

UNIT 2

SECTION C 3: Key

1. d.
2. a.
3. d.
4. c.
5. a.
6. c.
7. a.
8. b.
9. c.
10. b.
11. b.
12. b.

UNIT 3

SECTION C 3: Key

1. b.
2. a.
3. c.
4. a.
5. b.
6. b.
7. a.
8. c.
9. a.
10. b.

UNIT 4

SECTION C 3: Key

I
1. c.
2. d.
3. c.
4. d.
5. b.
6. c.
7. d.
8. c.
9. d.
10. c.
11. c.

II
1. b, d, c, a.
2. c, b, d, a.
3. b, e, d, a, f, c.
4. c, e, a, b, d.
5. d, a, c, b, e.

UNIT 5

SECTION C 3: Key.

I
1. c
2. b.
3. c.
4. c.

II
1. b, c, f, i, m, o.
2. g, j, k.
3. n, p.
4. h, l.
5. a, d, n, p.
6. o.
7. c, f, i, m.
8. e, g, j, k.
9. b, c.
10. a, d.
11. o.
12. e, g, j, k.
13. h, l.
14. a, d, n, p.
15. h, l.
16. b, c, f, i, m, o.

III

1. b, h.	4. a.	7. a, g, i.	10. a, e.
2. a, e.	5. d.	8. g, i.	
3. c, f.	6. j.	9. a, e.	

IV

1. f.	4. b.	7. i.	10. j.
2. h.	5. c.	8. g.	
3. a.	6. d.	9. e.	

UNIT 6

SECTION A: True-False Test.

F 1. Greece has no mountains.
T 2. Americans speak English.
T 3. New York is a very large city.
F 4. In Greece every worker has a car.
T 5. Three hundred sixty-five days is a year.
F 6. I want to eat a beer and drink a loaf of bread.
F 7. The women in America speak Greek.
T 8. Athens is bigger than Patras.
T 9. Rain is water.
T 10. Down by the sea it's cool in the evening.
T 11. Right is not left.
F 12. A farmer works in an office.
T 13. Here in America every large city has its station.
F 14. What time is it? — It's fifty.
F 15. A day always starts with rain.
T 16. A good husband always lives with his wife.
F 17. My son any my sister's son are uncles of mine.
F 18. Two and three make ten.
T 19. I see him every day but I don't know his name.
T 20. (Men and women) students read a lot of books.
F 21. Eight and four make five.
F 22. Winter starts in summer.
T 23. The weather is sometimes very bad.
F 24. In the summer it rains and snows.

c

- F 25. My father and mother are brothers.
- F 26. I have three children, one son and three daughters.
- F 27. American soldiers don't understand English.
- F 28. Greece is very large.
- F 29. Every doctor is married.
- T 30. Ships can go from one sea to the other.
- F 31. My grandfather is still a youngster.
- T 32. Snow is always cold.
- F 33. The day has three hours.
- F 34. My children have neither father nor mother.
- F 35. Water is always hot.
- F 36. My grandfather had no children.
- F 37. Sailors live in the country.
- T 38. Macedonia is in America.
- F 39. The houses in America don't have any water.
- T 40. War is no joke.
- T 41. Women work, too.
- F 42. A kilometer is ten miles.
- F 43. My wife's son is a brother of mine.
- F 44. In Macedonia they have a hard winter.
- T 45. Every year has three hundred sixty-six days.
- F 46. California is not a beautiful region.
- T 47. California has a good climate.
- F 48. My parents are still children.
- F 49. An employee works on a farm.
- T 50. In Greece they have very good cigarettes.
- F 51. Doctors in America are no good.
- F 52. Americans speak Italian rather than English.
- T 53. Salonica is a city in Macedonia.
- T 54. Hotels sometimes have restaurants.
- F 55. The Greeks are farmers or factory workers.
- F 56. In the Red Cross there are only teachers and aviators.
- F 57. Patras is near San Francisco.
- T 58. Six and four make ten.
- F 59. The sea is up in the mountains.
- T 60. My uncle and his son are relatives of mine.
- F 61. It's only seven kilometers from Athens to Salonica.
- F 62. The women of America are always small.
- F 63. Her husband isn't married.
- F 64. Nine and nine make fifty.

F 65. Salonica and Patras are two cities in America.
T 66. From New York to Italy we can go by boat.
F 67. In Patras they have snow and ice in the summer.
T 68. The winter is beautiful in Athens.
T 69. When it's night in San Francisco, it's day in Athens.
T 70. Three and three make six.
F 71. How's the weather? — It's three.
T 72. Athens is a very beautiful city.
T 73. It isn't always wartime.
F 74. When it rains, the streets are dry.
F 75. In New York it's hot in winter.
F 76. Americans speak Greek like the Greeks.
T 77. In Chicago it's windy in winter.
T 78. When I say yes, I don't mean no.
T 79. When we leave, we say "good-bye".
T 80. Soldiers sometimes go to the movies with pretty girls.

SECTION B: Key.

I

1. *kaliméra-sas ktrie.*
2. *ti-kánete?*
3. *polí-kala, efkharistó.*
4. *boró-na-sas-parusiáso ton-gírio-Cook?*
5. *chéro párapoli.*
6. *pú-in-o-stathmós parakaló?*
7. *o-stathmós in-aristerá.*
8. *dhén-gatálava.*
9. *millte-sighá parakaló.*
10. *thá-thela-na-pyó-enan-gafé.*

II

11. *me-sikhoríte-kiría, pú-ine-to-estiatório?*
12. *to-estiatório ine-dheksyá.*
13. *efkharistó-polí.*
14. *parakaló.*
15. *dhóste-mu-mya-bíra, k-ístera thélo-na-fáo kréaz-me-patátes*
16. *dhé-thélo-krasí, dhóste-mu-ghála i-neró.*
17. *échete-sigharéta ke-spírta?*

e

18. póso-káni?
19. póz-léte toilet eliniká?
20. tí-ora-íne?

III

21. ín-októ.
22. to-korítsi pái-me-to-stratyóti s-ton-ginimatóghrafo.
23. chérete, khárika párapoli.
24. me-léne-maría.
25. tí-boró-na-sas-prosféro?
26. to-yó-tu tone-léne-pétro.
27. íne-pandreménos-o-adherfó-sas?
28. óchi, dhén-íne.
29. s-tin-eládha dhé-milún-angliká.
30. tí-dhulyá-kánete?

IV

31. íme-yeorghós.
32. íne-kaló-pedhí.
33. ín-aeropóros.
34. dhé-dhulévi míte-s-tim-bóli míte-s-tin-eksochí, íne-se-vapóri.
35. pós-to-léne to-vapóri-pu-íste?
36. dhem-boró-na-sas-pó.
37. íst-amerikanós?
38. o-patéras-tu íne-ipálilo-se-ghrufío.
39. s-to-vapóri-mas íne-trakósyi-náftes.
40. dhyavázame-ena-soro-vivlía.

V

41. íkhate-kalí-dhulyá-eki-péra?
42. páme-mazí-s-ton-ginimatóghrafo.
43. apo-pyó-méros-tis-amerikís-íste?
44. pyós-edho milí-angliká?
45. pósa-mílya-íne ap-tin-athína-s-ti-saloníki?
46. í-zestí-aéridhes férnune-vrochés.
47. tí-keros-íne?
48. íne-kalós-kerós.
49. káni-zésti.
50. páno-s-ta-vuná chyonízi.

I

1. o-patéras k-i-mitéra-tu-níku ménune-s-tin-eksochí.
2. aftós-o-kírios-eki-péra íne-fílos-tu-pétru.
3. i-amerikaní-tóra milún-elinikā san-g-emás.
4. i-fíli-tu-yáni dhulévune-se-vapóri.
5. ta-pedhyá tis-adherfís-mu íne-mikrá.
6. énas-ap-tus-adherfús-mu ergházete-se-ksenodhochío.
7. páme-tóra-isya-brostá, k-ístera páme-aristerá
8. kondá-s-to-stathmó ín-ena-ksenodhochío.
9. pedhí! enan-gafé ke-dhyó-bíres parakaló.
10. dhóste-mu kréas psomí ke-krasí.

II

11. i-adherfí-mu echi-pedhyá.
12. o-thíos-tis dhén-echi-pedhyá.
13. ergházome-s-erghostásio.
14. i-ghonís-tus zún-akóma.
15. ménete-s-tin-eksochí?
16. dhuléri-káto-ki-s-tim-bóli.
17. dhulévume-se-khtíma.
18. ergházonde-se-ghrafío.
19. otan-ímuna-pedhí íksera-kalá-anglikā.
20. pó-saz-léne?

III

21. lipúme-polí ma-dhén-doné-kséro.
22. i-kóri-sas íne-polí-nóstimo-korítsi.
23. erghazómaste ke-dhyavázume-polí.
24. archízi-s-tis-pénde.
25. íme-náftis.
26. enas-fíloz-mu íne-stratyótis.
27. íne-fítítís?
28. dhén-íne-kalóz-yatrós.
29. íne-fítítria-ky-aftí.
30. eláte-na-sas-pó-en-astío.

g

IV

31. aftós-o-yatrós echi-pénde-spítya ke-tría-khtímata.
32. ksérete-ti-thyá-mu pu-méni-s-tin-athína?
33. dhén-íne-kakó-pedhí.
34. prín-ap-tom-bólemo ítane-dháskalos.
35. kséro-líglia-elinilcá.
36. févgho-to-vrádhi me-to-tréno.
37. eláte-mazí-mu.
38. s-tin-athína dhe-vréchi-ke-tóso-polí.
39. íne-steghní-i-dhrómi?
40. íne-paghonyá.

V

41. íste-romyós, dhén-ín-étsi?
42. eféłos íkhame-varí-chimóna.
43. ekhun-oréo-chimóna.
44. s-ti-thálasa echi-aéra.
45. edhó-s-ta-méri-mas dhén-gáni míte-zésti míte-krío.
46. dhe-mu-léte kírie, pós-íne-to-klíma-s-ti-makedhonía?
47. i-chimónes-tus íne-polí-kríi.
48. érkhom-ap-ti-salonílci ke-páo-s-tim-bátra.
49. i-dhrómi-sas ín-oréi.
50. i-kalifórnya ín-oréa-to-kalokéri, ma-pyó-oré-akóma to-chimóna.

UNIT 7

SECTION C3: Key.

I

1. *mu, mas.*
2. *tu, tis, tus.*
3. *mu.*
4. *mu, sas, tu.*
5. *sas.*
6. *mu, sas, tu, tis, mas, tus.*
7. *mu, sas, tu, tis, mas, tus.*
8. *mu, mas; sas.*
9. *mu, sas, tu, tis, mas, tus.*
10. *mu, sas, tu, tis, mas, tus; mu.*

II

1. *póz-léte* when *elinilcá*? 2. *póz-léte* never *elinilcá*? 3. *s-to-krevátimu kimúme-kalá.* 4. *ti-ora-févyi-to-tréno*? 5. *póte-thélete-na-fíyete*

h

ya-ti-salomíki? 6. érchete-káthe-méra s-tis-téseris. 7. kápote dhém-blirónune ya-tin-ipíresta. 8. s-aftó-to-ksenodhochío plirónete-ekató-dhrakhmés ke-dhén-gimáste-kalá. 9. dhóste-ta. 10. échete-dhomátio ya-dhío-átoma?

III

1. f.   4. i.   7. d.   10. e.
2. g.   5. c.   8. h.
3. j.   6. a.   9. b.

UNIT 8

SECTION C 3: Key.

I

1. katharízune; s-tu-ráfti. 2. kathíste. 3. ksenodhochío. 4. na-mu-pí. 5. s-tis-trís. 6. kimáste. 7. rotíste. 8. polí. 9. mu-ípate. 10. kalós; kalíteros.

II

1. b.   2. c.   3. b.   4. a.

III

1. kséro-mya-yinéka pu-pléni-ta-rúkha. 2. pίyene-s-to-estiatorió-tis. 3. prépi-na-páte-se-katharistírio. 4. váni-pánda to-klidhí-s-tin-dzépi-tu. 5. s-ta-kyóskya pulúne-lámes. 6. dhén-gatálava ti-íthele. 7. dhén-gzérune-típota. 8. prépi-na-sas-plirόso-tóra í-boró-na-sas-plirόso-ávrio? 9. to-pérno-pánda mazí-mu. 10. boríte-na-mu-yalísete ta-papútsya-mu? íne-vrómika.

UNIT 9

SECTION C 3: Key.

1. c.   2. c.   3. a.   4. d.   5. a.   6. d.   7. b.

II

1. *protimáte, protimái, protimúme, protimúne, protimúne.* 2. *tróte, trói, tróme, tróte, trói, tróme.* 3. *fíyete, fíyi, fíghume, fíghune.* 4. *bortte-na-ksekhásete, borí-na-ksekhási, borúme-na-ksekhásume, borúne-na-ksekhásune.* 5. *ergházeste, ergházete, erghazómaste, erghazónde.* 6. *kimáste, kimáte, kimúmaste, kimúnde.*

UNIT 10

SECTION C 3: Key.

II

1. *íne-mía.* 2. *i-kóri-mu íne-dheka-trió-khronóne.* 3. *to-dhomatió-mu íne-s-to-próto-pátoma.* 4. *ímaste eftakósya-eksínda-tésera-métra-psilá.* 5. *ap-ti-néa-yórki s-tin-athína íne-pénde-chilyádhes tetrakósya-éndeka-mílya.* 6. *aftó-to-kástro-eki-péra ín-ap-to-chílya-dhyakósya-peninda-eftá.* 7. *s-tin-eládha dhtnune-dheka-tis-ekató ya-tin-ipiresía.* 8. *to-dhomatió-mu íne-to-saranda-enyá.* 9. *s-aftó-to-ksenodhochío ménun-ekaton-íkosi-átoma, oghdhónda-okhtó-romyí ke-triánda-dhío-amerikaní.* 10. *téseri-súpes dhéka-ksi-dhrakhmés, tri-saláaes dhódheka-dhrakhmés, okhtó-avghá íkosi-téseriz-dhrakhmés, dhyó-kafédhes téseriz-dhrakhmés, ke-myá-bíra pénde-dhrakhmés. óla-mazí eksínda-mía-dhrakhmés.*

UNIT 11

SECTION C 3: Key.

I

1. *n-aghoráso.* 2. *na-fíghume.* 3. *mín-gzekhnáte.* 4. *na-tróo.* 5. *na-sas-to-dhíkso.* 6. *tha-taksidhévune.* 7. *tha-saz-dhó.* 8. *tha-párune.* 9. *tha-dhulévi.* 10. *tha-tone-vríte.*

II

1. g.
2. h.
3. m.
4. c.
5. f.
6. j.
7. i.
8. b.
9. e.
10. l.
11. d.
12. a.
13. k.

UNIT 12

SECTION A: True-False Test.

F 1. A taxi is not a car.
T 2. A wardrobe and chairs are furniture.
F 3. We always sleep in the bathroom.
F 4. We never go up high mountains.
F 5. The fourth floor comes before the third.
F 6. We go to stores at twelve o'clock at night.
T 7. Many go to war and never come back.
T 8. I do whatever I can to please my friend.
T 9. At night we light the light.
T 10. There are many ancient temples in Athens.
T 11. When they wake you up, you mustn't sleep any longer.
T 12. In Greece you pay for the service.
F 13. In winter our room must be cold.
T 14. All of us sleep better when it's noisy.
F 15. We need a little quiet sometimes.
T 16. You can put your key in your pocket.
T 17. When we're tired, we sit down for a little while.
T 18. When I like music, I enjoy listening to it.
T 19. One and two are numbers.
F 20. Ugly women don't always have ugly children.
F 21. Bootblacks don't shine shoes.
T 22. They clean suits at cleaning places.
T 23. When we wash our clothes, they're clean.
F 24. A tailor washes dirty clothes.
F 25. They sell chickens at barber shops.
T 26. A barber gives us a haircut and a shave.
F 27. Razor blades never cut.
F 28. Coffee-houses have no windows.
F 29. It's only five minutes up to the fortress. It's not any short distance.
F 30. A thousand people live in this room.
T 31. They give tips in Greece.
F 32. When a person is eighty years old, he has very little hair.
T 33. Shirts are white or colored.
F 34. Little children have white hair.
F 35. We're never sick in summer.
T 36. We sometimes get off the road.

k

F 37. Policemen never stop to rest.
T 38. They sell a lot of things at variety-stands.
T 39. When it's hot, we drink a good deal of water.
T 40. England St. is not a square.
T 41. In America people sometimes eat at drugstores.
F 42. When we're thirsty, we're hungry.
T 43. When a person is hungry, he can eat fish.
T 44. Old wine is good.
T 45. Brown is one color and blue is another.
F 46. We don't pay any checks at restaurants.
T 47. Wine can be red.
F 48. Americans don't eat steaks.
T 49. Many harbors have fine wharves.
T 50. Across from my house isn't near my door.
F 51. Our clocks always run well.
T 52. In the country there are many beautiful trees.
F 53. In America people don't go to church.
F 54. When I haven't any more socks, I go and buy three hundred pairs.

T 55. We're not always right.
F 56. The beds are hard in America.
T 57. Sixty minutes is an hour.
F 58. It's half past three and I thought that it was a quarter of three already.
F 59. A kilometer is a hundred meters.
F 60. Fat women don't get husbands.
T 61. In ancient Greece they didn't have ships.
F 62. I'll never forget my mother.
T 63. We never wear hats.
F 64. Museums are always closed.
T 65. Where do you order your shoes? — From the shoemaker.
F 66. I'm going to travel with my uncle who is no longer living.
T 67. Good taverns aren't always the best.
F 68. The meal isn't ready; come and eat.
T 69. In California they have fine fruit.
T 70. Living was cheaper before the war.
F 71. From Chicago to New York it's three hours' walk.
F 72. There are no boats in harbors.
F 73. When I'm poor, I lack nothing.
F 74. My coat is still new; I've had it for twenty years.

1

F 75. We eat our soup without spoons.
T 76. Mountains have peaks.
F 77. Today I'll iron my clothes and tomorrow I'll wash them.
F 78. In clothing stores they don't sell heavy cloth.
T 79. Shirts are long or short.
T 80. Many Americans come to Greece just for the ruins.

SECTION B: Key.

I

1. échete-dhomátio ya-dhío-átoma?
2. m-arési-to-dhekáksi s-to-próto-pátoma.
3. tha-saz-dhíkso-to-bányo.
4. dhé-m-arésune-ta-épipla.
5. to-dhomatió-sas echi-ílyo ky-aéra.
6. dhé-thélo-na-ksipnó-ti-níkhta.
7. aftó-to-ksenodhochío íne-krío-to-chimóna ke-zestó-to-kalokéri.
8. dhéka-tis-ekató plirónete ya-tin-ipiresía.
9. íne-ftinó.
10. mín-gzekhásete to-klidhí-sas.

II

11. ítan-arghá, ma-dhén-íthela-na-sas-ksipníso.
12. ta-papútsya-mu íne-vrómika.
13. boríte-na-mu-ta-yalísete?
14. s-tin-blatía ín-enas-astifílakas.
15. pú-plénun-edhó-ta-rúkha?
16. íne-kanéna-kyóski-edhó-péra?
17. kópste-mu-ta-malyá parakaló.
18. khriázome lámes ke-spírta.
19. to-kurtó íne-klistó.
20. kápote katharízume-ke-stolés.

III

21. min-gzérete-kanéna-farmakío-edhó-péra?
22. dhóste-mu súpa kréas frúta ke-tirí.
23. férte-mas áspro-krasí.

24. to-psomí ine-skliró ke-túto-to-kotópulo in-ekató-khronóne.
25. dhem-boró-na-fáo lákhana ke-saláta.
26. pedhí, lipune-tría-machérya ke-tría-pirúnya.
27. mín-dróte-polí-to-kalokéri.
28. s-tin-eládha prépi-na-plénete-ta-frúta.
29. mín-gzekhásete-to-tirí me-tim-bíra.
30. pedhí, to-logharyazmó parakaló.

IV

31. tí-tha-kámume-símera?
32. apo-dhó-isa-me-to-limáni ine-móno-dhéka-leftá.
33. to-kástro ine-trakósya-métra-psilá.
34. eláte-na-dhúme ta-erípia tu-archéu-naú.
35. mín-íste-kurazménos?
36. kathíste-s-ekíno-kí-to-trapézi.
37. t-aftokínita stamatúne kondá-s-tim-brokíméa.
38. póso-khronóne-íste?
39. íme-íkosi-trió-khronóne.
40. to-vapóri-mu in-ap-to-chílya-enyakósya-trianda-enyá.

V

41. khrázom-ena-soro-prámata, ena-kapeló pukámisa ke-iĵazma-ya-mya-foresyá.
42. páme-na-t-aghorásume s-aftó-to-emborikó.
43. efkharístos.
44. thélete-na-míliso-me-ton-ipálilo?
45. tí-aríthmó-forte?
46. tí-loyís-káltses-échete?
47. póso-kostízi aftó-to-kafetí-panofóri?
48. tí-ora-íne?
49. in-eksí-misi.
50. kyólas? prépi-ná-me-s-to-ksenodhochío-mu s-tis-eftá para-tétarto.

SECTION D: **Key.**

I

1. to-kreváti-mu ine-malakó.
2. dhem-boró-na-vró to-klidhí-tiz-dulápaz-mu.

n

3. kimáte kondá-s-to-paráthiro.
4. aftí-i-karékla íne-polí-sklirí.
5. to-méros íne-antíkri-s-to-bányo.
6. févgho-to-vrádhi s-tis-enyá.
7. thá-me-s-to-ksenodhochío s-tis-éndeka-ke-tétarto.
8. s-to-álo-ksenodhochío dhen-íkhane-típota.
9. thélo-aftó-to-dhomátio ya-ména ke-ya-ti-yinéka-mu.
10. íne-thórivos-ti-níkhta?

II

11. dhem-buló-típota, léi-o-kuréas.
12. s-to-kyóski vrískete-óti-thélete.
13. pyó-s-aftín-dim-bóli borí-na-mu-dhósi merikés-pliroforíes?
14. to-káno ya-na-sas-efkharistíso.
15. mi-vánete-pánda ta-vromiká-saz-rúkha páno-s-to-krevátti
16. páme-mazí káto-s-to-limáni.
17. íne-kerós-akóma.
18. boríte-na-mu-toné-férete-tóra ton-gafé-mu?
19. dhem-boríte-na-khásete-to-dhrómo.
20. tha-tone-vríte s-ena-kafenío s-tin-odhón-amerikís.

III

21. ksérete-pu-íne-kanena-kaló-estiatório?
22. s-tu-barba-yáni vrískete-ta-kalítera-krasyá.
23. s-tin-eládha dhe-férnune-ton-gafé mazí-me-to-fai.
24. pedhí, ti-ílsta parakaló.
25. símera ekhume-psári arní-psitó ke-brizóles.
26. dhé-thélo-paghotó, protimó-ghlikó.
27. íster-apo-tétyo-faí prépi-na-pyúm-ena-potíri-krasí.
28. dhóste-tu kaló-burbuár.
29. vréchi ke-dhém-borúme-na-páme-perípato.
30. páme-kalítera s-ton-ginimatóghrafo.

IV

31. eláte-n-anevúme s-tin-gorfí-tu-vunú.
32. yirízun-i-psarádhes me-tiz-várkes-tus.
33. dhen-ítane-kanéna-s-tin-eklisyá.

o

34. pú-íne-ta-fóta ? — dhém-boró-na-ta-dhó.
35. íne-makriá-apo-dhó ísa-me-to-mustó ?
36. ekhun-ena-soro-dhéndra s-to-khtíma-tus.
37. ekaton-evdhomínda-pénde.
38. íne-dhéka-chilyádhe-stratyótes-edhó.
39. chílya-okhtakósya-ikosi-éna.
40. aftós-o-yatrós echi-polá-ekatomíria.

V

41. boríte-na-mu-to-férete-amésos aftó-to-ghráma ?
42. elpízo-na-ne-tóra-s-tin-athína.
43. tha-me-vríte-s-to-ghrafío-mu s-tis-teserís-ímisi.
44. miló-elinikà, ma-dhém-boró-na-ta-dhyavàso.
45. boró-na-sas-prosféro-enan-gafé ?
46. yatí-dhen-ércheste-mazí-mas ?
47. dhem-binó-álo, ma-dhipsó-ligháki.
48. o-chimónaz-léi-s-ti-makedhonía íne-varís.
49. min-gzérete pu-echi-ta-ghrafía-tu-o-erithró-stavrós ?
50. théli-na-dhí-tu-singenís-tu pu-zúne-s-tin-eládha.

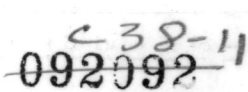